An Absolute Wreck

AN ABSOLUTE WRECK

THE LOSS OF THE
THOMAS W. LAWSON

John Hicks

Acknowledgments of words or images from other sources than the author are made, with grateful thanks, at the relevant point in the text, notes or captions.

Every reasonable effort has been made to trace and obtain permission from copyright holders, where appropriate, but if any items requiring clearance have unwittingly been included without it, amendments will be made at the earliest opportunity.

Copyright © John Hicks
First published in 2015 on behalf of the author by
Scotforth Books (www.scotforthbooks.com)
ISBN   978-1-909817-25-8
Typesetting and design by Carnegie Book Production, Lancaster.
Printed in the UK by Short Run Press Ltd

Contents

List of Maps

In these maps, and in the photograph at page 122, places and features referred to in the text are emphasised as appropriate.

List of Photographs

Acknowledgements

THIS BOOK HAS been so long in gestation that I must begin by recording my debt of gratitude to several members of my extended family who are not, sadly, here to read these words.

It was my father Charles, a boy of 10 at the time of the wreck, who died in 1963, who first told me the story of the *Thomas W. Lawson*, for the most part in outline, but with at least two invaluable pieces of personal recollection, one not recorded elsewhere, which have an important bearing on the issues discussed in the text, and who also left me his father Israel's gold medal and his mother Charlotte Ellen's key to the 1871 photograph of Augustus Smith and his St Agnes pilots (page 93).

William Lewis Hicks (always known as Lewis), who died in 1985, was the son of the Stephen Lewis who was a member of the St Agnes lifeboat crew on 13 December 1907. It was Lewis who first awakened my interest in the history of the family name, as developed in chapter 8, and gave me, among a wealth of other material, a copy of his invaluable map of the St Agnes graveyard, with a transcript of the inscriptions, and another key to that same 1871 photograph.

Four of the major figures in the story are Billy Cook Hicks, the pilot who was lost in the wreck, his son Freddy Cook, who rescued the schooner's master, Osbert Hicks, the cox of the rescue gig *Slippen*, and his son Jack, who wrote the fullest first-hand account of the lifeboat's involvement. I had the immeasurable advantage and joy, over the years, of many conversations about the wreck with Freddy Cook's son Joseph Thomas (Joe) and Jack's son Osbert (Ob), and learned much from them. It was also Ob who took me out in his boat to retrace both the last stage of the *Lawson's* drift into Shag Rock and, at the right state of the tide, the final rescue trip of the *Slippen,* including the journey of Freddy Cook and his companions across the Brow to the South Carn and then back with Captain Dow. Joe died in

2006 and Ob in 2011, and I am particularly sorry that I did not finish my work in time to show them the result.

For advice on the working of ships and boats in 1907, especially among the islands and rocks of the Scillies, and on tidal and other sea conditions, I am grateful not only to Ob but also to the legendary Matt Lethbridge junior, for many years coxswain of the St Mary's lifeboat, also now sadly dead, and to Kit Legg, happily still alive and active as the St Agnes fisherman.

My interest in the *Lawson* story from the family and island side is matched by that of Tom Hall from an American viewpoint, and I have been much helped in that regard, particularly when writing about Tom Lawson, the man, by conversations with him, by material which he has kindly supplied and by reading his own book on the subject.

One of the tasks which I undertook was to trace the descent of the watch and medals presented to the crew of the *Slippen* from their original owners to their present possessors, and for their help in that quest I gratefully thank Mandy Pearce, Deborah Carter-Clout, Marigold Barbanchon, the late Kathleen Stephenson and her daughter Hilary Nicholas, the late Frederick John Hicks, Gordon Willey, Dorothy Barker, Sheila Legg and Amanda Martin.

Mike Hicks, Mandy Pearce and Amanda Martin most kindly undertook the burden of reading and commenting on my typescript, for which I am very much in their debt, to which they have all added greatly in other ways – in particular Mike by the loan of the log book of the gig *Slippen*, Mandy by her recollection of conversations with her grandfather Freddy Cook Hicks and Amanda in her capacity as curator of the Isles of Scilly Museum, with its associated Isles of Scilly Family History Group

My requests for information and data from the Meteorological Office, Trinity House, the Royal National Lifeboat Institution, the Royal Observatory at Greenwich and the U.K Hydrographic Office invariably met with courteous and helpful responses.

For the transformation of my typescript into elegant book form I am indebted to Anna Goddard and her colleagues at Carnegie Publishing, of whom Penny Hayashi bore the brunt of my demanding correspondence.

Most of all my undying love and thanks go to my wife Mary for her encouragement to persevere, despite my sometimes painfully slow progress, for the enthusiasm and warmth with which she, much more ably than I, made personal friends of so many of my distantly related Scillonian cousins, and for everything which she has brought to our life together.

• 1 •

The Story

O<small>N THE AFTERNOON</small> of Friday, 13 December 1907, Israel Hicks was at the helm of an island gig on the run home from St Mary's to St Agnes, in the Isles of Scilly, when he heard the boom of signals fired from the Bishop Rock lighthouse, some five and a half miles ahead to the west-south-west. He and his crew kept a sharp look-out for the cause and very soon they made out, through the gathering gloom of the winter twilight, what looked like the largest sailing vessel they had ever seen, about three and a half miles to the west of them. Their own assessment of the position, given her size, her location and the weather conditions, confirmed the message of the lighthouse keepers' signals: she was in danger. They set off towards her.

Israel and his gig were there because he was retained by Trinity House as the relief boatman for the two offshore lighthouses in the Isles of Scilly – the Bishop Rock and Round Island lights. Round Island was due for relief that day, so he had set off in the morning from St Agnes to Hugh Town harbour, St Mary's, a row or sail of some two and a half miles. At Hugh Town he had taken on board the relief keeper, stores and mail for the lighthouse. Thus laden, the gig had next to make the journey from St Mary's to Round Island, a little over four miles to the north as the crow flies, but quite a bit further by the course she had to follow to avoid the islands, rocks and sandbanks on the way, although on the outward journey that day the flats which almost link Tresco to St Martin's at low spring tides were well covered, high tide being due at 10.51 am. Most of that leg was in

A visit to Round Island Lighthouse in about 1905.
© Gibsons of Scilly

sheltered waters, but the final stretch was more open; the lighthouse was at the northern extremity of the islands, and the wind that morning was freshening from Force 4 to Force 5 and coming round from the south to the south-west. At Round Island the gig lay offshore in the channel between the island and Camber Rock while stores, inward mail and the relief keeper's kit were hauled up by rope and pulley to the base of the lighthouse, some 40 metres (130 feet) above mean sea level, and the load for the return journey was lowered down into the boat. The relief keeper and the one coming off duty might use the same means of transfer, standing in a bight in the rope, although there were landing stages which were sometimes accessible. The gig and her crew then went back to Hugh Town and unloaded, after which they could set off for home.

There is no record of the composition of Israel's crew that day, but in view of what followed it is of some importance that, for reasons which will appear, we can be pretty sure that it included his wife's uncle, Osbert Hicks, and Grenfell Legg, a more distant relative of his wife's.

They were justified in their impression of the size of the vessel. She was in fact the *Thomas W. Lawson*, 5,218 gross registered tons, the largest fore-and-aft rigged sailing vessel of all time and the only seven-masted sailing vessel ever built. The *Lawson* had left Philadelphia on 15 November 1907, bound for London with a cargo of bulk oil. Buffeted by storms for much of her crossing of the Atlantic, with few sails left and an exhausted crew, she had that afternoon made, as her navigators thought, the open mouth of the English Channel, and with it comparative safety. They had seen to starboard the light of what they believed to be another craft and were keeping well clear of her. Too late they realised that it was not a ship's light, but the beam of the Bishop Rock lighthouse, and that they were therefore running into the rocks, shoals and islands of the Scillies instead of leaving them a safe distance to port. In that emergency the schooner was brought to and anchored. She was by then entering Broad Sound, between the rocks of Gunners Ledge and the shoals of Nundeeps.

The big schooner had been seen by coastguards and others as well as by the lighthouse keepers, the first report reaching the divisional officer of coastguards for the Isles of Scilly at 3.50 pm. The islanders were convinced that she was not in a safe anchorage. They expected the wind to veer round to the north-west and rise to gale force during the evening and night. There was a lifeboat station on St Mary's, the largest and much the most populous island, and another on St Agnes, which although tiny in comparison was the most south-westerly of the inhabited islands and so the nearest to the scene. On each island the decision was quickly made to launch the lifeboat. The St Agnes boat was away by about 4 pm and on St Mary's the launch was at 4.25. On that day sunset in the Scillies was at 4.24, so darkness was closing in as the lifeboats made their arduous way upwind towards the *Lawson*. Meanwhile Israel and his crew had been forced by the weather conditions to abandon their attempt to reach the schooner and had turned again towards St Agnes, which they reached after the lifeboat had left.

With the double advantage of an earlier start and a shorter journey the St Agnes lifeboat reached the *Lawson* first, at a little after 5 o'clock. One of her crew was a 17-year old lad, John Horace Hicks (Jack), on his first service in the boat. Some years later he gave perhaps the fullest and most graphic account of that crew's part in the night's events. He describes rowing for some 20 minutes before they were far enough out of Periglis (the westward-facing bay where the boathouse and slipway were sited) to get the sails up. Then they made sail, at first with some shelter from Annet, the uninhabited island which lies to the west of St Agnes, but after they had rounded Annet Head and the Haycocks, at the north end of Annet, they were beating directly into the wind, by now freshening all the time, as it blew in, unchecked, from the Atlantic. So they proceeded, tacking alternately north and south, but always gaining some westing, until they were beyond the Gunners Rock and could see the schooner. Jack remembered the coxswain, William George Mortimer, saying: "Lash yourselves in, every one of you, because I am easing for nothing". He also remembered that when the boat would go into a big sea, she would fill up with water, but that the safety valves were open and she would more or less empty herself.

The lifeboat's arrival alongside the *Lawson* is best told in Jack's own words: "So we went on and on and on, beating all the time, and eventually we got up to this huge ship, which proved to be a seven-masted American schooner. She was at anchor and we went straight to windward of her, and downed sails, downed mizzen and went alongside on oars. She was like a forest, all the masts one behind the other. It was from here to next week the length of her – enormous she was. By now it was dark, absolutely dark. We got alongside and it was very rough".

As the St Agnes lifeboat drew close enough to the *Lawson's* beam to speak her master, Captain George W Dow, came to the rail, and a crucial conversation ensued between him and the lifeboat coxswain. Jack gives it in direct speech, but even his memory, good as it evidently was, cannot have been word-perfect, and regard must also be had to other sources, in particular the evidence given by persons present to the coroner's jury only three days later.

It is clear that after opening greetings George Mortimer repeatedly pressed Captain Dow with the danger of his position and the necessity of accepting assistance from the lifeboat crew, or at least their strong advice not to stay where he was. Captain Dow as consistently refused, repeatedly stating that he was "alright"; he had two anchors out and had ridden out worse storms than this on the American side of the Atlantic. What particular form of assistance, if any, was discussed or contemplated on either side, or would have been feasible, and the master's motives for refusing help and rejecting the coxswain's advice, are not so clear and are discussed later.

What Captain Dow was willing to do was to take on board a pilot. The St Agnes lifeboat's crew included at least four, and probably five, licensed

Doing the Round Island relief. This photograph was taken in 1946, and the relief boat is not a gig, but the procedure is essentially that described in the text. The ladder and steps up from water level can just be picked out behind the boat, but are not being used. Photograph attributed to Mr Hills-Grove-Hills of the Island Air Services.

The original plans for Round Island, signed by James Douglass. The 'west landing' was never built. The 'south landing' is that shown in the previous photograph. © Trinity House

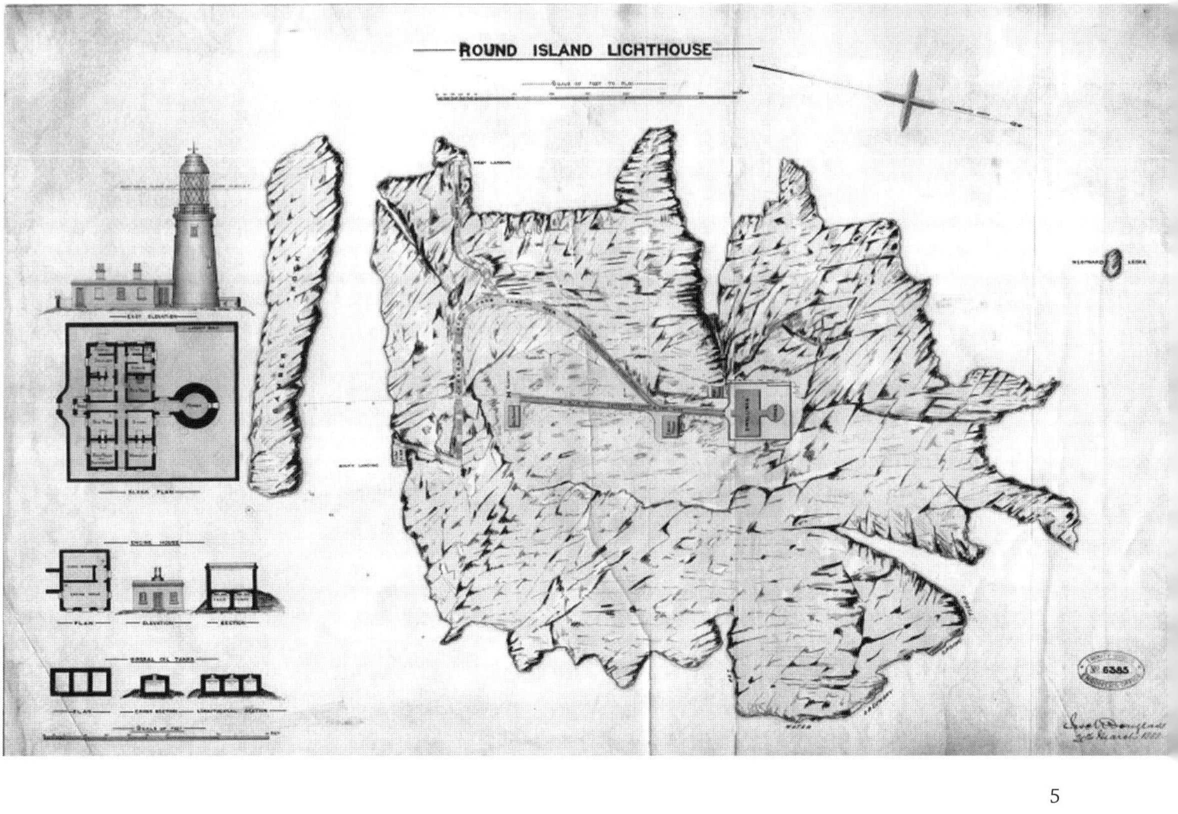

ROUND ISLAND LICHTHOUSE

Trinity House pilots. Abraham James Hicks was on this occasion at the head of their roster, but he was the second coxswain of the lifeboat and when his fellow-pilots turned to him he declined, on the ground that his duty lay in the boat while she was on life-saving service. Next in line was William Thomas Hicks, always called Billy Cook, and he accepted. A pilot would normally go aboard from alongside, up a rope ladder thrown over the edge of the deck, and that may at first have been contemplated, or even attempted, here, but it rapidly became clear that there was already too much sea for the lifeboat to come hard alongside in safety, so she dropped back into the lee of the schooner's stern. From there Billy Cook went aboard, and the lifeboat then paid out a long warp in order to lie astern as quietly as possible.

There the crew settled down to make as comfortable a stay of it as they could. The pilot arranged for cans of hot coffee and some biscuits to be sent down to them along the warp. They had oilskins and lifejackets on and for further warmth wrapped themselves in the sails in the bottom of the boat. Although the master had rejected their offer of assistance and emphatically asserted his confidence in the safety of his vessel, and although the wind was continuing to rise towards a full gale, making their prospects of a safe return to land increasingly more perilous as time passed, it manifestly never occurred to anyone that they should leave. The possibility is simply not mentioned in any of the accounts by the participants, contemporaneous or later. Whatever the master thought, they had no doubt that the schooner's crew were in danger and might well need their services at any moment; moreover one of their own number was now on board the vessel too.

About an hour after the St Agnes lifeboat had reached the *Lawson* the St Mary's boat arrived. Its crew held the same views as the St Agnes men did about the danger of the schooner's situation and the likely development of the storm, and a later account from their side has them conducting much the same exchanges on those subjects with the master as had occurred when the St Agnes boat arrived. Although that is not mentioned in the contemporaneous evidence something of the kind may well have happened, because it is clear that there was communication between the schooner and the lifeboat, and the St Mary's coxswain is unlikely to have refrained from expressing his concerns.

After a comparatively short stay the St Mary's lifeboat returned to her station in Hugh Town harbour, for two purposes. One was to repair her mast, because in manoeuvring under sail at the schooner's stern her coxswain had come too close under the vessel's huge counter and been dismasted as the lifeboat rose on a wave while the *Lawson's* stern came down. The other was to have a telegram sent, at Captain Dow's request, from Hugh Town to Falmouth asking for tugs. The relation between these two matters is not so clear. The coxswain's report to the coastguards on St Mary's was that he had been asked to return to wire for tugs; that was apparently said without reference to the loss of the mast, simply on the basis that there was no need for both lifeboats to stand by. George Mortimer's evidence at the inquest also gives the impression that the request for a telegram to be sent came before the mishap to the mast. There is, however, the suggestion elsewhere that the need for repairs was already in the air when the request for a telegram was made, and that possibility must be considered further when the master's role comes to be assessed in the round.

It is convenient to tie off those two strands before returning to the main thread of the story. The St Mary's lifeboat returned under oars and mizzen and was back in Hugh Town harbour between 7.30 and 8 pm. The telegram calling for tugs was sent to Falmouth. Later that night Falmouth reported that tugs had left at 10.20 pm, but they never arrived, apparently finding the conditions too fierce. The *Lyonesse*, the steamer which served the Isles of Scilly regularly from the mainland, was also telegraphed for at Penzance, but did not leave port because of the weather. The lifeboat crew worked through the evening and into the night to replace their broken mast. They had the boat seaworthy again by about midnight, but she was not re-launched.

Out in Broad Sound the evening wore on. As the wind continued to rise and veer conditions in the lifeboat, even in the lee of the *Lawson's* great bulk, became ever choppier. At a little before 9 pm a particularly large wave arrived, and a tremendous sea broke over them, filling the lifeboat "up to the gunwales", in Jack's words. The lifeboat was designed to live through such conditions, and in due course the water drained away through the valves, as previous incursions had done, but shortly afterwards the coxswain, checking how his crew had fared, exclaimed, as Jack recalled: "Something has happened here, boys". William Francis Hicks was in the bottom of the boat, unconscious. His crewmates did their best to revive him by shaking him, shouting at him and trying to force brandy down his throat, but to no avail, "he was just like a dead man".

There was a hurried consultation. Clearly something had to be done; or he might indeed die. They shouted up to the schooner for the pilot. Billy Cook came to the stern of the *Lawson* and another key conversation – and in some ways the most fateful of the night – took place. Again Jack gives a verbatim account of it, but again there is other evidence, in particular that at the inquest, and again these different versions need to be compared and discussed in detail later. What is clear is that the conclusion was that the lifeboat was to return to shore with William Francis, but without the pilot or the crew of the schooner, and that a flare would be burned if the *Lawson* later needed assistance.

The lifeboat therefore cast off, set a close-rigged lug, and ran before the wind back into Periglis. It was by now blowing at least a strong gale (force 9). Jack records that the three-inch galvanised tiller, five feet long, was bent from the force needed to hold the boat on course, and that when they landed they were so battered and soaked that his own mother did not recognise him. They took William Francis into one of the nearby cottages and sent to St Mary's for Dr Brushfield. It was 8.30 am before William Francis regained consciousness, but he made a full recovery from his collapse, which at the time was ascribed to a heart attack suffered when the boat was swamped. He never, however, went in the lifeboat again and we must return, later, to the question why he was there on this occasion.

The lifeboat was not at that stage re-launched, but the people of St Agnes, men, women and children, kept watch into the night, many from around the lighthouse. Despite the storm the sky was not continuously overcast; from time to time, indeed, the moon was visible at just after first quarter until it set at 2.11 am. They could see the riding lights of the *Lawson*, as indeed could the coastguards on St Mary's, and when there was moonlight it may even have been that the great bulk of the schooner herself could be made out. From time to time there were squalls of rain which blotted out the lights, but after each squall had passed they reappeared. At about 2.30 am there was another heavy squall, and again the lights disappeared. The gale was now at its height and this time, when visibility cleared, the *Lawson's* lights did not reappear.

No flare had been burned, and some of the watchers seem to have persuaded themselves that the lights had been blown out by the wind or that Captain Dow had slipped his cables and proceeded westward out to the open sea. Others feared, or more than feared, the worst, and for those on St Agnes that was confirmed when, after some time, they began to catch the stench of oil from the spilt cargo. It had by then, however, been concluded that there was nothing they could do until daybreak.

On the *Lawson*, while the anchors held, the very size of the vessel made conditions below deck comparatively sheltered, despite the increasing ferocity of the wind. On deck, the master and the pilot kept watch until the tide turned. High water was due at 11.27 pm, and as the tide set came round and the anchors still held both thought that the worst was over and the schooner was now safe. They went down to the cabin until an ominous change in wind noise and in the rhythm of pitch, roll and yaw brought them back on deck. The port anchor chain was hanging loose and the *Lawson* was dragging her starboard anchor. Captain Dow ordered everyone to put on life jackets "and every man for himself". He himself, the pilot, the mate, the engineer and the steward lashed themselves to the rigging of number 7 mast. Other members of the crew were elsewhere, several on the forecastle head.

The vessel struck broadside on, smashing in the starboard side, but was not aground, and so was repeatedly thrown against the rocks, and within fifteen minutes broke in two between masts 6 and 7. The engineer, Edward Rowe, was next to the pilot, and asked him whether there was any chance of getting ashore. "No", said Billy Cook. As the schooner progressively broke up and the masts collapsed the men, one by one, found themselves in the water, some thrown clear, some jumping, and some entangled in the rigging. Oil was gushing out of the ruptured holds, adding a further peril to those of the waves, the rocks and falling wreckage. Inevitably, most of them perished. But not quite all.

On St Agnes, as day approached, there was discussion about what could best be done to rescue any survivors there might be. That what could be done must be was not in question. The wind had backed to west by south and dropped from storm levels, but was still high (it was recorded as Force 7 when the morning reading was taken at 8 am), and there was a heavy swell running. The search would take them in among the rocks, given where the schooner had struck, which they expected to have been at or near the north-west tip of Annet. The consensus was that in those conditions a gig was better for that sort of work than the lifeboat; it was lighter and handier and drew less water. The best gig on the island for such a job was the *Slippen*. It was decided that at first light she should be manned and launched.

Sunrise that day was not until 8.15. By soon after 7 am, however, the *Slippen* was already in the water. Eight men were needed – six oars, a cox and a bowman. Little is said in the first-hand accounts about how they were chosen; Israel's evidence at the inquest was that "after a little difficulty" they got a crew together. Osbert Hicks was by common consent made cox, as the acknowledged master boatman of the island. Family tradition has it that Osbert's younger son, young Jack, upon whose account of the lifeboat trip we have already drawn, stepped into the gig, but was ordered out again by his father. "Fred and I are going", he said (Fred being an older son). "Whether we come back is in the balance, and your mother is not to be left without a man in the house". It is clear that Frederick Charles Hicks (always called Freddy Cook), the son of the pilot, Billy Cook, insisted on going in the hope of finding his father, although as a young, fit man, already well used to handling boats, he would have had a good claim to a place in any event.

The schooner had struck on Shag Rock, some 250 yards off shore to the west of Annet. The gig's crew managed to get ashore on Annet at about 8 am and found a body and a quantity of wreckage but not, at first, any survivors. They divided into parties to search the island and one party, hearing calls, followed them to find a seaman sheltering beneath a rock. He was George Allen, the only Englishman in the crew, who had taken this chance of a home voyage after five years at sea. He was badly injured and in pain, but wished them to search for three of his shipmates, whom he had seen nearby, he thought still alive, at first light. A further search was made, and two more bodies found, but no-one else alive. George Allen was taken to the *Slippen* and brought back to St Agnes, by now only intermittently conscious. He was taken to Israel Hicks' farmhouse at Lower Town, and Dr Brushfield was brought over in the St Mary's lifeboat to attend him, but he had broken several ribs, and in addition to those injuries and the effects of exposure had swallowed oil, and the doctor did not hold out much hope of his recovery. In the event he survived the next night but died on the following day.

The passage to and from Annet and the search had occupied the whole morning and more, but it was decided to make a further attempt, and the *Slippen* put out again at about 2.30. This time they searched around the Hellweather rocks, to the south of Annet, and there Israel spotted a man who proved to be the schooner's engineer, Edward Rowe. He was on the South Carn, an isolated rock with no landing possible, but they threw him a rope and pulled him through the surf to the gig. He told them that Captain Dow was out of sight on the same rock, but helpless. How he had reached it or got out of the water Rowe did not know, but he had discovered him in the night and had been able to drag him up into a position of comparative safety, above the high-water mark. The engineer himself was badly battered and had swallowed some seawater and oil, but was nevertheless in remarkably good condition for a man who had undergone such an ordeal.

Spurred on by the hope that the master too could be rescued the gig's crew landed Edward Rowe on St Agnes, collected a life jacket from the lifeboat house and some rope, and returned to the scene. High tide had been due at 12.03, so it was by now past half-tide on the ebb, and although the South Carn itself remained inaccessible, just to the east the flatter stretches of The Brow were emerging, a jumble of rocks forming one of the largest continuous expanses of the Hellweathers above water at low tide, some 250 yards by 150. Osbert found a point on the far (inshore) side where he could bring the *Slippen* in without being holed and managed to land four or more men, including Freddy Cook. These men scrambled across the rocks and seaweed to the nearest point to the South Carn, still some 25 yards away across a deep gully. Freddy Cook put on the life jacket, fastened a line round his waist, and set out to swim across, taking another rope's end with him. Somehow he managed to cross the swirling waters and find a footing on the South Carn. Captain Dow was there, where the engineer had left him. He weighed nearly 18 stones, had a fractured arm and broken ribs and was quite unable to move himself unaided. Freddy Cook, who was not a large man, roped him up and managed to get him to the edge of the gully, so that the others could pull them both across. Then, between them, they got him back across the rocks and into the gig. It was nearly dark by the time they set off home to St Agnes.

The *Slippen* had now landed the only three survivors. They were all housed at Lower Town farmhouse that night, and after George Allen unhappily died the next day the other two remained on St Agnes until nursed back to health, Edward Rowe quite quickly and Captain Dow over a longer period. The latter remained in the care of Israel's wife, Charlotte Ellen, but she also had her husband and five children, one sickly, to look after, so her sister, Agnes Hicks, not only helped with the nursing of the master but took the engineer into her own home.

On the day of the *Slippen's* rescues the St Mary's lifeboat, after twice bringing over the doctor to St Agnes, had made an unsuccessful search for other survivors, and on the following day, Sunday, by which time the wind had dropped almost to a calm (Force 1) that lifeboat and several gigs from throughout the islands combed Annet and the rocks again, recovering further bodies, but finding no-one else alive.

Remarkably, there was an inquest on the dead men the day after that, Monday. It was held in Lower Town farmhouse, so that Captain Dow's evidence could be taken at his bedside. In addition to George Allen there were five bodies recovered from the rocks, three identifiable and two not. Much of the earliest evidence now available of the events of the 13th and 14th is to be found in newspaper reports of that inquest.

The President and Congress of the United States of America awarded to Freddy Cook a gold watch and to each other member of the *Slippen's* crew a gold medal "in recognition of his heroic services in effecting the rescue of the captain and two men of the American Schooner Thomas W. Lawson Wrecked off Scilly Islands Eng Dec. 14, 1907". The lifeboats' part in the events of the night does not appear in the official record of either the St Mary's or the St Agnes station; by the stringent criteria of the Royal National Lifeboat Institution they had rendered "no service" to the *Thomas W. Lawson* or her crew. But the RNLI did, nevertheless, award Freddy Cook Hicks its silver medal. Edward Rowe gave Agnes Hicks a gold signet ring.

Those are the bare bones of the story, much of it as it was imprinted in the memory of Israel's son Charles, a boy of ten at the time, and first passed on by him to his own teen-aged son, the present author, thirty or forty years later. But there is much more still to be explained, both about the background (on both sides of the Atlantic) to those events and about the often conflicting evidence of what really happened. And there are many questions to be asked about the decisions made on that eventful night, the reasons behind them and what would have been the outcome had they been different.

· 2 ·

The East Coast Trade

THE STORY TOLD IN CHAPTER ONE brings climactically together a great American sailing vessel and the close-knit community which inhabited a small, remote British island. If we are to capture its full flavour we need some understanding of the history behind each. This chapter describes the sailing tradition into which the *Thomas W Lawson* was launched and of which it was, in its own way, the ultimate incarnation.

To embark upon it requires a brief explanation of vocabulary. Nowadays "ship" is a general word for anything larger than a boat which travels on the surface of the sea, but in the days of sail it had a much more precise, limited, meaning. A ship was a vessel with three or more masts, square-rigged overall (apart, as went without saying, from the jibs). "Square-rigged" means that the sails were approximately rectangular in shape and hung from "yards" – straight horizontal spars slung centrally in front of each mast and, in their neutral position, lying square across the axis of the vessel. In contrast, sails attached at their leading edge to a mast or stay and, in their neutral position, lying aft from that attachment along the vessel's axis, are called "fore-and-aft" sails, and a schooner was a vessel with two or more masts, rigged fore-and-aft overall (for a more precise definition, and for all the technical terms used in the next few paragraphs, see the Glossary in Appendix 1).

Ships and schooners are simply described, but there were also hybrids and variations. A brig was like a ship, but with only two masts. A barque was like a ship, except for fore-and-aft sails on the the aftermost mast (in

The Cutty Sark with sails set. Photograph taken at sea by Captain Woodget with a camera balanced on two of the ship's boats lashed together. © State Library of Victoria.

a three-master called the mizzen). A barquentine was like a ship, except for fore-and-aft sails on two or more of the aftermost masts. A brigantine was like a brig, except for fore-and aft sails on the aftermost mast. A topsail schooner was like a schooner, except for square-rigged topsails on one or more of the foremost masts.

The significance of that visit to old-time sailors' lore is that it is the beginning of an explanation why the *Thomas W Lawson* was a schooner. A sailing vessel is being pushed through the water by its sails, which are in turn being pushed by the wind. The forces developed, particularly those on the masts, are very great, and they would break under the strain if not stayed by rigging. One great advantage of square-rigged sails is that there can be permanent stays running centrally aft from the masts, and therefore carrying the force directly driving the vessel forward; such stays do not interfere in any way with trimming the sails to the wind, whereas a fore-and-aft sail has to cross the centre line every time the vessel tacks or gybes, ruling out any standing rigging in the whole arc described by the boom. Moreover gybing (or wearing ship) is much more troublefree for square-rigged than fore-and-aft sails.

On the other hand square-rigged sails need a wind in a favourable quarter; they are very inefficient when beating against a head wind, at which a fore-and-aft rig is much better. So ships showed to best advantage on the really long-distance routes, where courses could be set in each direction which took advantage of every favourable wind. For example, clippers like the *Cutty Sark* (the apotheosis of the three-masted ship), when engaged in the wool trade between London and Sidney, could circumnavigate the globe, running before the prevailing westerlies for the whole of their passage through the Southern Ocean and having the Trade Winds at worst not much forward of abeam for much of their time in the Atlantic. Where rather more time facing a head wind was likely, or when masts multiplied, barques and barquentines were favoured. Finally, there were some comparatively short "there and back" trades where the prevailing winds were such that one of the legs was normally upwind, and there schooners came into their own.

A prime example of that was the east coast of the United States, where there was a heavy coastwise trade in bulk cargoes such as lumber, coal and (later) ice, stone and lime, and where the prevailing south-westerlies blew parallel to much of the shore line. There is an extensive literature devoted to that trade, and this chapter owes a great deal to two monographs in particular: *New England Coasting Schooners* (Charles S Morgan, in *The American Neptune,* Vol 23 (1963), pp 5–21, and pictorial supplement), and *The Operation and Management of the Great New England Schooners, 1870–1900* (W J Lewis Parker, National Maritime Museum, Greenwich, 1972. pp 17–24). Despite his title, however, Morgan points out that not all the vessels he describes confined themselves to the coastal trade; some alternated successfully between that and long transoceanic voyages.

Small fore-and-aft-rigged vessels had been used in the east coast trade from the time of independence, if not before,[1] and shipbuilding and ship-

....

1   *New England Coasting Schooners* (Charles S Morgan, in *The American Neptune,* Vol 23 (1963),

The three-masted wooden schooner Lavinia Campbell, 738 tons, built 1883.
© *Historic New England*

owning industries grew up to supply and run them, boosted by statutory protection. From 1789 only US-registered vessels could engage in coastal transportation,[2] and from 1817 they also had to be US-built.[3] Until the Civil War (1861–1865) the United States was also a major participant in shipbuilding and shipowning for international trade, but that was an open, unprotected market, and for various reasons the Civil War left America uncompetitive, especially in comparison with Britain, and its deepwater fleet and shipyards collapsed,[4] leaving only the coastal trade. That, by contrast, flourished.

---

pp 5–21, and pictorial supplement), at p.5.

2   Morgan (note 1 above), at p.5.

3   *The Operation and Management of the Great New England Schooners, 1870–1900* (W J Lewis Parker, National Maritime Museum, Greenwich, 1972. pp 17–24), at p.17.

4   Morgan (note 1 above), at p.5, and Parker (note 3 above), at p. 17.

The five masted wooden schooner Cora F Cressy, 2089 net tons. built 1902. Painting by Solon Badger; on display in the Maine Maritime Museum, Bath, Maine

Initially east coast schooners were nearly all two-masters. Apart from a few built for speed during the War of Independence three-masters did not appear on the scene until the late 1820s (for example the *Pocahontas*, 380 tons, in 1827[5]) but from the 1850s they became increasingly prevalent as commercial pressures led to the building of larger and larger vessels. Before 1850 most east coast schooners were of less than 100 registered tons, and very few reached 150 tons.[6] Between 1850 and 1860, however, vessels of more than 300 tons became common.[7] Registered tonnage (which is what we shall always be referring to unless otherwise stated), is a measure of capacity (100 cubic feet per registered ton), not weight, and a schooner might be able to carry something between 140 and 180 (Imperial) tons weight of a bulk cargo such as coal for each 100 registered tons.

From the close of the Civil War the industry resumed its expansion, and the progression in size continued, the largest three-master built in 1870

....

5   Morgan (note 1 above), at p.7.
6   Ibid., at p.7.
7   Ibid., at p.8.

being of 518 tons[8] and the largest ever (the *Bradford C French*, launched in 1884) of 920 tons.[9] By then, however, the difficulty of handling such large sails as were needed had produced two changes.

The first was the introduction of auxiliary power. In 1879 a steam wind-lass was installed on the *Charles A Briggs*, a 758-ton three-master.[10] It hoisted sails, raised the anchor, pumped the bilges and powered derricks to load and discharge cargo. The use of steam power for these purposes spread rapidly among the larger schooners, although manually operated vessels continued to be used as well. In the comparison, earlier, between the relative attractions of square and fore-and-aft rig, the only factor consid-ered was that of performance in relation to wind direction. The advent of auxiliary power, however, greatly enhanced a schooner's already existing advantage in another respect: it could be sailed by a smaller crew than a wholly or partly square-rigged vessel of the same tonnage.

The second change began almost simultaneously. The same year which saw the first use of auxiliary power also saw the laying-down of the keel of the first four-masted schooner, the *William L White* (996 tons), launched in 1880.[11]

Not surprisingly these two changes, continuing growth in trade, and the pressures from economies of scale, led to a further surge in average tonnage. From 1881 vessels got larger year by year and hull by hull. The first 1,000 tonner was launched in 1882[12] and by 1897 four-masters had reached their practical limit of some 2,000 tons, the largest ever being the *Frank A. Palmer* (2,015 tons).[13]

Meanwhile the progression to five-masters had occurred, and after a perhaps premature start, they established themselves as a significant element in the total fleet. The first, the *Governor Ames* (1,764 tons) had been built as early as 1880, contemporaneously with the earliest four-master, but had acquired a reputation as a failure, and it was ten years before there was another.[14] After that, however, their popularity grew

....

8   Morgan (note 1 above), at p.11.
9   Ibid., at p.11.
10   Ibid., at p.10.
11   Ibid., at p.12.
12   Ibid., at p.12.
13   Ibid., at p.13.
14   Ibid., at p.13.

rapidly, and ultimately 56 were built.[15] There is less information in the main sources about their size, but it can be conjectured that many of them were probably between 2,000 and 2,600 tons.

This history of successive increases in the number of masts, to enable larger and larger vessels to be built, inevitably raises the issue whether there were any, and if so what, reasons why that should come to a halt, and when. Perhaps the most obvious first question is whether the ports served by this trade had sufficiently deep berths to take larger vessels. Here the schooners had yet another advantage over square-riggers, in that ton for ton they drew less water, and the number of five-masters built and successfully operated shows that this cannot have been a significant inhibiting factor for them. When the question arose whether to go further, however, it began to have an effect, albeit chiefly an indirect one. It was not so much that schooners of 3,500 tons or so, as the six-masters were,[16] could not find berths, but that in many docks they took the ground at low tide, and since the bottom was never completely level and such vessels were very long, that imposed enormous strains on the hull.[17] That had two consequences. The first was that designers using wood, the material in which, until now, east coast schooners had, almost without exception, been built, had to resort to almost unbelievable expedients to provide keels of sufficient strength: "Six tiers of 15 x 15 timber formed the keelson, with 'sister' keelsons on either side of three or four tiers of similar stuff".[18] The second, of direct relevance to the story of the *T.W. Lawson* (as was indeed the availability of deep berths), was that experiments began in the use of steel.

Another difficulty, perhaps not quite so obvious, but again a matter to which we shall have to return when considering the characteristics of the *Lawson*, was that the continuing increase in the number of masts, and in length, was beginning to imperil what we have seen was one of the main advantages of the schooner rig, namely its superior ability to tack when sailing upwind. The length of a six-master made her very slow to come round into and through the wind, increasing the chance that she would lose all way in the process, and the decreasing proportion of her sail area carried in the jibs reduced their ability to speed the turn.

....

15   Ibid., at p.14.
16   Ibid., at p.14.
17   Ibid., at p.15.
18   Ibid., at p.15.

Despite these obstacles six-masters were built and used profitably – ten in all between 1900 and 1909,[19] and we shall find in the next chapter a claim to the building of the first of them which provides a direct link with the *Lawson* herself.

Much has been written about the building, ownership, cargoes, operating systems and profitability of the New England schooner, but we shall confine ourselves here to a few points particularly relevant to our main interest. As to the place of construction, Maine came to enjoy a very large predominance,[20] its shipyards built most of the largest schooners, and many of more modest size. But its experience was overwhelmingly in timber, and in addition the steel-built *T.W. Lawson* was conceived and financed in Boston, so that contract went to a Massachusetts yard.

As to ownership, nearly all east coast schooners were run individually as separate commercial entities, rather than being units of a shipping fleet. The ownership of vessels of all kinds was by international custom, and in many cases by national law, held in sixty-fourth shares. Construction was financed by the sale of such shares, often to many different investors. The builders themselves often took some. Other owners fell into two categories, the 'dry' owners, who held their shares solely as an investment, and others in shipping-related trades or occupations, such as chandlers and sailmakers, whose shares entitled them to provide services to the vessel at a profit, and in particular the captain[21] himself, who (at least until the late 1890s) was commonly required to take eight shares himself and find owners for another eight.[22] To pick up, again, an aspect of particular relevance to our story, it became fashionable for someone to take a large enough interest to have the privilege of naming the vessel after himself, his wife or his daughter.[23]

Some indication has already been given of the range of bulk cargoes carried at various times. At different periods and for different capacities particular trades might dominate, and for the largest vessels, when the *T.W. Lawson* was built, coal was in that position.

Until not long before then the operating system most widely in use had been a complex affair. Out of the gross earnings of a voyage were paid the

19 Morgan (note 1 above), at p.14.
20 Parker (note 3 above), at p.19.
21 See the Glossary at Appendix 1 for this and all technical terms.
22 Parker (note 3 above), at p.22.
23 Ibid., at p.23.

port charges, and the balance was divided into two halves – the captain's and the 'vessel's'. The captain paid the crew's wages and subsistence and kept the rest of his half. From the 'vessel's' half' came sails, chandlery, towage and any other 'capital' expenditure, before the remaining profit was distributed as a dividend to the owners.[24] That, however, became outmoded for the very largest schooners built in the last phase, the masters[25] of which were more likely to receive a fixed wage plus 5 per cent of the gross earnings, without being liable for any outgoings.

As to profitability, a share in a schooner was clearly a speculative investment. How speculative depended heavily upon whether the hull was insured, which seems from the little we know to have been far from universal – the *T.W. Lawson* herself was not covered, and Parker rather revealingly writes that insurance, "if carried", took 7 per cent on a new vessel, and as much as 12 per cent on the depreciated value of an old one.[26] At those rates the net earnings before insurance had to be well over those figures before any dividend could be of much attraction to owners. The profitability of an uninsured schooner obviously depended heavily on its life-span; the average was in the teens of years, which was long enough to give a good return in most instances, but quite a number were lost much earlier – 23 of the 181 four-masters built before 1900 did not last four years,[27] and if uninsured must have cost their owners a great deal of money.

For at least one schooner we have enough information to do the sums. The *Charles P. Notman* cost a little under $64,500 in 1894. She sank a little more than five years later in collision with a steamer. Her lifetime earnings, including a "settlement" on her loss (it is not specified whether from insurance or from a claim against the steamer), amounted to about $122,500, 190 per cent of that cost.[28] At the time returns seem to have been quantified simply by dividing that figure by the vessel's life, giving 36 per cent, but that cannot be compared with what would nowadays be regarded as the true return on a discounted cash flow basis. Making the simplifying assumptions that the "settlement" was at a depreciated value of 70 per cent of cost, and that the remaining receipts, from freight profits, had been

....

24   Ibid., at p.22.
25   See the Glossary at Appendix 1.
26   Parker (note 3 above), at p.23.
27   Ibid., at p.23.
28   Ibid., at p.23.

earned at a steady rate over the vessel's life, we arrive at a figure of about 20 per cent per annum.

Seagoing sailing vessels all over the world inevitably succumbed in time to the competition of steam. Hardly any new east coast schooners were built between 1909 and 1915, although many of those already afloat struggled on. The first World War produced a belated revival; freight rates rose to levels at which the survivors made a killing and it even became profitable to start building again, so that large numbers of new schooners were built, although the boom was so short-lived that many came off the stocks too late to earn a living.[29] By 1920 the schooner fleet was virtually worthless.[30]

It was a sad ending to a proud tradition. Of many tributes it suffices to quote one: "The great schooner was the last technical achievement of the builders of wooden ships. Notable advances were made in model and rig, but particularly the latter. These made the American great schooner the most weatherly and economical sailing vessel in the world".[31] Although she was atypical in some respects, in others the *Thomas W. Lawson* represents the pinnacle of that tradition, and to her we turn, introduced by one who was, in his own way, another towering figure, her eponymous begetter and financier.

....

29   Morgan (note 1 above), at p.21.
30   Parker (note 3 above), at p.24.
31   *American Maritime Industries* (John Hutchins, Harvard University Press, 1941), as quoted by Morgan (note 1 above), at p.21.

• 3 •

The Man

Thomas William Lawson was born on 16 February 1857 in Charlestown, Massachusetts. His father was a working carpenter. While Tom, as he was commonly called, was little more than a baby the family moved to Cambridgeport, a neighbourhood in Cambridge, Massachusetts, where he grew up,[1] but his father died in the Civil War, leaving him as the only son among four children.[2]

His career began at the age of 12 in an episode often recounted, and no doubt much embellished with repetition. His own account to his daughter Dorothy[3] was that one morning he started off as usual, as if for school, with his books under his arm, but instead walked the four miles into Boston, wanting to help support his family, but also fascinated by the "world of gold". Sitting on a bench outside the old State House, with a view over the harbour, he noticed a sign "Office Boy Wanted" in a bank window opposite. Inside he found a young man shovelling gold coins into scales and then tipping them, in $5,000 lots, into canvas bags. The banker then appeared and said "What can I do for you, little boy", and in a few minutes he was taken on at $3 a week of six eight-hour days. He had difficulties, however, in reconciling that commitment with the fact that he was still supposed

....

1   *The Luck of the Lawsons* (Alton H. Blackington, in *Yankee Yarns*, Dodd, Mead, 1954, pp. 1–30), at p.l.

2   *Thomas W. Lawson – Eccentric Millionaire Stockbroker* (Tom Hall, in *The Scillonian*, No. 254, pp. 137–143) at p. 139.

3   Dorothy Lawson McCall, in *The Copper King's Daughter* (Binfords & Mort [Portland, OR], 1972), at p. 2.

Thomas Lawson at his state office in Boston, Massachusetts, reading stock market prices from the ticker tape. Reproduced with permission, Thomas (Tad) William Lawson McCall Jr.

to be at school, and next week confessed that fact to the banker, who took him home and made what Tom called "a more business-like bargain" with his mother, under which the banker was to see that he had afternoon instruction, so that his education would not be prejudiced.

In another account[4] he was even younger, only 11, and the employers were not bankers but stockbrokers. The latter difference may be more apparent than real, because it was common for financial businesses to use both titles. We are, however, given the name and address of the firm (Amory, Stevens & Co. of 39 State Street), accounts are given of incidents there which concern broking rather than banking, and a stockbroker is

....

4   Blackington (note 1 above), at p. 4.

certainly what Lawson himself became. He began speculating early, making $60,000 by his seventeenth birthday and losing it all again shortly afterwards.[5] He started again, however; by the age of 20 he was probably worth several hundred thousand dollars, by 30 a million and by the year 1900 some 50 million.[6]

At the age of 21 he married.[7] He and Augusta (Jeannie) Goodwillie had gone to school together and he had fallen in love with her. As his daughter tells the story she was a beautiful girl with other admirers, one particularly favoured, and when she came home from Boston each day the two young men would be waiting on opposite corners of the crossing where the trolley stopped.[8] Although it was Tom she usually chose to walk her home she had left his proposal in the air, and his rival was persistent, so one day he delivered an ultimatum: next time, if she crossed to his corner, he would take that as his answer, but if she went to the other side she would never see him again. Next day she walked home on his arm, and the wedding soon followed. They had five children over the next ten years and then a sixth eight years later.

Lawson was a devoted husband and father. He was also becoming a very wealthy man (albeit with vicissitudes, to which we must return). Those two attributes come together in the next story. Dorothy, the youngest of the first five children, remembered a childhood

Jeannie Goodwillie as a girl. Reproduced with permission, Thomas (Tad) William Lawson McCall Jr.

living first in Winchester, eight miles north of Boston, and later in Boston itself.[9] Summers were spent on Cape Cod, in the early days at Duxbury

....

5   Ibid., at p. 7.
6   *Journalistic Advocates and Muckrakers: Three Centuries of Crusading Writers* (Ed Applegate, Jefferson [North Carolina] and McFarland & Company [London], 1997), at p.102.
7   Applegate (note 6 above), at p. 102.
8   McCall (note 3 above), at p.8.
9   Ibid., at pp.8, 35.

and later at Cohasset. As Alton H. Blackington tells it, in *The Luck of the Lawsons*, it was on a drive from Cohasset, along the South Shore, that Tom and Jeannie stopped one day on a hill, in the Scituate neighbourhood some 25 miles south of Boston, with a view over the Otis farm to the shore and the ocean beyond, and Jeannie said: "I wish we could build a house on top of this hill, and have a nice white fence and some rambler roses".[10] Dorothy sets that in 1901,[11] but a later author in 1899.[12]

His wife's wish was Lawson's command, but was transformed in his hands into something altogether grander. He immediately acquired not just that hilltop, but the whole farm and much surrounding land, to form an estate of some 350 acres, on which he built not just any house but a lavishly furnished and decorated mansion of 22 rooms, with two separate guest houses, staff cottages, a windmill, an 800 ft stable and riding hall for his string of up to 100 thoroughbreds, and kennels. There were indeed a white fence and rambler roses, but also, to meet other interests of Jeannie's, a special strain of carnations ($30,000) and a large pipe organ with water-driven bellows ($100,000). The whole complex was developed at breakneck speed, and given the name "Dreamwold".[13] Sadly Jeannie herself died not long afterwards, in 1905.

As a link between the figures in that story and those which will appear as we turn to look, first, into Lawson's financial affairs generally and then, in later chapters, into the economics of the schooner which bore his name, it is worth noting here how the value of the sums referred to compared with sterling at the time and with both currencies now. The U.S. cent had started life as the equivalent of a British halfpenny, at a time when there were 12 pence in each shilling and 20 shillings in the pound, so at 100 cents the dollar was worth 4s.2d. (or 21 new pence). Upon independence the dollar was officially defined in terms which made it worth slightly less in terms of sterling,[14] and since both currencies were linked to gold the exchange rate remained essentially unchanged until the United Kingdom abandoned the gold standard in 1931. During the whole of Lawson's life, therefore, it is sufficiently accurate, in round terms, to treat £1 as worth $5. As to

....

10   Blackington (note 1 above), at p. 8.
11   McCall (note 3 above), at p.53.
12   Hall (note 2 above).
13   Blackington (note 1 above), at pp.8–9.
14   Coinage Act of 1792.

internal values both currencies were, in comparison with modern rates of inflation, comparatively stable until the First World War, and it would be an unnecessary complication to distinguish between dates or to attempt greater accuracy than simply to multiply dollars by about 25 and pounds by about 75 to give current (2014) equivalents.[15] If Blackington is to be believed Jeannie's carnations therefore cost about $750,000 or £450,000 in today's money and her pipe organ $2,500,000 or £1,500,000.

What was the source of all the money lavished on Dreamwold, and elsewhere, and how much was Lawson really worth? As we have seen, he was a stockbroker by occupation, but stockbrokers do not make large fortunes from their commission; his millions came from trading in stocks on his own account. That may have been in whole or part from straightforwardly shrewd or lucky judgments as to future market movements, and other legitimate activities, but in the cutthroat trading world of his day the really big killings were made by market manipulation, for example by ostentatiously buying in large quantities of a stock while feeding the press and market gossip with "news" and rumours of that company's glittering commercial prospects, the two activities, often boosted by fictitious transactions on the trading floor, combining to send the price to stratospheric levels, at which the manipulator sells, leaving the buyers to watch it fall back to its natural level as the "prospects" evaporate, often to their ruin. There is no doubt that Lawson was operating close to the heart of that world, and equally no doubt that he made large sums of money, but there was fierce controversy at the time as to whether or not he was himself one of the deep-dyed villains of the piece, or at least culpably involved with those who were.

The image of himself which he vigorously projected was one of injured innocence. He was a prolific author, and two full-length works of his, in contrasting genres, can be taken as examples of his style and methods. In 1904 and 1905 he wrote for *Everybody's Magazine* a series of articles under the title *Frenzied Finance*, which in 1906 he published as a book of 409 pages, with three lengthy appendices devoted largely to meeting criticisms of the original articles or of his own conduct in the events described.[16] His own account of his motives is contained in an advance advertisement of the series:

....

15   For ease of later reference this passage is reprinted in Appendix 2.
16   *Frenzied Finance – the Crime of Amalgamated* (Thomas W. Lawson, William Heinemann [London], 1906).

27

"I have unwittingly been made the instrument by which thousands upon thousands of investors in America and Europe have been plundered. I wish them to know my position as to the past, that they may acquit me of intentional wrongdoing; as to the present, that they may know that I am doing all in my power to right the wrongs that have been committed; and as to the future, that they may see how I propose to compel restitution".[17]

It is impracticable to include here even a tiny fraction of the wealth of often highly technical detail contained in such a work, but Lawson provided his own summary at the beginning of the first chapter:

"AMALGAMATED COPPER was begotten in 1898, born in 1899, and in the first five years of its existence plundered the public to the extent of over one hundred millions of dollars.

It was a creature of that incubator of trust and corporation frauds, the State of New Jersey, and was organized ostensibly to mine, manufacture, buy, sell, and deal in copper, one of the staples, the necessities, of civilization.

It is a corporation with $155,000,000 capital, 1,550,000 shares of the par value of $100 each.

Its entire stock was sold to the public at an average of $115 per share ($100 to $130), and in 1903 the price had declined to $33 per share.

From its inception it was known as a "Standard Oil" creature, because its birthplace was the National City Bank of New York (the "Standard Oil" bank), and its parents the leading "Standard Oil" lights, Henry H. Rogers, William Rockefeller, and James Stillman.

It has from its birth to present writing been responsible for more hell than any other trust or financial thing since the world began. Because of it the people have sustained incalculable losses and have suffered untold miseries."

His admission of involvement and his self-exculpation follow almost immediately:

....

17 Applegate (note 6 above), at p.103.

> "I laid out the plans upon which Amalgamated was constructed, and, had they been followed, there would have been reared a great financial edifice, immensely profitable, permanently prosperous, one of the world's big institutions."

The central claim, supported by a wealth of complex detail, and accompanied by accounts of a host of introductory and related villainies by supporting characters, was that "the system", embodied in this instance by Rogers, acting on behalf of himself and Rockefeller, and with the connivance of Stillman, had used Lawson as an unwitting "catspaw" to make such an overwhelming success of the flotation of Amalgamated Copper that they had been able, by various fraudulent manoeuvres, to make enormous undisclosed profits, both out of the acquisition of the mines which were the company's underlying assets, and also out of the frenzied trading in the newly issued stock, initially at a large premium and then on a catastrophic slide down to a larger discount. Lawson also claims that he used up all his legitimate earnings from the flotation, and more, in a vain attempt to support the price.

The articles and book attracted enormous attention. They were, of course, highly defamatory of a number of persons, and it is an interesting insight into changing attitudes that a major London house should have been prepared to issue a work which for that reason no modern publisher would touch. Several of those named (although not, apparently, any of the three central characters) sued Lawson, but none successfully.[18]

Lawson's other major book on this theme was, by contrast, a novel, *Friday, the Thirteenth*.[19] The title immediately betrays one of his other notorious characteristics – intense superstition. He never traded on the day of that title, but that was far from being the only manifestation of this trait; the stories of his other superstitious bugbears are legion. There is no room for them here, but the theme will briefly recur when we come to look in more detail at the night of the wreck.

Friday, the Thirteenth is the highly melodramatic story of Bob Brownley, a young stockbroker, who uses all his legitimate trading skills to help a beautiful girl make enough money to rescue her father from potential ruin and disgrace, and wins her love, only to be defeated on the brink of final success,

....

18   Ibid., at p.104.
19   *Friday, the Thirteenth* (Thomas W. Lawson, Doubleday, Page & Company [New York], 1907).

and be himself beggared, by the machinations of "the system". He then resorts to "the system's" own methods and, at the climax of the first half of the book, pulls off an enormous coup at their expense, but at the cost of the sanity of his fiancée, reduced to second childhood by her horror at the suffering he has in the process inflicted on hundreds of innocent investors and traders, and by the suicide of her father, for whom this rescue has come too late. He marries her none the less, and the second half of the book, after recounting his attempts to restore her mental health, interspersed with some further stock exchange incidents, and a good deal of what is clearly Lawson's own analysis of the structural deficiencies which permit such events, culminates in a mirror-image trading climax, Brownley's ruthless triumph on the trading floor now coinciding with news of the recovery of his wife – but when he rushes home to share that joy with her he finds that this time the shock of what he has done has killed her.

The picture of himself painted by Lawson in these and other writings was controverted by his detractors, who charged him with committing the very same sins as those of which he accused "the system". Some of them, for example Denis Donohoe, are in turn counter-attacked by Lawson in one of the appendices to *Frenzied Finance* already mentioned, entitled "The Enemies I have Made".[20] The most extended attack, one in Lawson's own vein, is C.F. King's *The Light of Four Candles*,[21] an autobiographical book of 510 pages, which in somewhat similar detail to *Frenzied Finance* recounts repeated, and ultimately successful, underhand attacks by Lawson on the author's own business, which he describes at one point as "the greatest individual finance house in America".[22] At page 360, having quoted a long advertisement by Lawson, in the form of an open letter to the District Attorney, accusing unnamed persons of defrauding the public of vast sums by manipulating stock prices through fictitious trading, King comments that "the methods [the letter] describes as being pursued are the exact methods used by Lawson himself in his own campaigns".

It is not within the scope or competence of this account to judge exactly where the truth lay, but two matters can perhaps be noted in Lawson's favour. The first is that the title of King's book reflects the fact that it was written from a prison cell, where he was awaiting trial for larceny. Notwithstanding

....

20 Lawson (note 16 above), at p. 493.
21 *The Light of Four Candles* (C.F. King, published by the author [Boston], 1908)
22 Ibid., at p. 8.

its protestations of innocence the book itself recounts how, when his financial empire collapsed, King fled the country, eventually returning after lengthy travels in Europe and Ceylon to be arrested. At the subsequent trial he gave and called no evidence and was in the event convicted on 27 counts.[23] By contrast Lawson was never successfully sued or prosecuted for that kind of wrongdoing (he was, more than once, reduced to near or actual insolvency by his trading debts, but that is on a different moral level).

The second point to note in Lawson's favour is that he features, without any evident irony, as one of the persons who are the subjects, and are characterised by the title, of what seems to have been an independent investigatory work, already cited several times above: *Journalistic Advocates and Muckrakers: Three Centuries of Crusading Writers*,[24] which recounts how he successfully campaigned for investigations into the market practices he criticised, leading first to a New York State enquiry into the life insurance business, later to a Federal committee on stock markets and eventually to the Securities Act of 1933, which established the Securities and Exchange Commission.[25]

Lawson's energies were by no means fully extended by his trading and family interests, intensely as he pursued them. Among other activities he kept and raced a large string of thoroughbreds. Of more direct interest here, however, is his involvement in nautical affairs, which brought him into contact with two persons of central importance to the story of the schooner which bore his name.

The first was Bowdoin B. Crowninshield, who in 1901 designed, and supervised the building for Lawson of the *Independence*, a large,[26] unconventional[27] racing yacht. In October 1900 Sir Thomas Lipton had announced the second of his five challenges to the New York Yacht Club, the holders of the America's Cup, the premier trophy in the sport. Lawson's ambition

....

23 Newspaper cuttings pasted into the present author's copy of *The Light of Four Candles* (note 21 above).
24 Applegate (note 6 above), generally.
25 Ibid., at pp.104/5.
26 Crowninshield, in a letter to Lawson of 7 August 1901 (see note 41 below) describes her as a "ninety footer", and Doug Riggs, in *Keelhauled* (Simon & Schuster, 1986) says that she was "enormous (140 ft)" (p. 59). The former was no doubt a waterline measurement (that being the then America's Cup limit) and the latter perhaps an overall length.
27 In the sources quoted in note 26 above Crowninshield describes her as a "considerable departure" from any previously constructed yacht of her size, and Riggs as a "racing 'scow' with a very flat body, a huge sail spread, [and] a deep fin keel".

was to enter *Independence* as the defender. He failed, for two reasons. The more mundane was that *Independence*, although potentially very fast, did not handle well in match race conditions, and was outclassed in trials by the other contenders, *Columbia* (the eventual, and successful, defender) and *Constitution*.[28] As a Bostonian and non-member of the New York Yacht Club, however, Lawson chose to fasten upon, and ventilate with great publicity, a second reason – his dispute with NYYC as to the terms upon which she could, if chosen, be entered. The Deed of Gift which governed the award of the Cup specified, as he acknowledged in a letter to the NYYC on 25 April 1901, that the defender must be "made the representative of the challenged club", and he professed himself willing to comply with that requirement, but the club then wrote that the vessel "must be qualified to fly the flag of the NYYC" (30 April 1901), which he disputed (1 May 1901), and later that it must either be registered in the name of a member or chartered to a member for not less than two months (10 May 1901).[29] The dispute then reached near-farcical levels of hairsplitting, because it seems that Lawson professed himself willing to meet this requirement if asked by NYYC, but alleged that they refused to ask.[30] The upshot was that in September 1901, just three months after she had been completed at a cost of $200,000,[31] *Independence* was on Lawson's instructions decommissioned and broken up.[32]

Lawson's second important maritime connection, this time not in yacht racing but in the shipping world described in Chapter 2, was with Captain John G. Crowley. There were two Crowley brothers, but Captain Arthur Crowley was still a sea-going ship's master, in which capacity he will play a significant part in the next chapter, whereas John had turned his attention and energies to ship-owning. In 1903 he wrote: "I built the first of my big five-masters, the *John B. Prescott*, in 1899, and the first six-master that was ever floated, the *George W. Wells*, the year before last".[33] When and how Lawson first met him is not recorded, but he also was based in Boston, so they may already have been well known to each other when in 1902

....

28   Riggs (see note 26 above), at p.60.
29   *The Lawson History of the America's Cup*, by Winfield M. Thompson and Thomas W. Lawson (Lawson, 1902).
30   Ibid.
31   Riggs (see note 26 above), at p.174.
32   Thompson and Lawson (note 29 above).
33   *Munsey's Magazine* (February 1903), as quoted by Douglas Lawson in *The Boston Sunday Globe* (11 December 1955).

they, with Captain Arthur, formed the Coastwise Transportation Company, Lawson being the president,[34] with a large financial interest,[35] and Captain John, in Douglas Lawson's words, the "treasurer and operating head"[36] or, as another writer puts it, the "moving spirit".[37]

One of the first tasks of Coastwise Transportation, and perhaps the reason for its incorporation, was to take over a project already in train – the fulfilment of Crowley's ambition to commission and operate the largest schooner afloat. Such a project had an immediate appeal to someone of Lawson's temperament, and although he had no personal expertise in the field his influence is evident at several points. His financial contribution was clearly sufficient to make naming the vessel for him an apparently undisputed acknowledgment. Although in one account Crowley had from the outset decided that she was to be a seven-master[38] another gives Lawson the casting vote and has him vacillating to a late stage between six masts and seven.[39] And, perhaps most importantly, it seems to have been through his connection that Crowninshield was introduced as the designer. His son Douglas describes him as having an "intense admiration" for Crowninshield,[40] and their relationship apparently survived a very fraught correspondence between July and September 1901, during which Crowninshield complained bitterly of exclusion from the management of *Independence* and of an allegation by Lawson's aide, Clapp, that his fees for work in connection with her were "exorbitant", and must be reduced.[41]

The story of the design and construction of the *Thomas W Lawson* belongs to the next chapter, and we must here return briefly to the life of the man whose name she bore. At its height his fortune was said in one source to have made him a "thirty-times millionaire",[42] in another to have amounted

....

34 Douglas Lawson, in *The Boston Sunday Globe* (11 December 1955 and 8 January 1956).
35 According to Blackington (note 1 above), at p.15, he was the largest shareholder. As to his interest in the *Thomas W Lawson* see the next chapter.
36 Lawson (note 34 above).
37 'Ships that made history' (Frank C. Bowen in *Shipbuilding and Shipping Record*, 19 February 1953)
38 'The last Voyage of the Thomas W. Lawson' (Thomas Hornsby in *Nautical Research Journal*, April 1953)
39 Blackington, (note 1 above), at pp.15–16.
40 Lawson (note 34 above).
41 The Crowninshield papers, Phillips Library, Peabody Essex Museum, Salem, Massachusetts.
42 McCall (note 3 above), at p.1

to some $35 million,[43] and in a third to have reached some $50 million.[44] The speculative nature of his business must have entailed some large movements up and down, as during the Amalgamated Copper episode, but his lifestyle remained that of a very rich man for many years. His last years, however, were ones of decline. Given his intense streak of superstition, it is not surprising to find a dramatic story of how that all began:

> "[In 1917] another incident occurred which illustrates the faith Tom Lawson had in his watch, and how helpless he became without it. Lawson had made a statement to the press that, having obtained advance knowledge of what President Woodrow Wilson was going to say to Congress, he had cleaned up in the market. Summoned to appear before an investigating committee to explain the leak, Lawson bumped into Secretary Tumulty, also on his way to the committee room.
>
> Tumulty, glancing at his watch, saw that it had stopped. He called, 'What time is it, Mr. Lawson?' And Lawson, reaching in his pocket, found to his horror that he had forgotten his lucky timepiece; then he recollected having left it on the mantel of the living room at 'Dreamwold'. He was so distracted, friends thought he had suffered a stroke, but he went before the committee nevertheless. The outcome of that hearing, as is well known, dealt a body blow to the Lawson interests. Shaky, perspiring and faltering in his answers, the financier went to pieces and made an extremely poor impression.
>
> From that day, Lawson's power declined. Wall Street ceased to fear him. ... the collapse of the Lawson fortune started that day ..."[45]

In stark contrast to that colourful account Lawson's daughter writes of her father's later years in terms only of declining health, and makes no reference to financial losses.[46] No doubt health did play a part in his business failures, but failures on a massive scale there must have been, because there is no doubt that Dreamwold and virtually all his other assets had to be sold to pay his debts, and that in 1925 he died in poverty, if not insolvent.[47]

....

43　Blackington (note 1 above), at p.10.
44　Applegate (note 6 above), at p.102.
45　Blackington (note 1 above), at pp.16–17.
46　McCall (note 3 above), at pp.179–189.
47　Recorded in many sources, e.g. http://www.swiftpapers.com/biographies/Thomas-William-Lawson-34276.html.

· 4 ·

The Schooner

C HAPTER TWO ENDED with the warning that although the *Thomas W Lawson* was widely regarded, and is very naturally categorised, as the ultimate East Coast schooner she was in some respects a departure from that tradition, and it is an instructive approach to her genesis to ask how and why. An obvious answer to the "how" is that the traditional schooner was wooden, whereas she was built of steel. That was indeed significant, and gave her important advantages, to which we must return, but she was not unique in that respect, and it will be revealing to look first at what may seem a more subtle, or even recondite, difference, namely her lines.

Here the "why" comes first, and is revealed in evidence which Capt. John Crowley gave to a Congressional committee in 1904:

> When we built the *Lawson* two years ago we built her at a cost of $258,000, and fitted her up for foreign business, and at the same time we contracted for the schooner *William L Douglas*, a steel vessel, at a cost of $220,000 … . These vessels were adapted for the foreign trade. We expected at the time to run them in the foreign trade to Manila and those parts, but after we got them built we could not run them, and the only way we can run them today is in the coastwise business.[1]

So the *Lawson* was not, after all, built for the East coast trade, and Crowley was aggrieved at having been forced to use her there. What was his

....

1   Quoted in *Stranger in Truth than in Fiction: The American Seven-Masted Schooners*, by Erik
     A.R. Ronnberg, Jr in *Nautical Research Journal*, Vol. 38, No. 1, March 1993, at p.13.

grievance? That brings us back to another theme introduced in Chapter 2, namely the uncompetitiveness of American shipping in the open market, and the protectionist legislation under which the New England schooners flourished. Although the prohibition on foreign competition was in that chapter discussed by reference to coastal transportation, to which alone it applied when enacted, its precise legislative wording was of course framed more generally, in terms of trade between one part of United States territory and another, and that seemed to open up a new dimension when, having defeated Spain in 1898, the US acquired control of the Philippines. The general expectation was that the Philippines would become US territory, and specifically that American ships trading between them and the US mainland would have the same protection as those in the coastal trade.

It was in that expectation that the *Lawson* and the *Douglas* were "adapted for the foreign trade". By the time the *Lawson* was launched on 17 July 1902, however, basic legislation for the future government of the Philippines had only just been passed,[2] in terms which could not have any effect of assistance to Crowley before 1904, and by the time he gave his evidence that had already receded to 1906.[3]

But meanwhile his expectation had, according to a detailed study of the design progression by Erik A.R. Ronnberg,[4] had a decisive effect on her lines. The first design sketch, dated 28 February 1901, calls, in Ronnberg's words "for a steel version of a very conventional wooden schooner's hull". That soon changed, however. Through a succession of revisions the hull design bore by 15 June what Ronnberg calls "a close resemblance to the large barques and ships of the European grain and nitrate fleets", and in its final form on 12 July made yet further concessions to carrying capacity at the expense of elegance and sharpness of entry. To a layman's eye the most obvious difference between the first sketch and the final design is the steepening and filling out of the bow, but perhaps the most telling as an indicator of the extent to which at this stage attention to the requirements of the East coast trade was being ignored is an increase in depth of 5'2".

Crowninshield's role in all this work is of some interest. He has commonly been criticised as simply not qualified, by training or experience, to undertake the design of a vessel of the *Lawson's* size and construction, and it is

....

2   Philippine Organic Act 1902.
3   Ronnberg, in *Stranger in Truth than in Fiction* (see note 1, above), at p. 15.
4   Ibid., at pp.6–8.

The Thomas W. Lawson under construction, with the designer, B. B. Crowninshield observing (and serving as a standard against which to register the scale of the hull as a whole and of the anchors in particular). Picture courtesy of Tom Hall.

true that his previous work had largely been confined to small racing and cruising yachts, plus a fishing schooner and Lawson's *Independence*. One answer to this is that although she was the first, the *Lawson* was far from being the last large schooner for which Crowninshield was responsible, so the owners whose money was at risk had clearly come to regard him as a safe pair of hands. Another is that this criticism has no weight unless it can be shown that the *Lawson* was in fact faultily designed. But Ronnberg has convincingly demonstrated that the drawings were supported by a mass of detailed tables, graphs and calculations, predicting the vessel's reaction to a wide range of loading and sailing conditions.[5] The care and thoroughness with which they were prepared suggest the work of a conscientious

....

5   Ibid., at p.8.

The Thomas W Lawson under sail, apparently in ballast, given the great height of hull above water, and said to be on her maiden voyage. © Historic New England

and competent professional, fully equal to the task in hand. At least part of the explanation, Ronnberg suggests, is that by this time Crowninshield's practice had reached the stage at which he could be largely what would nowadays be called a "front" and "ideas" man, employing others to do the detailed drawing and calculations. Most of the *Lawson* drawings are in fact initialled by "R.C.S.", identified by Ronnberg as Robert Coffin Simpson, who had obtained a degree in naval architecture and marine engineering in 1900 and whose subsequent career evidences a sound, if unshowy, mastery of his craft.[6] It appears from Crowninshield's books of account that Simpson was in fact what we should nowadays call a free-lance, albeit engaged full-time

....

6   Ronnberg (note 3 above), at p.10.

on Crowninshield's work; he is charged a rent and the expenses incurred on his behalf and credited with commission earned.[7]

Given that as built she had the lines of a large barque and was intended for the Manila trade, which might have been thought typical square-rigger territory, why did the *Lawson* remain a schooner? Part of the answer, no doubt, was that schooners were what the Crowleys knew how to build and run. Part, no doubt, was that both John Crowley and Lawson wanted the glory of being associated with the first seven-master ever built – a ship or barque on the same hull would (judging by the handful of such vessels of comparable tonnage with the *Lawson*) have had fewer masts. Part may have been Crowninshield's lack of experience of anything other than fore-and-afters, although had that been the only consideration he could if necessary have been jettisoned.

Ronnberg, however, makes the very interesting observation that many West coast schooners could and did make transpacific trading voyages, albeit with a rig adapted to the conditions, to the extent of including either a square running foresail or square topsails on two or more masts.[8] That suggests the possibility that the retention of a basically schooner configuration was not just a matter of habit, desire for publicity or inexperience, but involved also an informed and hard-headed assessment of its potential, if suitably modified. It is, however, in the absence of evidence, only a possibility, and against it must be set the fact that no such modification was made or, so far as we know, contemplated, when the decision was made to commit her to an Atlantic crossing in 1907, although that did involve restoring the topmasts and topsails which had earlier been discarded, so there could have been a change of rig without too much disruption or extra expense.

As already noted the other way in which the *Lawson* was atypical of East coast schooners, although in this instance not unique, was her construction. Chapter 2 included a description of the lengths to which designers of wooden six-masters had to go in increasing the dimensions of the keel and its reinforcements in order to obtain anything like adequate stiffness. That, and other features of wooden vessels of that size, not only reduced alarmingly the overall volume available for cargo, but also made the shape

....

7   The Crowninshield Papers, Peabody Essex Museum, Salem, Mass.
8   Ronnberg (note 3 above), at pp.36–37.

The Thomas W Lawson, apparently beginning to tack, given the alignment of the sails and the angle of the wake. © Historic New England

of the hold much more complex, and therefore less convenient for loading, packing and unloading. A steel schooner of the same tonnage was not only stronger and stiffer, but also had a hold in the shape of a large, simple, unobstructed box. It was a little more expensive to build than a comparable wooden vessel, but more than compensated for that in speed of construction, greater and more efficient carrying capacity, and lower maintenance costs.

As we have seen, the design period lasted from 28 February to 12 July 1901, but on 25 June the contract for building the vessel had already been signed by the Fore River Ship & Engine Company of Quincy, Massachusetts, some 15 miles south of Boston, a yard specialising in steel construction,[9]

....

9   Ronnberg (note 3 above), at p.17.

The Thomas W Lawson, deeply laden, in Boston harbour, 1906 or 1907. No photograph of her fully laden under sail has been found, but even moored the contrast in hull profile with the two preceding photographs is marked.

and the keel seems to have been laid very soon after that.[10] The Fore River company prided itself on the speed and quality of its steelwork. The plates were riveted, not welded, and the rivet holes were matched by meticulous adherence to the drawings, not by "offering up" and marking.[11] Progress was uninterrupted, and she was launched on 12 July 1902 and commissioned, ready for sailing trials, on 8 September.

The statistics of the *Lawson's* dimensions and capacity are impressive, although her notoriety is such that they appear in a multitude of sources and with almost as many variations. The one certain fact is that her registered tonnage was 5,218 gross, 4,914 net. Her maximum deadweight tonnage, or carrying capacity, is variously put at between 8,000 and 11,000 (U.S.) tons (the latter probably an exaggeration).[12] Her length and beam also

....

10   Thomas Hall, in *The T.W. Lawson: the fate of the world's only seven-masted schooner* (Orchid Hill Publishing, St John, U.S.V.I., 2002) at p.24.

11   Ronnberg (note 3 above), at p.17.

12   The American, or "short" ton is 2,000 lb, so the equivalent range in Imperial or "long" tons of 2,240 lb would be approximately 7,000 to 10,000 The metric tonne of 1,000 kg is, at 2,205 lb, so close to the long ton that at these tolerances it can take the same values. Because it is often uncertain which ton is meant metric equivalents are not usually given in subsequent references to weight by tons, but if they are known or assumed to be short tons the multiplier is about 0.9, while if they are known or assumed to be long tons no adjustment is necessary.

vary in different accounts. One puts the length at 375'6", but that seems to be a mistake, since the others cluster closer together at 395'0", 395'4" and 404'3" (120m to 122m). The beam is usually given as 50'0" (15.2m), but in one source as 49'3". According to Ronnberg her depth, as built, was 35'2" (10.7m).[13] She had a double bottom, or second skin, 4' (1.22m) inside the outer hull plates.

Those were the dimensions of her hull. To them must be added the principal spars. There was a steel bowsprit, 85' (26m) long. The lower masts were also of steel, 135' (41m) in length (of which 20' (6.1m) was below deck), all stepped before launch. Most sources have them all of 32" (81cm) diameter, but Crowninshield himself says the foremast was 33" (84cm) and the others 30" (76cm).[14] Above them rose the topmasts, of Oregon pine, all (except the foretopmast, which was some 7' (2.1M) longer), 58' (18M) long, tapering from 18" (46cm) to 10" (25cm).[15] Allowing for the overlap that gave a total height of 175' (53m) to 182' (55m) from step to truck, of which 155' to 162' would therefore have been above deck. She was gaff rigged, and the booms and gaffs were also of Oregon pine, the booms being 45' (14m) long except for the spanker,[16] which was 75' (23m). Her overall length from the tip of the bowsprit to that of the housed spanker boom was some 500' (152m). Set lengthwise in a large football stadium (Association, Rugby or American), her hull would have overlapped the playing area by 50' (15m) or so at each end and her bowsprit and boom would have extended well out over the stands.

To drive the schooner there was a sail area of over 43,000 square feet (4,000m²). The sails were made of the best and heaviest sailcloth, weighing some 18 tons in all.

Then there was her machinery and equipment. Although propulsion was entirely by sail the *Lawson* was in other respects highly mechanised. The steam-powered machinery was installed before the vessel was launched,

....

13   Ronnberg (note 3 above), at p.13.

14   B.B. Crowninshield in *Fore-and-Afters* (Houghton Mifflin Company, Boston, 1940) at pp 54, 55.

15   Frank C. Bowen in *Ships that made history, No. 172*, published in the *Shipbuilding and Shipping Record*, February 19, 1953, at p. 248.

16   Much of the space in what has been published about the *Lawson* is occupied by an inconclusive, and sometimes fanciful, debate about what her masts were called, which does not merit attention here. Where it is necessary to refer to individual masts they are identified simply by number or in accordance with the names used by her first master, Captain Arthur Crowley: fore, main, mizzen, 4, 5, 6 and spanker.

the boilers and main hoisting engines being housed in two engine rooms on deck, one fore and one aft. The winches there raised and lowered the gaff (lower) sails, the forestaysail and the jibs. Other winches, on the open deck, handled the lighter topsails and topmast staysails or, in port, the cargo, and there was a windlass under the foredeck for the two 10,000-lb (4,500kg) stockless anchors. Steam power also worked the pumps, capable of shifting six tons of water per minute. The steering was also mechanically powered, and there was electric lighting throughout, a telephone system and steam heating to the crew's quarters.[17]

We have already seen that construction cost $258,000 and that Thomas W. Lawson was a major financier, but again there are variations in the sources as to the exact extent of his involvement. Lawson himself wrote an "epitaph for his lost namesake" in the *Boston Sunday Post* of 15 December 1907 in which he described himself simply as "the largest owner", but elsewhere in the same edition he is quoted as saying to a reporter, more specifically, that he had $110,000 invested in her. The *New York Times* and the *Philadelphia Public Ledger* of the same date, using what looks like a common informant, both put his loss at, or near, $150,000. The papers differ also as to the form of his investment, the *Boston Sunday Post* describing it as stock in the Coastwise Transportation Company, while the *New York Times* and the *Philadelphia Public Ledger* have him and his family owning shares in the vessel herself. The former seems clearly to be the correct version, because when particulars of ownership had to be listed so that the *Lawson* could be registered for the foreign trade in November 1907 the Coastwise Transportation Company is recorded as owning 61/64.[18]

Ownership of the remaining 3/64 probably varied over time. A contract dated 10 December 1901, arising out of the dissolution on 20 September 1901 of a partnership between Crowninshield and one Frank N. Tandy, records that the commission for the design and construction of "the seven-masted schooner for Captain John O. Crowley" is to be in part payment for a 1/64 share in the vessel, the balance being paid by Crowninshield, and that the share is to be his personal property.[19] The presence of the

....

17 *Mechanical Equipment of a Seven-Masted Schooner*, in *Marine Engineering*, November 1902, pp.560–565.

18 *The Last Voyage of the Thomas W Lawson* (Thomas Hornsby, in *Nautical Research Journal*, April 1953, at p. 58.

19 The Crowninshield Papers (note 7 above).

designer among the initial owners is within the tradition, described in chapter 2, of participation by persons in shipping-related occupations, but by 1907 connections of that kind seem to have disappeared, so individual shares or half-shares were probably just being traded as investments. The *Philadelphia Public Ledger* report cited above states that "the *Lawson*, while owned principally in New England, had several shareholders in this city", whom it names, including the vessel's Philadelphia agent, but that was either baseless rumour or out of date, since the recorded particulars listed in November 1907 show just four private persons as the minority share-holders, two owning 1/128 each, both from Massachusetts, and two 1/64 each, one from Maryland and one from Chicago.[20]

One important dimension, namely draught, was omitted from the list given earlier in this chapter and has been postponed until now, in part because it is not fixed, but varies with loading, and in part for the connected reason that in the case of the *Lawson* it cannot sensibly be discussed except in conjunction with the subjects of ballast and handling. The primary provi-sion for ballast was the 4' double bottom already described, which with the addition of fore and aft peak tanks held just over 1,000 tons of water; with that ballast she drew 12' (3.7m).[21] By contrast, when fully laden, her draught is variously described as (among other figures) 25'6", 27'3", 28'6½" and 29'10" (from 7.8m to 9.1m). Draught varies, of course, with the temperature and salinity of the supporting water, but the main reason for this range of values is undoubtedly how "fully" the vessel was laden. The two last, and largest, figures cited above do come from sources which give draught and cargo tonnage together. The 28'6½" is an average of 28'3" forward and 28'10" aft on 29 May 2005, when "the Lawson came in with 8,018 long tons of coal",[22] while Crowninshield himself states that "when fully loaded with the 9,200 tons of coal that she once carried to Boston she drew 29'10".[23] The "once" plainly implies that that was exceptional, so the 11,000 tons claimed elsewhere[24] seems unreliable, even if it is in short tons and Crowninshield is (as he probably was) using long tons.

The great depth drawn fully laden, and the width of the gap between

....

20   Hornsby (note 18 above), at p. 58.
21   Bowen (note 15 above), at p. 248.
22   Ronnberg (note 3 above), at p.19.
23   Crowninshield (note 14 above), at pp 54, 55.
24   Undated extract from *American Neptune*, supplied by Mr Colin Mumford.

that and the draught in ballast, had two important consequences. As to the former, we have already noted the extent to which the *Lawson's* design generally, and this aspect in particular, were influenced by the intention to "run [her] in the foreign trade to Manila and those parts". Although she carried on an active and profitable trade between the main East coast ports during her early working years she must clearly in many of their berths and approaches have been working at the extreme limit of availability, and it seems likely that her draught must have excluded her from some which she would otherwise have served, or forced her to work at less than full capacity if she was to visit them.

As to the difference of 13 to 18 feet (4m to 5.5m) between draught in ballast and fully laden, one of the most striking features of contemporary comments on the *Lawson's* handling is the violence of the contrast between those which praise her to the skies and those which haven't a good word to say. They might as well be talking about two different vessels. And the truth is that, in an important sense, they are. As those who knew her best make clear, her performance unladen bore little or no relationship to that with a full cargo. When light she presented to the wind an enormous area of flat, vertical side and below the surface a fairly shallow and rounded profile offering less resistance to leeward drift than when deeper in the water. It is understandable that commentators who knew her best in that mode, or chose to centre their attention on it, described her as "like a beached whale" and "at best a slow sailor",[25] or "extremely unhandy" and "a brute to handle".[26]

What she was designed for, however, was to carry a full cargo, and in that mode she came into her own. Crowninshield himself wrote that "[w]hen loaded she handled like a yacht, in fact much better than some yachts",[27] and Dow, her last master, said that she could be easily handled.[28] Axel Larsen, who served as her second or first officer on several voyages, described her as "the most comfortable ship on the coast" and, in comments echoed by others, as "nearly always dry on her deck" and very fast: "In her career as a coal carrier, when she was loaded and we had a good stiff breeze, she would pass anything afloat, and it used to amuse us to see a steamer ahead, and

....

25   Ibid.
26   Bowen (note 15 above), at p. 248.
27   Crowninshield (note 14 above), at pp 54, 55.
28   Quoted by Ronnberg (note 3 above), at p. 41.

she would always pass her."[29] A Wikipedia entry gives her "speed" (presumably meaning top speed) as 16 knots.

Even at her best, however, she could not entirely escape one consequence of her enormous length and comparatively narrow beam. We noted in chapter 2 that by the time the progression in schooner size reached the era of six-masters difficulties in tacking were beginning to reach worrisome levels, and explained why that should be so. The *Lawson*, not surprisingly, displayed those difficulties to a high degree. Larsen, indeed, states flatly that "it was impossible to tack ship",[30] although that seems to be an exaggeration, not borne out by other accounts. Crowninshield, in particular, gives a circumstantial and convincing first-hand description of how on her first trip, with no cargo, in a light breeze, she successfully tacked (although it took ten minutes), but the next morning, in an even lighter air, she "simply would not do it", and had to wear around, losing almost half a mile dead to leeward.[31]

In references to the *Lawson* much is, of course, made of the special place in marine history which she occupies by virtue of her sheer size, and various claims to primacy have been made, The basic facts of her dimensions have been given above, but has she any rivals for a place in the record books? Our first mention of her in chapter 1 described her as "the largest fore-and-aft rigged sailing vessel of all time", and measuring size in the usually accepted way by registered tonnage that is incontestably true, but is it all that can be said?

At the time the *Lawson* was lost her closest rival in this respect was the *Preussen*. She was the largest full-rigged ship ever built, and the only one with five masts. Built in 1902, she sailed in the nitrate trade until run down by a steamer in 1910. In some respects she has claims to surpass the *Lawson*. She was longer and wider and had a greater sail area. Moreover she had no auxiliary engine. But in the crucial measure of registered tonnage she fell short – 5,081 against the *Lawson*'s 5,218.[32] And as we have noted the *Lawson*'s engines played no part in her propulsion. So, despite the *Preussen*, it can truly be said of the *Lawson* that during her life she was the largest vessel propelled purely by sail that was, or ever had been, afloat.

The vessel which requires the qualification "during her life" in the last

....

29   Ronnberg (note 3 above), at p. 41.
30   Ibid., at p. 41.
31   Crowninshield (note 14 above), at pp 54, 55.
32   Sailing Ships website.

sentence is the *France II*. A five-masted barque, built in 1911, and working until she drifted aground and was abandoned in 1922, she had a registered tonnage of 5,633, and was therefore larger than the *Lawson*. In the context of record claims, however, there is the curiosity that she was built with auxiliary diesel propulsion, but had her engines removed in 1919.[33] It was therefore only in the last four years of her life that she deprived the *Lawson* of the ultimate crown, and despite that it is still true that the *Lawson* remains the largest vessel ever built which, throughout her life, had no means of self-propulsion other than sail. It is tempting to add "and will probably always remain so", but the modern enthusiasm for recreational replicas has already produced, in the *Royal Clipper*, something very close to the *Preussen* in size and sail plan,[34] so it may be unwise to make such predictions.

As a tailpiece to those reflections it is instructive to compare the size of these giants of over 5,000 registered tons with that of the clippers which inform most persons' image of the classic sailing vessel – three-masted ships like the *Ariel* (853 tons), *Taiping* (767 tons) and *Cutty Sark* (963 tons). But what is perhaps even more unexpected is their relative hull shapes. The clippers are thought of as the greyhounds of the deep, but of those three (perhaps the most famous) only the *Cutty Sark* compares in length/beam ratio (7.8/1) with the *Lawson* (7.9/1), the *Preussen* (7.6/1) and the *France II* (7.3/1).[35] The *Ariel* (5.8/1) and the *Taiping* (5.9/1) look surprisingly broad-beamed in comparison.

Another interesting comparison, this time between the *Lawson* and large vessels of competing types – ships and barques like the *Preussen* and *France II*, and steamers – concerns crew size, already mentioned as one of the advantages of the schooner design, especially when incorporating auxiliary engine power for sail handling. On her last voyage the *Lawson* had what was for a long haul a quite usual crew of 18, comprising master, first and second mate, engineer, two firemen, ten seamen, steward and cabin boy.[36] For shorter coastwise runs under sail 16 sufficed.[37] By way of contrast the *France II* required a crew of 47 and even the much smaller *Cutty Sark* one of about

....

33 Ibid.
34 Star Clipper website.
35 Sailing Ships website.
36 *New York Times,* 15 December 1907.
37 Bowen (note 15 above), at p. 248.

The east and gulf coasts of the USA, from Port Arthur to Philadelphia. © DM Solutions Group Inc., Millennium House, Open Street Map and Open Street Map Contributors

Philadelphia

Charleston

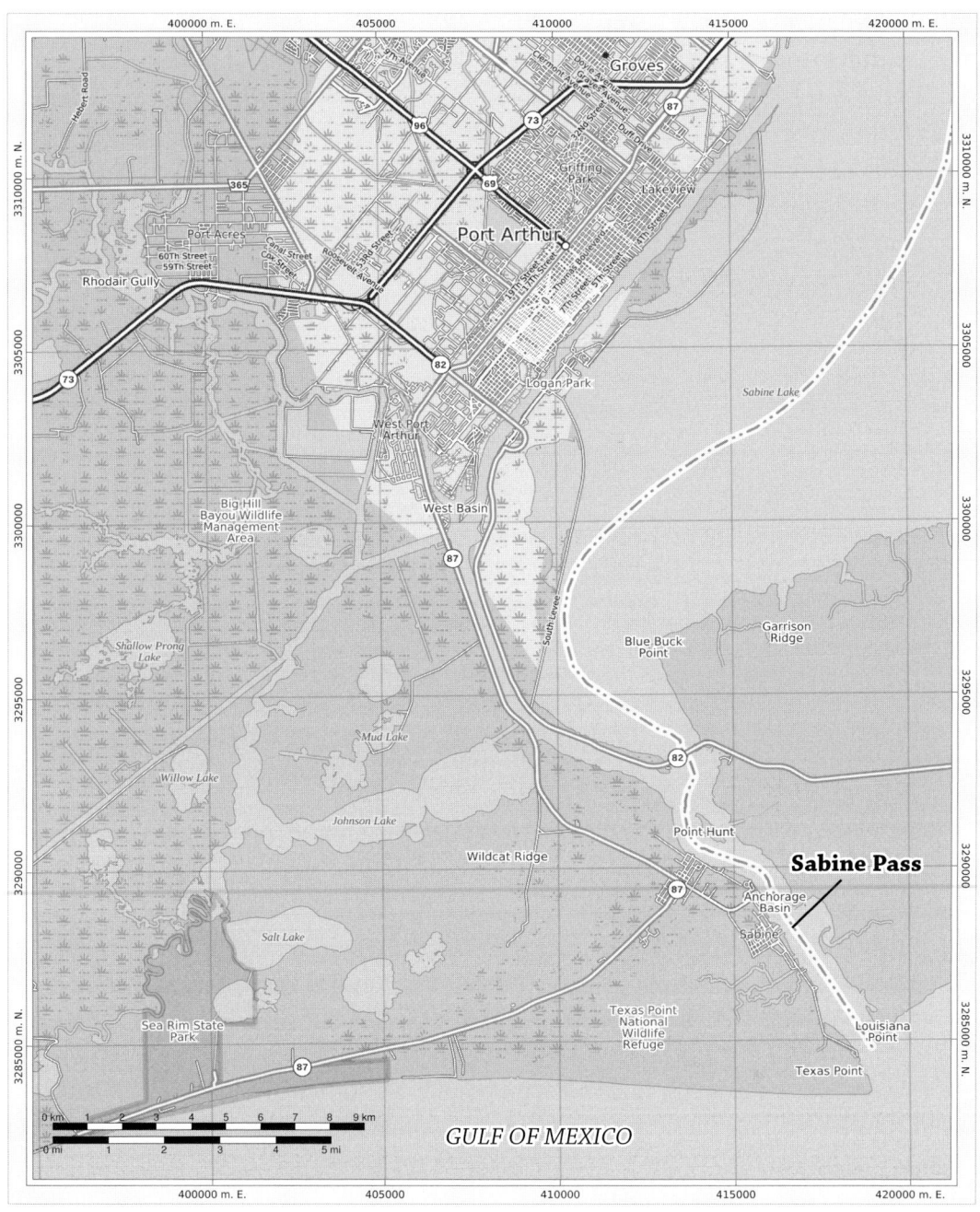

Port Arthur and Sabine Pass © DM Solutions Group Inc., Millennium House, Open Street
Map and Open Street Map Contributors

26,[38] while steamers of a comparable size would have had crews of 35 to 50.[39]

That leads naturally into a consideration of the *Lawson's* profitability. As Ronnberg points out, there are no primary records specific to this vessel, although the annual reports of Coastwise Transportation show that the company as a whole was thriving up to 1907.[40] There are, however, a number of assertions in the literature which, although unsourced, are sufficiently consistent to paint a reasonably persuasive picture. They range from the very general "phenomenal profits [in the oil trade]",[41] through "dividends of 66 per cent of her cost in her first three years of operation",[42] and "capable of yielding a return of about $75,000 a year"[43] to the most specific, that at the time of her loss she was "under charter which brought her owners a return of $78,000".[44] The last two figures are very close. Since her cost was, as we have seen, some $258,000, the one before that equates to an average of nearly $57,000 per annum, and although that is somewhat lower we shall see that there may be reasons why the first years were the leanest.

It remains to describe in outline the *Lawson's* trading activities from the outset until the preparations for her final voyage. There are two certainties about those activities. The first is that for a period after her working life began she was wholly, or almost wholly, engaged in the coastwise coal-carrying trade, much of it from the Chesapeake and Delaware ports to Boston, and that her master during at least the earlier part of that period was Captain Arthur Crowley.[45] The second certainty is that in 1906 she was converted into an oil tanker by the Newport News Shipbuilding Co, wooden bulkheads being built into her hold to divide it into a series of fourteen tanks, and that thereafter she worked exclusively as such, for the most part under tow, and wholly or mainly between Port Arthur, Texas and Marcus Hook, Pennsylvania.[46] The Wikipedia entry for the *Lawson* adds the fascinating detail that the (hollow) steel masts were adapted to use as vents for the oil gasses.

The reason for the transition from coal-carrying to the oil trade is also

....

38   www.cuttysark.org.uk.
39   *Shipwrecks of the Isles of Scilly* (Richard Larn, Thomas & Lochar, 1993), at p. 56.
40   Ronnberg (note 3 above), at p. 27.
41   *The Fate of the World's Largest Schooner* (R. Barry O'Brien, September 1953).
42   *The Thomas W Lawson – the first or last of the great sailing bulk carriers* (anon).
43   Hornsby (note 18 above), at p.56.
44   *New York Times* and *The Philadelphia Enquirer,* 15 December 1907.
45   Hornsby (note 18 above), at p.56.
46   Ibid.,at p.56.

plain. Freight rates for coal were dropping and oil was rapidly growing in importance. Crowninshield describes how "coal rates had dropped below sixty cents and long waits at both ends became the rule".[47] What is less clear is when, and in what stages, the change occurred. Many accounts simply take it for granted that there was just one clean break, marked by the conversion in 1906. It seems likely, however, that in truth the *Lawson* had moved from coal to oil before then, albeit that until her conversion the oil would have had to be carried as "case oil", in casks, drums or other containers. There are, however, widely different versions of the date of that change. The Wikipedia entry puts it only a year after her commissioning, in 1903, when "Crowley withdrew her from the coal trade" and "had the topmasts, gaff booms and all other wooden spars removed and ... chartered her out as a sea-going barge for the transportation of case oil". The *New York Times* of 15 December 1907 sets it later: "For three years ... she was used steadily in the coastwise soft coal trade", but then "was leased ... two years ago to the Sun Oil Company". The word "leased" implies a time charter, which other sources put at five years.

The *New York Times* account, being almost contemporary, seems the more reliable, and the later date (also spoken to elsewhere) the more likely. Moreover, although other sources confirm the removal of the topmasts there must be more doubt over whether the *Lawson* was ever made completely unsailable, which would have been the case had "all [her] wooden spars" gone. Certainly in April 1907 she was far from being a mere "sea-going barge", as we shall see in a moment, but whether that was because she never had been or because her sailing ability was restored in the 1906 conversion is less clear, as is the question whether her topmasts were rerigged as part of that conversion or after the decision had been made to cross the Atlantic.[48]

In the early spring of 1907, therefore, we have a picture of the great schooner's settling into a comfortable and profitable, but distinctly unglamorous, middle-aged routine, on a long-term time charter to a major oil company, and spending her time, usually under tow, carrying bulk oil from the charterer's Texan outlet at Sabine Pass, Port Arthur, deep in the Gulf of Mexico, out past New Orleans, round the Florida Keys, up the Atlantic seaboard, into Delaware Bay and up the Delaware River to the refineries at

....

47   Crowninshield (note 14 above), at pp 54, 55.
48   The *Nautical Gazette* of 19 December 1907, at p. 405, simply says it was done "recently".

Marcus Hook, Pennsylvania, on the South-West edge of Philadelphia. Her next run in that trade, however, was far from routine, and the story of it also serves to explain the presence of Edward Rowe as her engineer at the time of her loss .

It is a story which begins when she was being loaded at Sabine Pass in March 1907. According to reports in the files of Atlantic Mutual Insurance she listed so badly that it was necessary to discharge her cargo, after which she was surveyed, and the offending bulkheads were to be caulked before she resumed loading.

Rowe's account is much more dramatic, and gives him a central role.[49] The vessel had, he says, capsized, rolling over on her port beam ends and completely blocking the channel, with ten steamers upstream unable to get out and nothing able to get in. He was summoned to the scene by Arthur Crowley, which suggests that he was already employed by Coastwise Transportation, although he does not say so. He concluded that the cause was that what he called six "giant valves", now under water, had wrongly been left closed, and set about opening them, after which the schooner began to right herself. "An hour later everyone could see that the *Lawson's* masts were coming upright, and within a short time the schooner was erect. Although the capsizing had strained and ruined her wooden 12" x 12" bulkheads it was decided to continue with her loading and sail for Philadelphia." Rowe was appointed chief engineer.

The voyage began, as planned, under tow, the tug being the large and powerful *Paul Jones*, but on 1 April, off Cape Canaveral, "a hurricane hit, and the tow line eventually had to be cut. The crew ... broke out their storm sails and were able to reach Delaware Breakwater, while the *Paul Jones*, terribly battered, staggered into the harbor of Charleston, S.C.",[50] The significance of the two points of arrival is that the tug had to make for the nearest port with adequate repairing facilities, whereas the *Lawson* was evidently able to continue unassisted over some days, under sail, effectively to her intended destination, without any recorded damage beyond that already suffered from her capsize at Sabine Pass, as recorded sightings on 6, 7 and 9 April testify.[51]

....

49   *Boston Herald*, 9 January 1972.
50   *Boston Herald*, 9 January 1972. The arrival of the *Paul Jones* in Charleston on 3 April is
       recorded in *Lloyd's List*.
51   *Lloyd's List*; Atlantic Mutual Insurance archives.

• 5 •

Setting Sail

J UST AS ONE CHANGE in freight rates had driven the *Lawson's* move from coal to oil, so another induced the decision to send her across the Atlantic, but this time the spur was not a fall in her earnings. Indeed, Captain Arthur Crowley is quoted by Lawson's son Douglas as saying, in the latter's words, that the schooner "had been so successful operating coastwise that he broke with his brother and my father when they determined to put her in the overseas trade".[1] This time the motive was the lure of exceptionally high earnings elsewhere. The newspaper report of the impending voyage has no doubts about that: "Freight rates to Europe are almost prohibitive now, especially for tankers, owing to a war going on between the Standard Oil Company and Russian interests for control of tank steamships. As a result of this struggle ... freight rates have increased from 35 to 45 shillings (£1.75 to £2.25). Owners of tank steamships are reaping a harvest at the premium rates offered for their vessels".[2] Making every proper allowance for the difference in length of haul (a factor of perhaps between seven and nine), the contrast between those figures and the 60 cents (2s.6d., or 12.5 new pence) which had driven the *Lawson* out of the coal trade is stark.

But who made the decision? Arthur Crowley, in the quotation above, attributed it to his brother John and Lawson, as the moving spirits of the owners, Coastwise Transportation. But we have already seen that by now

....

1   *The Boston Sunday Globe* 8 January 1956.
2   *Philadelphia Public Ledger* 14 November 1907.

the schooner was under charter to Sun Oil, and the newspaper article last quoted treats the decision as theirs.[3] Both may well be correct, in the sense that while it was for the charterers to take the initiative, and it was they who would initially receive the vessel's earnings, the conditions of the charter may well have required the owners' consent to such a change, while higher rates may have yielded a benefit to them as well, either under the terms of the charter itself or by way of an inducement offered for their consent to going "off-route".

Several accounts of the final voyage speak of the *Lawson's* being on charter, not to Sun Oil but to Standard Oil or its subsidiary Anglo-American Oil Company, but here again that may well be no contradiction; a time charterer like Sun might well have had power, at least with the owners' consent, to "sub-let" by voyage charter and Standard Oil, involved in the struggle for transatlantic capacity described above, was not only an obvious customer, but one which when contracting for a tanker's full capacity would probably expect to do so by way of charterparty rather than bill of lading.

Having at some point lost her topmasts, and having functioned largely under tow for some time, the *Lawson* clearly needed to be brought back into full sailing order, topsails included, and all accounts of her final voyage take that result as read, but there is surprisingly little material about when and where it was achieved. Two accounts which claim some precision are late, unsourced and contradictory. The Wikipedia entry for the *Lawson* states that in the 1906 conversion to a tanker she was "retrofitted for sail", whereas O'Brien's account is plainly consistent only with its having happened after the decision to go overseas had been made: "Her charterers ... suddenly conceived the idea ... of rerigging her completely and sending her across the Atlantic ...".[4] The only contemporary reference (in the *Nautical Gazette,* 19 December 1907) is vaguer: "Recently her topmasts were set up again, and the Sun Co. started her across the Atlantic ...", but tends to support the later date.

The cargo was, of course, oil, and since the vessel had in 1906 been converted into a tanker it might be thought obvious that the oil would be carried in bulk, but there have been persistent assertions in the literature

....

3   *Philadelphia Public Ledger* 8 January 1956.
4   *The Fate of the World's Largest Schooner* (R. Barry O'Brien, September 1953).

that it was "case oil"[5] or "in barrels",[6] Moreover there is also a local tradition in the Isles of Scilly that the oil was in wooden barrels, many of which were salvaged by islanders and cut down for use as planters, and the Isles of Scilly Museum at one time displayed a barrel head as being from the wreck.[7] The preponderance of the most reliable accounts, however, and the commercial absurdity of expensively wasting the vessel's bulk-carrying capacity, point conclusively to oil in bulk. The best and most immediate contemporary evidence is the record of ships' movements in the *Philadelphia Public Ledger*, which on 14 November 1907 has, under "Freights and Charters": "Schooner Thomas W Lawson 50,000 barrels gas oil in bulk, hence London, private terms", but there are other credible sources to similar effect.[8] It is also what the surviving engineer, Edward Rowe, said in interview in 1964,[9] and although his recollections were, as we shall see, often unreliable, it is difficult to see how he could have been mistaken on such a point. Even more tellingly, because not directly addressed to the issue, he described how during the crossing "we were forced to pump the oil from No. 6 tank, to bring her stern up out of the water". The cause of the confusion may have been reports, such as that quoted above, in which "barrel" was used (as it still is) simply as a measure of quantity, but was mistakenly taken to describe the mode of carriage. There may well have been a few drums or barrels washed ashore in the Isles of Scilly (the *Lawson* would, for example, have always needed her own supply of lubricating oil), but that was not how the cargo was carried.

As to quantity, we have that reference to 50,000 barrels, which at 42 US gallons to the barrel equates to 2,100,000 gallons, and others to "over two million gallons" or 2,250,000 gallons,[10] as well as an almost certainly mistaken one to 60,000 barrels',[11] but there is one figure which is repeated

....

5   Frank C. Bowen in *Ships that made history, No. 172*, published in the *Shipbuilding and Shipping Record*, February 19, 1953, at p. 248, and *Lloyd's List*, 14 December 1907.

6   *Wreck and Rescue round the Cornish Coast* by Cyril Noall and Grahame Farr (D Bradford Barton Ltd, Truro 1964) at p. 84, and Wikipedia entry for *Thomas W Lawson (ship)*.

7   Author's personal observation.

8   *New York Times,* 15 December 1907; *Maine Coast Fisherman*, September 1951; *The Loss of the Thomas W Lawson 14th December 1907* by Richard Gillis in 'Sea Miscellany', 1968.

9   *The Last Voyage of the "Thomas W Lawson"* in *The Yankee*, December 1964, at p. 90.

10 *The Thomas W Lawson – the first or last of the great sailing bulk carriers* (anon).

11 *The Loss of the Thomas W Lawson 14th December 1907* by Richard Gillis in 'Sea Miscellany', 1968.

in several places and is so precise (2,003,063 gallons) that it seems likely to derive from primary documents.[12]

But what sort of oil? That is not only of general interest, by way of an insight into the nature of the commodities being exported to Europe at that time; it also affects both our calculation of the weight of the cargo and our understanding of the conditions on the surface of the water into which those on board were plunged when the vessel struck the rocks and her tanks were breached. Here again the sources differ, referring variously to light paraffin oil,[13] petroleum,[14] gas oil,[15] lubricating oil[16] and engine oil[17], The one certainty seems to be that it was not crude, both because it is not mentioned in the above list and because the *Lawson* was loading from a refinery port, not one serving an oil field. If we exclude lubricating oil, as the odd one out and also the least likely to be traded in such quantities, we are left with a cluster of rather similar hydrocarbons toward the volatile end of the liquid spectrum, and perhaps including some examples of overlapping nomenclature. If we take a specific gravity of 0.8 (roughly halfway between what we would now call petrol (US gasoline) and diesel) that gives a weight for 2,003,063 US gallons of 5,970 Imperial ("long") tons, 6,066 tonnes or 6,687 US ("short") tons, rather less than some of the contemporary reports claim,[18] and a good deal below the vessel's maximum deadweight capacity as a collier, but perhaps near the capacity of her tanks and probably as much as was thought safe for a transatlantic voyage in winter.

One might expect accounts of the wreck to have much to say about money, and on Lawson's personal stake and (uninsured) loss they do. To that we shall return, but there is surprisingly little about the value of the

....

12 *New York Times,* 15 December 1907; John Bunker in the *Maine Coast Fisherman*, September 1951; *The Last Voyage of the Thomas W Lawson* (Thomas Hornsby, in *Nautical Research Journal*, April 1953, at p.58); *Boston Herald*, 9 January 1972.

13 Wikipedia entry for *Thomas W Lawson (ship)*.

14 *Cornishman*, 19 December 1907; *Wreck and Rescue round the Cornish Coast* by Cyril Noall and Grahame Farr (D Bradford Barton Ltd, Truro 1964) at p. 84; *The Loss of the Thomas W Lawson 14th December 1907* by Richard Gillis in 'Sea Miscellany', 1968.

15 *Philadelphia Public Ledger* 14 November 1907; *New York Times,* 15 December 1907.

16 *New England Coasting Schooners* (Charles S Morgan, in *The American Neptune*, Vol 23 (1963), at p.16); *The Yankee*, December 1964.

17 John Bunker in the *Maine Coast Fisherman*, September 1951; *The Thomas W Lawson – the first or last of the great sailing bulk carriers* (anon).

18 For example 7,000 tons in *The Cornishman*, 19 December 1907.

cargo, and the two figures we have are so far apart that one or both must simply lack all credence. The *Western Morning News* of 16 December 1907 (with associated publications) gives $200,000 (essentially 10 cents per US gallon), whereas Thomas Hornsby, in *Nautical Research Journal,* April 1953, at p.58, has $71,000 (3.55 cents per gallon). No 1907 prices for comparable products have been found on the web, and the bracket there between American crude (1.7 cents per gallon) and UK retail petrol (13.5d per Imperial gallon, equating to 23.5 cents per US gallon) is too wide to be decisive, although the crude price does suggest that 3.55 cents is probably too low for a refined oil of any kind. The clue may lie in the freight rate of 45 shillings already mentioned. Assuming that that is per long ton of cargo it equates to 3.35 cents per US gallon, which suggests that Hornsby was perhaps confusing freight with value and that the *Western Morning News'* $200K was about right. That would be some $5M or £3M in 2014 money, and the *Lawson's* voyage would, if completed, have earned in freight the equivalent of nearly $1.7M or £1.1M.

The *Lawson* was to be loaded in, and sail from, Philadelphia. She was reported as passing the Delaware Bay breakwater at 2.50 on Saturday 9 November 1907, inbound from New York and as an arrival in the port of Philadelphia on Sunday 10 November, under Captain Gardiner.[19] According to Rowe her reason for being in New York was that steel bulkheads had to be installed at the Brooklyn dry dock to replace the wooden ones which had sprung when the schooner capsized in the incident described at the end of the last chapter.[20] He tells that as if it occupied the whole of the time since the April voyage, but six months would have been an inordinately long time for such a job, and the Atlantic Mutual Insurance archives show that the *Lawson* was working during the summer; indeed, on 28 June she was in Sabine Pass again, suffering an almost carbon-copy repetition of the March mishap, although this time the piling of the dock prevented her from falling on her beam ends. Again the cargo had to be discharged and again a survey blamed leaky bulkheads, so it seems likely that it was not until after that incident that they were replaced by steel. The autumn visit to New York may then have combined that with the final fitting-out before the Atlantic crossing.

....

19 *Philadelphia Enquirer* and *Philadelphia Public Ledger*, 10 and 11 November 1907.
20 *Boston Herald*, 9 January 1972.

Captain George W Dow as a young man.
Photograph courtesy of David M. Quinn.

Although Captain Gardiner had brought the schooner into Philadelphia, and may have been her master ever since she became a tanker,[21] he was not to be in command for the Atlantic crossing. Whether he was offered the job and declined, or was not considered suitable, or was out of the running for other reasons, does not emerge. The new master was George W. Dow of Melrose, Massachusetts. George Washington Dow had been born in 1847, so was now 60 years of age.[22] He had been born on a farm in Tremont, Mount Desert Island, Maine, but when he was eight his father and uncle had moved to North Hancock, Maine and supplemented their small farming income by seafaring, his father being master of the schooner *Fulcrum*.

George himself had been a seaman all his working life, having started as a cabin boy of 12 and obtained a master's ticket at the age of 21. He had married Johanna (Jennie) Bush in July 1870, and they had had four children, of whom two were still alive in 1907. The family had moved from Hancock, first to Ellsworth, Maine, and in about 1884 to Melrose, Massachusetts. Captain Dow was clearly a capable officer, and by 1907 a very experienced one. In his early days he had served on and commanded brigs and barques, but more often schooners. Then, for some seven years until 1883 he was master of the schooner *Stampede*. Having spent over a year on shore during the illness and death of his son Ellery he next entered the service of John S Emery and Company of Boston, with whom he remained until 1905, commanding first the barque *Gem* for two

21   *The Last Voyage of the Thomas W Lawson* (Thomas Hornsby, in *Nautical Research Journal*, April 1953, at p. 56.

22   Apart from his year of birth the details of Captain Dow's background are taken from *Leviathan's Master* by David M Quinn (iUniverse, August 19, 2009). It describes itself as a work of historical fiction, but is written by the captain's great-great-nephew, who has kindly confirmed that the facts for which it is cited here are authentic.

years, then the schooner *Albert L.* Butler and finally, from 1891, the barque *Auburndale*. He is described in one account as "one of the best-known and most popular navigators along the Atlantic coast".[23] It is not clear from that history whether he had any significant transoceanic work, but one source does describe him as "an experienced deep water mariner,[24] and the fact that, as we shall see, he was called out of semi-retirement to skipper the *Lawson* on her first Atlantic crossing speaks for itself. His long service in command of the *Auburndale* may explain, but certainly does not justify, Rowe's waspish dismissal of him as "an old square-rigger master", who "wouldn't take advice from schooner men" (presumably meaning, or including, Rowe himself).[25]

Since 1905 Captain Dow had not sought any further command, and although not formally retired he might never have gone to sea again had he not been recruited by the owners or charterers of the *Lawson* (probably the former, who would certainly have known of him) in 1907. It is not known why he, in particular, was chosen, or indeed whether he was the first choice, although clearly a well-qualified one. His motives for accepting must also be a matter of speculation, but likely ones are not hard to find. In terms of reputation it was the crown and summit of his career, the remuneration was no doubt attractive for a man conscious of the need for a nest-egg of comfortable proportions, and after two years on shore he may well have begun to miss being at sea.

The *Lawson* had for some time had as her regular first officer Axel Larsen, whose recollections of her handling and speed were quoted in the preceding chapter, but he "decided, shortly before the sailing, to turn over the mate's job to someone else".[26] The "someone else" whom George Dow wanted, and secured, as his chief mate was B.P. Libby, aged 34, of Marlborough, Massachusetts. Libby was reluctant, because he had left the sea, had a wife and five children, and had a good position ashore, but he felt under a debt of gratitude to Dow, having originally gone to sea in the *Auburndale* and owed much to the older man's help in his rise to be her first mate. He and the second mate, O. Crocker, aged

....

23 *Boston Herald* (note 20 above).

24 *The Luck of the Lawsons* (Alton H. Blackington, in *Yankee Yarns*, Dodd, Mead, 1954, at p. 21.

25 *Boston Herald* (note 20 above).

26 John Bunker in the *Maine Coast Fisherman* of September 1951; to similar effect ("on the eve of her departure") is *Stranger in Truth than in Fiction: The American Seven-Masted Schooners*, by Erik A.R. Ronnberg, Jr in *Nautical Research Journal*, Vol. 38, No. 1, March 1993, at p.13.

40, of New York, reported aboard on 4 November 1907.[27]

We have already met the engineer, Edward L. Rowe, and shall do so again. He was 34 or 35 years old and gave as his home town Wiscasset, Maine. Leaving seamen aside for the moment, the other crew members were the steward, George Miller, 37, of Boston, the cabin boy, Mark Sanson or Lamson, 17, of Brooklyn, New York, and the firemen (Rowe's engine-room staff) John Krase or Kiase, 38, and Z. Olanssen or V. Olanson, 36, both from Sweden.[28]

How far any of the above, apart from Libby and Rowe, had any previous association with either the schooner or Captain Dow does not appear, but the remainder of the crew, the seamen or deck hands, must almost certainly have been recruited ad hoc from the dockside. One of the curiosities of the story, to an outsider's eyes, is that none of them is identified in the crew list as boatswain, or bo'sun. Whether or not, once aboard and assessed for capabilities, one of them was accorded any status of seniority or supervisory role does not appear, nor, if not, whether that was general in the East coast trade or peculiar to the *Lawson* or to Captain Dow.

What is known is that their recruitment was not trouble-free. Only four of them signed on in the ordinary course of events and made the voyage: Gustav Englund, or England, 28, from Norway or Finland, John Lunde, or Hunde, 25, from Norway, Gustav Bohnke, 27, from Berlin, Germany, and George W. Allen, 27.[29] We have met George Allen in chapter 1 as, all too briefly, a survivor of the wreck, and as the only English member of the crew. In some English papers he is described as being from Battersea, or as coming home to visit his aunt there, and in one of the crew lists his home is indeed given as London. In the others it is "Bradford, England", but that may have been a misreading of "Battersea" by an American journalist unfamiliar with London neighbourhoods.

Another six "jumped ship" while Dow was ashore completing the last formalities to clear the vessel for departure. They were M.E. and A.A. Wiklund (brothers), from Sweden, John E. Burgess from Portland, Maine, William O'Brien from Dublin, Ireland, J. Edwards from Barbados and

....

27   Hornsby (note 21 above), at p. 58.
28   The sources for this information are three crew lists, all ostensibly based on the original held by the U.S. Shipping Commissioner in Philadelphia, but varying in spelling and other details: *Philadelphia Enquirer*, 15 December 1907; New *York Times,* 15 December 1907; *Boston Herald*, 9 January 1972.
29   Crew lists (note 28 above).

George H. Smith from Yarmouth, Nova Scotia.[30] It has naturally been speculated, given the fate of the schooner, that they distrusted her ability to make the voyage safely, and one source does add that they left "because they asserted that the vessel was unsafe".[31] Other accounts, however, do not support that, giving as their reason simply that they "became dissatisfied" or "did not like their quarters".[32] Since they had already signed on and come aboard it seems probable that they were in law deserters, but there is no report that anything was done about that, and had it been they would no doubt, once they heard the news from England, have thought any likely penalty a small price to pay for their lives.

At the very last minute, therefore, after the vessel had already cleared, Captain Dow had hurriedly to find six replacements – "a true pier head jump".[33] They were Ole Olsen, 21, from Denmark, P.A. Burke, 25, from Tonawanda, New York, A. Garridon, or L. Gorridon, 22, from Caracas, Venezuela, N. Petersen, 24, from Riga, then in Russia, A. Petersen, 26, from Denmark, and Anton, or Anten, Andrade, from Austria.[34]

It is no surprise that seafarers in general were at that time, as they still are, a cosmopolitan bunch, but is perhaps more worthy of note that so many nationalities and languages were combined in a single crew, that on an American vessel so many were from northern Europe, and that to all appearances that situation was accepted as a matter of course. They must all, presumably, have had a sufficient command of English to understand and carry out orders to some acceptable standard of speed and accuracy. Apart from the six officers and cabin crew only one other was from the U.S.A. Eight were from lands bordering on the Baltic Sea, but they were from five different countries (or six if Englund was Finnish), two from other European countries (Austria and the U.K.) and one from South America. If the deserters are included that adds one more American, two more Swedes and one more U.K. citizen (as Irishmen then were), but also two further countries of origin – Barbados and Canada.

....

30 *New York Times,* 15 December 1907; *The Last Voyage of the Thomas W Lawson* (Thomas Hornsby, in *Nautical Research Journal,* April 1953, at p.58.

31 *New York Times,* 15 December 1907.

32 *The Last Voyage of the Thomas W Lawson* (Thomas Hornsby, in *Nautical Research Journal,* April 1953, at p.58; *Philadelphia Enquirer,* 15 December 1907.

33 *The Last Voyage of the Thomas W Lawson* (Thomas Hornsby, in *Nautical Research Journal,* April 1953, at p.58.

34 Crew lists (note 28 above).

As to pay, we are told only that the first mate signed on at $80 per month and that the rate for ordinary seamen was $30 per month.[35]

Thus manned, the *Lawson* set sail. In stories of the wreck various dates of departure are given, ranging from 1 to 28 November 1907. The two extremes can be discounted. The apparent exactness of the former, indeed, perhaps unfairly ascribes to Crowninshield, its source, somewhat greater precision than he was claiming when he wrote that it "took her six weeks to cross the Atlantic",[36] although even allowing some latitude that was a substantial overstatement. There is, however, no room for any width of interpretation in the document which asserts the latter date. It is a manuscript signed by Edward Rowe on 17 March 1954 and prepared because he was "irked at the incomplete way he was often quoted by writers".[37] He writes that "we disconnected the pipelines and cast her ropes off from the dock in Philadelphia about the 27th of November 1907. What makes me certain of this date is a check I cashed that morning before we sailed, dated the 27th November. I'm certain of the date on the check." He has her reaching the open sea late on the following day.

He does not, however, assert that in 1954 he still had the 1907 cheque, and for all his certainty he simply cannot be correct. The other dates given cluster between 15 and 20 November, and that variation can be accounted for by the fact that different versions are speaking of different stages in the process, from "clearance" by the port authorities to reaching the open sea, a journey of some 100 (statute) miles. They are, crucially, supported by contemporary reports in publications whose raison d'être was the reliable recording of shipping movements, and in the following paragraphs those reports are distinguished from other, secondary, sources by the phrase "The records show that …".

The records show that the *Lawson* was cleared on 15 November.[38] That is reported as having been done by the Philadelphia port authorities, and Captain Dow had to attend for that purpose at their office on Chestnut Street,[39] whereas the cargo would have been loaded from the storage tanks at the Marcus Hook refinery, 17 miles or so downstream. Whether the port

....

35 Hornsby (note 21 above), at p. 58.
36 B.B. Crowninshield in *Fore-and-Afters* (Houghton Mifflin Company, Boston, 1940) at p 55.
37 *The Yankee* (note 9 above), at p. 90.
38 *Philadelphia Public Ledger*, *Philadelphia Enquirer* and *Lloyd's List* (which uses the word "sailed").
39 Hornsby (note 21 above), at p. 58.

authority's jurisdiction at that time included Marcus Hook, or whether the schooner came upstream after loading to sign on the deck crew and obtain clearance does not appear, but the latter seems the more likely, because seamen looking for work would congregate in the dock area. After clearance and, if that came later, the signing on of the six crew replacements, she was taken under tow downstream on 16 November by the tug *Paraguay*.[40]

The records show that on 17 November the *Lawson* was anchored at Deep Water Point, which is on the southern (Delaware) shore of Delaware Bay, as it opens out from the river, some 30 miles short of the open sea.[41]

At some point or points she grounded. There are four accounts of that, but each contains contradictions within itself or with the others or with known facts or probabilities, so it is very difficult to conclude with any assurance how many such events there were, or when and where they occurred. What should be the most authoritative is that in the Atlantic Mutual Insurance archives, which reads as follows: "Newcastle, Del. Nov 19th. Sch. Thos. W. Lawson ... is aground above here apparently to eastward of channel. She is in tow of steamer Toledo and tug Bristol which took her in tow at Deepwater Point to take her to sea. ... (Later) Schooner is now afloat and proceeding down in tow." One of the two accounts by Edward Rowe (the one given in 1944) also places the grounding under tow at Newcastle.[42] The difficulty with that is that Newcastle (or New Castle), Delaware, is on the river, well over 30 miles <u>upstream</u> of Deepwater Point, where the *Lawson* had already anchored two days before that entry.

A third account, in the report by the *New York Times* of the wreck, places the grounding in the Delaware River, when the schooner would still be under tow, and states that "a dozen tugs were required" before she floated off.[43] The fourth comes in the 1954 account by Edward Rowe cited in dealing with the date of departure above. He has the *Lawson* already under sail in Delaware Bay, identifies the site as the Brandywine Shoal, south of the lighthouse of that name, only a few miles short of the open sea, and states that "with the coming flood tide, we floated unassisted".[44]

....

40　Ibid.
41　*Philadelphia Enquirer* (the date given in the text is that of the event recorded; it is reported in the issue dated one day later).
42　*The Luck of the Lawsons* (Alton H. Blackington, in *Yankee Yarns*, Dodd, Mead, 1954, pp. 1–30), at p. 22.
43　*New York Times*, 15 December 1907.
44　*The Yankee* (note 9 above), at p. 90.

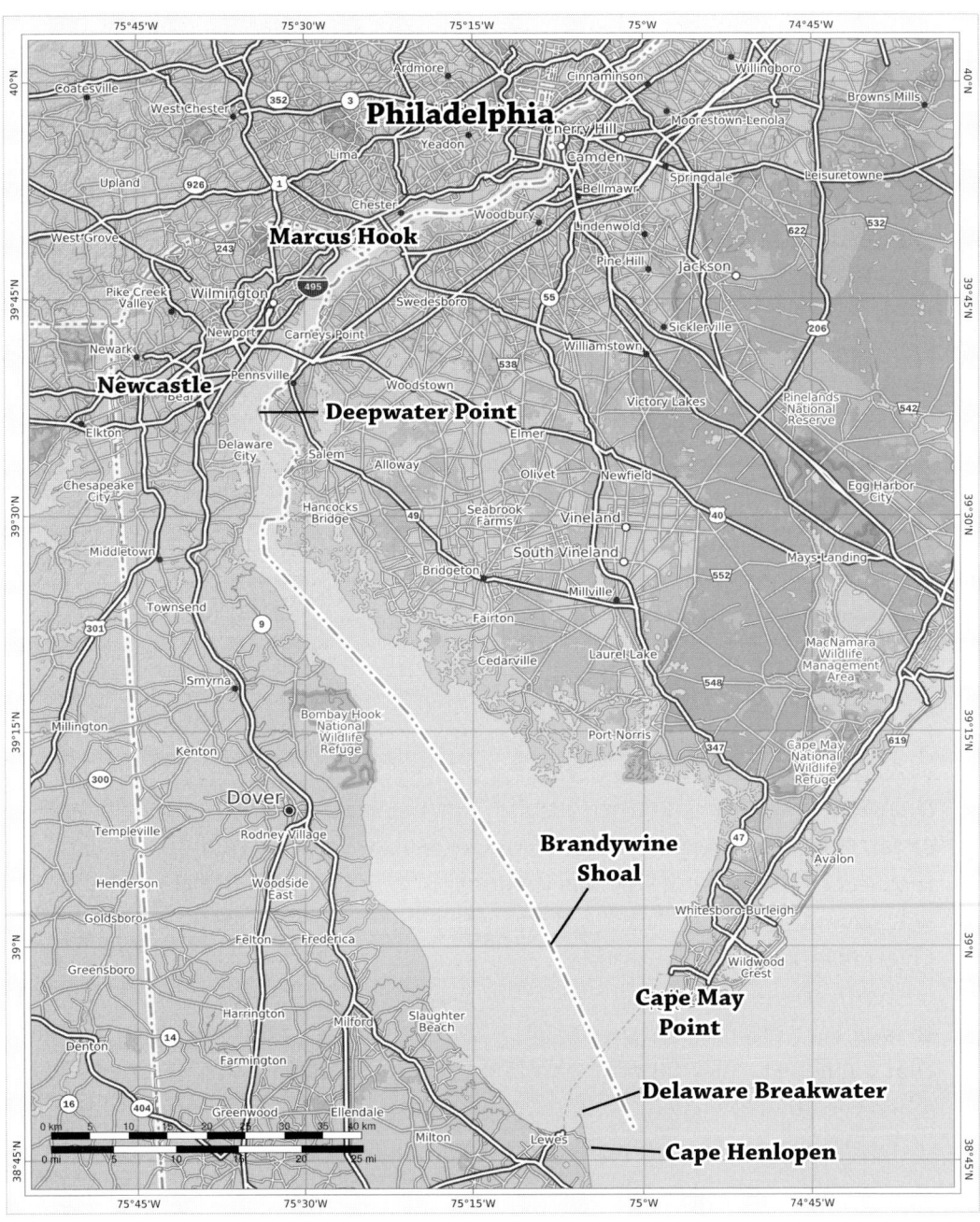

The Delaware river and bay from Philadelphia to their mouth. © DM Solutions Group Inc., Millennium House, Open Street Map and Open Street Map Contributors

That there should have been three groundings does seem beyond belief, not only in terms of its inherent improbability, but also in the internal contradictions of the insurers' file entry, in the fact that each of Rowe's versions treats this as a single event, and finally in the unlikelihood that such a "hat-trick" would have gone unremarked, both at the time and in the spate of publicity which followed the wreck. If there was only one then either the *New York Times* was approximately right (except perhaps for the number of tugs), Rowe (1954) entirely wrong, and the insurers' file and Rowe (1944) right only in the references to the schooner's being in tow, or else Rowe (1954) is approximately right (except for the reference to being under sail, as to which see the next paragraph), the *New York Times* entirely wrong, and the insurers' file right only in the date, and in the reference to a new tow from Deepwater Point. Another, more remote, possibility is that despite the improbabilities, and Rowe's failure to remember both at the same time, there were two groundings, each approximately as described respectively by the *New York Times* and Rowe (1954), and that the insurers have conflated elements from both.

The records show that on 19 November the *Lawson* "passed Delaware breakwater (in tow)".[45] The two "gateposts" which mark the mouth of Delaware Bay are Cape May on the northern (New Jersey) shore and Cape Henlopen on the southern (Delaware) shore. Near Cape Henlopen are the Delaware breakwaters, passing which was the customary mark of entering or leaving the bay from or into the open sea. So, notwithstanding Rowe's recollection to the contrary, the schooner was still in tow at that point, but will have parted from her tug very soon after, have passed under sail the Overfalls lightship, the traditional local end-point for measuring transatlantic distances, and at last been fully embarked upon her Atlantic crossing. It is not surprising that many later accounts fix on 19 November, when that happened, or 20 November, when it was officially reported, as the date when the *Lawson* "sailed".[46]

....

45 *Philadelphia Enquirer* (the date given in the text is that of the event recorded; it is reported in the issue dated one day later).

46 *The Thomas W Lawson – the first or last of the great sailing bulk carriers* (anon); *The Fate of the World's Largest Schooner* (R. Barry O'Brien, September 1953); *Cornishman*, 19 December 1907; *The Seven-masted Steel Schooner Thomas W. Lawson, 1902–1907* (William Armstrong Fairburn, in *Merchant Sail*, 1953; *The Loss of the Thomas W Lawson 14th December 1907* by Richard Gillis in 'Sea Miscellany', 1968; Captain Dow to *The Western Morning News*, 16 December 1907.

• 6 •

The Voyage

T HERE WAS AT LEAST ONE further official report of what was believed
to be a sighting before the *Lawson* made her fateful landfall. The *New York Maritime Register* for 27 November (repeated on 4 and 11 December) reads, after the usual identification of the *Lawson* by ship's name, master, origin and destination: "Supposed spoken November 21". *Lloyds List*, on or about 3 December, has what must be the same encounter, recorded as "A seven-masted schooner (probably [sic] the Thomas W. Lawson) ... Nov. 21 by the *Caribee* (S) at New York".

Douglas Lawson, in his account, wrote that she was "reported by the Antwerp passenger liner *Barnsmore* ... in fine shape, under full sail, off the Grand Banks".[1] He does not give a source or date, but this, if authentic, must be a different and later sighting than that on 21 November; the open sea immediately outside New York is only some 130 nautical miles from the Overfalls lightship, whereas the distance to the Grand Banks (off Newfoundland) is more like 1,400 to 1,500.

For the rest, since the log went down with the schooner and was never recovered, we are left with the recollections of survivors, of whom, as we have seen in Chapter 1, only two lived long enough to give any recorded account of the voyage – Captain Dow and the engineer, Edward Rowe. There is very little by way of independent evidence against which to check the detail of what they say, although there is no doubt about the broad

....

1   *The Boston Sunday Globe* 8 January 1956.

truth that the *Lawson* encountered severe storms and suffered substantial damage to her sails and on-deck boats.

There are, however, two approaches, of very different kinds, which taken together give some measure of a cross-check on the narratives. In the first place the route followed by sailing vessels from the east coast of North America to the English Channel was normally close to a great circle (see the Admiralty's *Ocean Passages of the World*), and we know the great circle (shortest) distance from the Overfalls lightship to the Bishop's Rock lighthouse and how long the crossing took. The distance is 2,906 nautical miles. From 19 November to 13 December is 24 days and although, to be exact, we should also add up to, say, eight hours if the schooner passed the Overfalls earlier on 19 November than the Bishop's Rock on 13 December we also have to subtract five hours for the time difference, so just 24 days of 24 hours is sufficiently exact. That gives an average speed of something over 5 knots – how much over depending on how far off the great circle was the *Lawson's* planned route and how far off her planned route she was blown during the storms. The average speed tells us nothing exact, and indeed by common consent she was going much faster, in favourable conditions, for some of the time before storms struck, but allowing for that it helps to provide a very rough check on approximately where the vessel could have been at particular times.

Secondly, we have the (British) Meteorological Office's weather charts for the North Atlantic for the whole period of the crossing, showing isobars, weather fronts, reports of wind speed and direction, and other meteorological data received from shipping – the last, of course, clustered most thickly along the main shipping lanes.

Much the earliest accounts by Dow and Rowe, and to that extent the most likely to be reliable, are those appearing in the local press in the days immediately following the wreck, and taken either from interviews with newspaper correspondents or from Rowe's evidence at the inquest held on Monday, 16 November 1907. The latter has the added weight of having been given on oath to an official tribunal, but both are of course, quite short and general, because the crossing itself was not the main focus of anyone's attention.

The Western Morning News of 16 December carried interviews with both men. Unless, surprisingly, its (unnamed) correspondent was one of the rescuers or Dr Brushfield, who could perhaps have obtained some sort of response on the very day of the rescue, those interviews must presumably have taken place on the next day, Sunday, 15 December. Captain Dow, who was "hardly able to converse", said that they had had "the very worst of passages. I have never seen such weather in my life. It was awful, and blowing something wicked." Rowe is reported as saying: "We had a rough passage throughout a week ago. Last Monday, Tuesday, and Wednesday we met a southerly gale. It smashed up the liferaft and lifeboat, the hatches and cabin door, and strained the ship. We lost half our sails as well." There is an obvious punctuation error, in that the full stop should follow "throughout", but correcting that raises the question whether there should then be a comma after "ago", and thus opens up an ambiguity as to whether the "Monday" was 2 or 9 December.

The *Cornishman*, a weekly, does not disclose in its edition of Thursday, 19 December 1907, the source of its information. At one point it states, without attribution, that "Some ten days ago the vessel encountered very bad weather and lost a great deal of canvas. A couple of boats were also washed away,and the decks swept". Elsewhere it quotes both Dow and Rowe to essentially the same effect as in The Western Morning News' interviews above, except that Rowe's southerly gale here starts, fairly clearly, on 9 December and that he adds: "We drove on before the wind under almost bare poles."

At the inquest Rowe said that they had been in two gales, and had lost one whole set of sails, leaving six good sails, besides storm sails. The gales had also carried away their lifeboat and smashed the liferaft, leaving them only one small boat.[2] Captain Dow gave brief evidence about the wreck but, so far as reported, none about the voyage.

Captain Dow no doubt reported more fully to his owners, but no record of that has emerged, and he seems to have found the subject too painful to discuss at any length in public. There are elements in apparently factual, but unattributed, accounts of the voyage by later writers which, so far as they cannot be traced to Rowe, may possibly originate from Dow, but may equally well be pure invention.

Edward Rowe poses the reverse problem. He was far from reticent on the subject; the challenge, in his case, is to reconcile his various accounts

....

2 *The Western Morning News*, 16 December 1907; *The Western Weekly News*, 21 December 1907.

Edward L. Rowe. Reprinted from the December 1964 issue of Yankee Magazine, *with permission of Yankee Publishing Inc., Dublin, NH, USA*

with each other and with the known facts, so far as the latter are available. Apart from his contemporary evidence, noted above, there are three later narratives from him which can be dated with greater or less accuracy, and are quoted below, and various statements in books or periodicals either attributed to him or of which he is the probable source, but which are not separately relied on here, because it seems likely that most, if not all, of them are unacknowledged derivatives of the same material.

The earliest of the three narratives was given orally to Alton H. Blackington on 12 October 1944, nearly 37 years after the event, and, in the version now available, published in 1954.[3] In this account Rowe has the date of departure correctly at 19 November and states that once free of the tugs in open sea, the schooner "stood on the starboard tack with a strong east wind", but that on 22 November the wind came about more strongly from the north west, "Blowing ... like the very devil. We had all sails set and were making close to twenty knots." Topsails and spankers were taken in, leaving the courses (the big sails attached to the fixed masts) and the jibs. "In a few hours the wind was blowing half a gale and fairly shrieking through the rigging." The more the gale increased, the faster they went, and off the Grand Banks were passing British tramp steamers one after another.

....

3   *The Luck of the Lawsons* (Alton H. Blackington, in *Yankee Yarns*, Dodd, Mead, 1954, pp. 1–30), at pp 22–24.

He claims that the wind speed "seemed like one hundred miles an hour, and suddenly one of the sails ripped with a terrific crack and let go, followed soon after by others ... leaving just the trysail on the foremast and the mainsail." For the first time, Rowe says, the *Lawson* began to ship water. Number six hatch was smashed in and the pumproom flooded. Then both trysail and mainsail carried away, but with her high freeboard and towering masts she was still, he claims, making six to seven knots. He has this state of affairs continuing until 12 December, when the winds died down and new trysails were rigged, but the calmer weather brought thick fog. That takes us, of course, to the eve of landfall.

The second of these narratives is the most circumstantial. It was the product of conversations with Captain William P. Coughlin over some two years, and incorporated in a manuscript signed by Rowe on 17 March 1954. What claims to be the first publication was issued in 1964.[4] It begins with the "certain", but clearly incorrect, assertion (discussed in the last chapter) that the *Lawson* left the dockside on 27 November and reached the open sea late the next day. Since in this account Rowe ostensibly records the passage of time with meticulous care the summary which now follows states at each stage, in brackets, first the date reached on Rowe's timetable, starting from 28 November, and secondly that based on the true sailing date of 19 November.

In this account the schooner "stood off to the eastward on the port tack, the wind south west, a comfortable sailing breeze" (which is not only contrary to the earlier version, but self-contradictory, since a vessel sailing east under a south-west wind is on the starboard tack). Early next morning (29 or 20 November) the wind shifted to the north west, increasing steadily to about seventy miles an hour, building up in no time a mountain of sea. The heavy sea continued rolling up on their quarter all the way across the Grand Banks and beyond, "a living gale". "Old Tom" was "making steamship time", overtaking a number of steamers that day and night. A little before midnight every lower sail blew from the bolt ropes except the spanker, which was furled to the boom, as were the head sails, "never loosed from their stops". Seas were running over her, all along the decks. At daylight the next morning (30 or 21 November) the work boat was ripped from her fastenings.

....

4   *The Last Voyage of the "Thomas W Lawson"* in The Yankee, December 1964, from p. 90.

The *Lawson*, Rowe continues, ran free for three days under bare poles, logging 15 to 18 knots in hurricane force wind from the north west. At the end of the third day (1 December or 22 November) a giant comber climbed up and over her quarter, breaking open No. 6 hatch. The weight of water flooding into and filling the after holds settled the stern, so that the decks aft were all awash. A sea from astern lifted the lifeboat from its fastenings, smashing it on deck into a wreck against the pilot house. The oil from No. 6 tank was pumped out, to bring the stern up out of the water.

On the fifth day, he says, the gale moderated. (Here Rowe's chronology creaks; to make narrative sense this should be the fifth day of the storm, 3 December, but to make what follows fit a landfall on 13 December he needs to treat it as the fifth day out, 2 December. From here on the dates follow the latter convention.) The sea abated somewhat, but left a heavy ground swell, which kept up for days. The crew were able to set storm sails. Thick weather then set in and by nightfall there was a heavy fog, with no visibility for the next five days, On the tenth day (7 December or 28 November) the glass was tumbling fast, and by nightfall another violent northwester was on them. In the attempt to save the foresail by dousing it the foresheet got adrift and the foreboom smashed against the engine house structure and smokestack, demolishing them. "We were now making knots towards the British Isles under storm or trysails, our spanker and head sails still furled."

In this narrative Rowe moves immediately (without any suggestion that the weather eased) from that situation to landfall on what he correctly accepts was 13 December, although he also calls it the 14th day out, which from 28 November would have been 11 December or, from 19 November, 2 December.

What purports to be Rowe's third narrative is much more cursory, and whether it is truly independent is made more doubtful by the fact that, although not published until 1972, it again claims to be "For the first time, as told by the sole survivor, the true story".[5] It is stated to have been given by Rowe to the author, Edward Rowe Snow, "half a century" after the schooner foundered, which would date it in about 1957. The relevant passage is short enough to be quoted:

....

5   *The Sinking of the Thomas W. Lawson* (Edward Rowe Snow, in the *Boston Herald*, 9 January 1972), from p.31.

When we found ourselves out beyond Delaware Breakwater we stood off on a starboard tack. The wind came round north west and we ran with a free sheet. Harder and harder the wind blew. The only sails we took in were: the spanker and topsails. The weather increased, and by the time we were on the Grand Banks she had lost all her main sails. ... Higher and higher went the wind, in that hurricane, and we were being pushed across the ocean at 14, 15 and even 16 knots. Passing steamers of all types, we were practically under bare poles. Three days later, after the wind had hit 100 miles an hour, we ran out of the worst of the hurricane. Then we got the triangular storm sail up. Actually we had sailed right out of the storm because of our speed. On Dec. 12, a Thursday, the *Lawson* made soundings as she approached the English Channel in the fog.

These three narratives, although each presented as "at last, the true story", contain some frankly incredible embellishments, such as the more extreme wind and boat speeds and, most outrageously, the image of the schooner overtaking steamers while practically under bare poles. And the apparently precise chronology of the fullest and most circumstantial is fatally compromised by starting nine days too late, and therefore shortening the crossing time by over one third and requiring an impossibly fast average speed. Moreover there are fundamental contradictions among them and between them and Rowe's evidence at the inquest, most notably as to whether there was one storm (1944 and 1957) or two (the inquest and 1954) and, if two, whether the second was another north-wester (1954) or southerly (the inquest).

It is therefore necessary to consider how far a reliable reconstruction of the *Lawson's* final voyage can be built up if Rowe's accounts are checked against the matters referred to in the first five paragraphs of this chapter.

In the Met. Office weather charts of that era a wind arrow, with surrounding figures for other weather features, indicates a ship's report. The chart for 19 November 1907 has a wind arrow a little off the coast outside Delaware Bay showing a wind of 18 to 22 knots (force 5, a "fresh breeze") from due north. On 20 November, roughly half way to New York, there is a north-easter of force 3 (a "gentle breeze"), and on 21 November New York is bracketed by wind arrows, all showing south-east winds of force 4 or 5. None of that accords either with Rowe's (1944) "strong east wind" or with his (1954) south-westerly, and overall it implies much slower progress than the impression which he gives. For the first 24 hours or more the *Lawson* would at best have been close hauled and for some of the time having to tack, the exact sequence depending on whether she held out directly north-east for the Grand Banks or more closely followed the coast-line as it curves from north-north-east to north on the run to New York.

The sighting by the *Caribee* off New York on 21 November is cautiously recorded as "supposed" or "probably", but gains credibility from the fact that there was, after all, only one seven-masted schooner afloat. When checked against any of Rowe's versions that may seem to involve implausibly slow progress, but given what we have now learned of the true wind conditions is not impossible to accept. If the sighting was close inshore the distance run would have been some 130 (nautical) miles, while on a course set more directly for the Grand Banks the location "off New York" could imply anything between that and 170 miles. The time elapsed can be anything from 40 to 56 hours, since we do not know the time of day at either end, giving a very wide bracket of possible averages between 2.3 and 4.3 knots, and the top end of that is within the range of possibilities for the schooner in such conditions. As will later appear, however, such a comparatively slow start would make it more difficult to achieve the sort of average necessary to be in what appears to be the only possibility of a first storm, if there were two, so whether the *Caribee's* "supposition" was justified must remain an open question.

The other possible sighting, by the *Barnsmore* off the Grand Banks, is undated, and at odds with Rowe's three references to that part of the crossing, which all speak of gale conditions and loss of sails, whereas according to Douglas Lawson the *Barnsmore* reported the schooner as being "in fine shape, under full sail". If we were to allow for a possible range of average speed between 4 and 15 knots the 1,100 to 1,200 nautical miles from off New York to the Grand Banks would have taken anything between three and twelve days, taking us from 21 November to between 24 November and 3 December, but the later date would implausibly leave only ten days for the rest of the crossing, and despite the differences between these two sources (Rowe and Douglas Lawson) they are both consistent with a fast passage over that earlier leg. On the other hand 24 November would require racing speed throughout, so the most likely date for the *Lawson* to have been over or off the Grand Banks is probably between 25 and 27 November (8 to 12 knots). The Met. Office weather charts show winds there on the 25th as northerly, force 6, on the 26th as southerly, force 5, and on the 27th as SSE, force 6. And even if the search is widened to earlier and later dates, including an allowance for the fact that the *Caribee* may have been mistaken and that the schooner may have passed New York before the "supposed" sighting on 21 November, there is simply no sign of gale force winds in the Grand Banks area at any time when the *Lawson* could have been crossing it.

When and where, then, did the schooner encounter the storm or storms from which she undoubtedly suffered? On the Beaufort scale, in the vocabulary set out in Appendix 5, force 7 (32–38 mph) is a "near gale" or "high wind", force 8 (39–46 mph) a "gale" or "fresh gale", force 9 (47–54 mph) a "severe gale" or "strong gale", force 10 (55–63 mph) a "storm" or "whole gale", force 11 (64–72 mph) a "violent storm" and force 12 (over 72 mph) a "hurricane". We need, therefore, to find wind speeds in that range at times and places consistent with the *Lawson's* departure and arrival dates and her sailing capabilities.

On 21 November there were two weather systems in the North Atlantic with winds of force 9 to 10. One was a small one centred at about 42°N, 60°W, some 300 (statute) miles off the coast of Nova Scotia. But (i) the *Lawson* would have needed to make an average of 13 to 18 knots from dropping her tugs to have reached that point, which does not seem possible in the wind conditions already considered, (ii) that would also have been inconsistent with the supposed sighting by the *Caribee,* (iii) the storm was too short-lived (there is no sign of it on 20 or 22 November) to accord with any of the descriptions by Dow or Rowe, and (iv) it is too early in the voyage even for Rowe's first reference to such conditions. So that can be discounted as one of the storms we are looking for. The other weather system was larger and more persistent, but so far east (the nearest report of a force 9 wind was at 48°N, 32°W, about two thirds of the way across the Atlantic) as to be out of the question.

During the following days the first of these storms died quickly away and the other moved even further east. The next time winds reached the speeds we are looking for was on 25 November, when a depression west of Ireland deepened and extended its influence as far west as 42°W, where at 47°N there was a report of a WNW force 8. That is just over 1,500 (nautical) miles out from the Overfalls lightship, requiring an average speed of 10 to 11 knots, but if we discount the *Caribee's* supposed sighting that was well within the *Lawson's* capabilities, and even if we accept that sighting the average from there would not have had to be more than 14–15 knots, which is by no means impossible. High winds from that depression continued until 28 November (N force 9 on 26 November at 52°N, 37°W, NNE force 9 on 27 November at 50°N, 27°W and W force 7 on 28 November at 49°N, 21°W), and as we shall see it is the only serious candidate for the first storm to strike the *Lawson*, if there were two.

As those co-ordinates, in each case at its western edge, indicate, however, it was moving eastwards at such a pace that it seems unlikely, for four reasons, that the schooner stayed within it for its full duration. The first reason is that to do so she would have had to maintain and then improve on her average speed to date, and despite Rowe's graphic image of sailing "right out of the storm because of our speed" the loss of sails must have slowed her down. The second is that if, as Rowe states, and as is inherently likely, she was, once she had lost most of her sails, largely reduced to running before the wind, its direction on 26 and 27 November would have prevented her from gaining much, if any, easting. The third is that to have kept within the storm until 28 November would have brought her within 610 (nautical) miles or so of the Bishop Rock, with 15 days still to account for, a very unlikely situation. The fourth is that only a scenario in which she drops back to the west of that weather system provides any opportunity for the period of relative calm and fog between storms of which Rowe tells in his 1954 manuscript.

Although nothing in this part of the story is entirely straightforward, it does seem to be more likely than not that the *Lawson* did indeed encounter, and suffer significant damage, in this storm, although she was probably in it for a day or so at the most.

During the period from 28 November to 3 December there were no high winds anywhere near where the *Lawson* could have been, and that is consistent with Rowe's five days of respite in his 1954 manuscript, although as usual he over-eggs his pudding by having heavy fog, with no visibility, for the whole of that time, whereas there was no fog in the charts which the schooner could have encountered on 1 or 2 December. There was a bank of fog moving eastwards at the forward edge of an occluded front from 28 to 30 November, but even if the *Lawson's* experience of the storm was of the shortest duration consistent with the damage suffered that bank would not have caught up with her before 30 November, in latitude 30°–35°W. There was a more short-lived bank in latitude 30°–40°W on 3 December, but it was mostly north of 50°N and she had probably been blown too far south to meet it. So she may well have been in fog once, and possibly twice, but not for long.

On 4 December the picture changed again. A large area of W to NW, force 9, winds developed between 47° and 55°N and 10° and 45°W. On 5 and 6 December the wind was W to WNW and dropped to force 7 to 8 , but on 7 December it rose to 9 and backed to SSW to WSW, and on 8 December, having veered back to W to WNW, it was as high as force 9 to 10. It stayed in that quarter on 9 and 10 December, dropping to force 7 to 9 on the first of those days and 7 to 8 on the second, before ceasing, at force 5 to 7, to count as a storm on 11 and 12 December, and backing again by the latter date to SW. The exact area of the highest winds varied somewhat during that period, and in particular extended at times further south, in which direction the *Lawson* may have been blown during the first storm, but it was essentially stationary, and included for at least part of the time the last section of her route to her landfall. It is true that the dates are somewhat earlier than was the impression given by the contemporary newspaper reports, but in contrast to the complexities of the earlier part of the investigation there seems here to be a relatively straightforward conclusion: this was the storm, or more probably the second of the two storms, which the *Lawson* met on her last voyage, and which caused the damage evident when she arrived at the unintended destination described in the next chapter.

Before turning to that, however, something can briefly be added about the final error of navigation which brought her to that destination, leading her officers to believe that they were safely out in the English Channel and that the light which they saw must therefore be a ship's light. They must, of course, have been sailing by dead reckoning, and that is inherently imprecise, especially in storm conditions, but they knew that and would have taken it into account. What needs explaining is not just that they were not exactly where their dead reckoning indicated, but that they were well north of the margin of error for which they would have allowed. It is significant that they were not alone in that. The navigators of the *Schiller* (wrecked in 1875) believed that they were eight miles south of the Bishop, those of the *Earl of Lonsdale* (1885) at least ten miles, of the *Independence* (1881) fifteen miles, of the *Minnehaha* (1910) at least seven miles, of the *Susanna* (1913) enough to be "well clear" and of the *Isabo* (1937) thirteen miles.

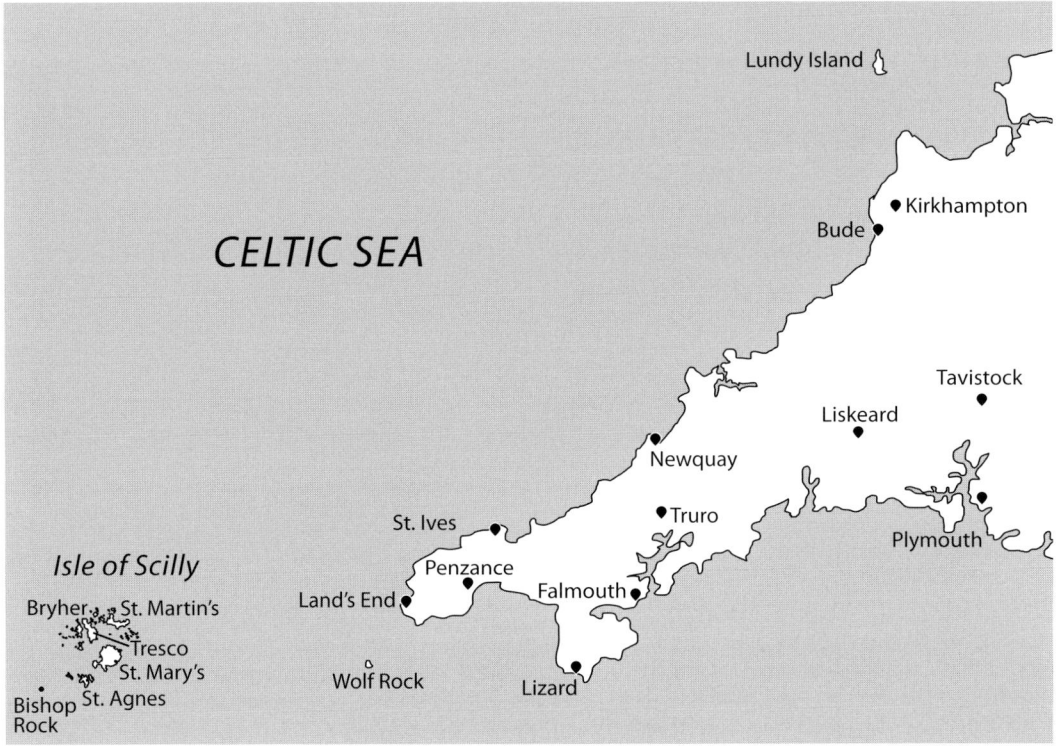

The Isles of Scilly in context.

It has been suggested[6] that the explanation is failure to take account of the Rennell current, which in certain conditions can set round the Bay of Biscay and then north-west across the entrance of the Channel, and can reach a velocity of one knot.

....

6   By Juliet du Boulay in *Wrecks in the Isles of Scilly* (self-published, 1960) at pp. 99–100.

· 7 ·

The Islands

T HE ISLES OF SCILLY are a group of islands centred some 28 (statute) miles west-south-west (more exactly bearing 251°) of Land's End, the most south-westerly point of Cornwall, and therefore of mainland Great Britain,[1] and are accordingly themselves the most south-westerly inhabited plots of metropolitan British soil. Their geology is plainly a continuation of that which surfaces in the granitic intrusions of Devon and Cornwall – Dartmoor, Bodmin Moor, St Austell, Carnmenellis and Penwith – but the land bridge which presumably once joined them to the mainland has been submerged by a progressively rising sea level for at least 11,000 years or so, perhaps creating originally a single main island. However, by at latest about 7,000 BC a channel had already opened between St Agnes and everything to the North and East. The final encroachment of (still shallow) water to create the current little archipelago may not have been complete until historical times. There are currently five inhabited islands (St Mary's, Tresco, St Martin's, St Agnes and Bryher), plus dozens of smaller islets, some populated in the past, and hundreds of rocks.

For at least 4,000 years human beings have lived there. There are remains of huts and other dwellings from the Bronze Age (3,300–1,200 BC) onwards and, much more impressively, of massive stone barrows, probably housing lavish grave goods, constructed between 2,600 and 4,000 years ago (2,000 to 600 BC). The apparent disproportion between the economic and cultural

....

1   Map on facing page.

standards evidenced by the modest habitations for the living, as compared with the lavish provision for the dead, and the much greater concentration of chambered barrows on the islands than in mainland Cornwall (indeed, in terms of findings, there are more even in absolute number) has fostered suggestions that there may have lain here some reality behind the Greek mythology of the Islands of the Blest or, maybe more plausibly, the Celtic legends of a land of the dead called Avalon.[2] Perhaps, it is supposed, there was a practice of bringing here for burial wealthy and high-ranking members of mainland communities.

What is much more persistently and plausibly speculated, although without any definitive resolution, is that the isles of Scilly can be identified with the Cassiterides (meaning tin islands), reputedly discovered and exploited by the Phoenicians. That would have involved sailing the length of the Mediterranean, out through the Pillars of Hercules (the Straits of Gibraltar), and then northwards over 1,100 miles by the most direct route, to which must be added another 450 or more if, as in the early years at least must have been much more likely, they hugged the coast for as long as they could. The Phoenicians kept the origin of their tin a closely guarded secret, but by the time Rome was becoming dominant there clearly was an established trade in the metal from Cornwall, and once Caesar had subdued Gaul, if not before, that trade followed a route which crossed the English Channel and continued overland to the Mediterranean coast. In the sources for that information, again, there are tantalising references to the Cassiterides as islands where tin is found.[3]

During the Roman occupation of southern Britain, from the invasion under Claudius in 43 AD until the withdrawal of the legions, traditionally dated 410 AD, references to the islands are sparse, and chiefly concern their use as a destination for exiled rebels or heretics, but pottery, brooches and other remains from that period have been found.[4] Reliable evidence is even harder to come by for the interregnum which followed, or for the period of Anglo-Saxon invasion which was beginning as the Romans left, but probably did not reach the Isles of Scilly until the ninth century.

The heartland of the Roman Empire had become progressively Christianised from the time of Constantine's Edict of Milan in 313 AD, but

....

2   *The Fortunate Islands* (R.L. Rowley, Rowley Publications, 8th ed. 1990), at p.5.
3   Ibid., at pp 8–14.
4   Ibid., at pp. 22, 24.

there is no evidence of Christianity in the Isles of Scilly in Roman times, and the Anglo-Saxon invaders were of course originally pagans, although themselves increasingly Christian after the arrival of Augustine in 597 AD. At some stage monks arrived in the islands. Their influence is apparent in the one glimpse we have of the Isles of Scilly during the time of Viking raids on Britain from 793 AD onwards. It comes in the form of an account in the *Heimskringla* collection of Old Norse sagas of a visit by Olaf Tryggveson:

> After Olaf had spent three years in Vendland, his wife, Geira, fell sick and died. He felt so much sorrow from her death that he could no longer bear to stay in Vendland, and set out to plunder in 984. He raided from Frisland to the Hebrides, until after four years he landed on one of the Scilly Isles. He heard of a seer who lived there. Desiring to test the seer, he sent one of his men to pose as Olaf. But the seer was not fooled. So Olaf himself went to see the hermit, now convinced he was a real fortune teller. And the seer told him:

> "Thou wilt become a renowned king, and do celebrated deeds. Many men wilt thou bring to faith and baptism, and both to thy own and others' good; and that thou mayst have no doubt of the truth of this answer, listen to these tokens. When thou comest to thy ships many of thy people will conspire against thee, and then a battle will follow in which many of thy men will fall, and thou wilt be wounded almost to death, and carried upon a shield to thy ship; yet after seven days thou shalt be well of thy wounds, and immediately thou shalt let thyself be baptised."

> After the meeting Olaf was attacked by a group of mutineers, and what the seer had foretold happened. So Olaf let himself be baptised by St. Ælfheah of Canterbury in 994.[5]

Soon after the Norman conquest in 1066 written records start to be more prolific, and it becomes a matter of selecting what is of relevance and interest in such a short summary as this must be. By 1114 there was a priory on Tresco, and in that year it was placed under the control of Tavistock Abbey, in Devon, which gave successive Abbots an importance in the life of the islands until the dissolution of the monasteries in 1539. The ruins of the priory buildings suggest a substantial establishment, and

....

5   *Wikipedia* entry for Olaf 1 of Norway.

the Abbey claimed all shipwrecks and tithes in the islands and had significant landholdings. The rest of the land was held by a succession of "lords",
described as "feudal", which seems to imply that they held it freehold.[6] They
would have done so directly from the Crown until the islands became part
of the estate of the Duchy of Cornwall upon its creation in 1337, and from
the Duchy after that.

The value of the holding can be gathered from records showing the
islands to be worth, yearly, in 1349 £18.19s.4½d, and in 1548 £26.13s.4d,
apparently in terms chiefly of the rents which could be extracted from
tenants. Those sums, with 2014 equivalents of about £11,000 and £7,200
respectively, look broadly comparable, but are at odds with one of 40 shillings in 1478 (£1,230 in 2014 money), which must presumably have been
measuring something different. Even the higher figures are pitiably low,
but they accord with what seems to have been the contemporary reputation
of the islands as a wretched, impoverished backwater.[7] A tiny glimpse into
population levels, and into the perils of island life, comes in the following
passage from the notes of a visit, probably in 1540, by the antiquary John
Leland:

> The Isle of S. Agnes was desolatid by this chaunce in recenti hominum
> memoria. The hole numbre of V householdes that were yn this isle cam to
> a mariage or a fest in S. Mary Isle, and going homewarde were al drownid.[8]

The period of feudal tenure ended in 1549 with the attainder for piracy and
execution of the last person to hold the islands in that way, Lord Admiral
Seymour,[9] so that his lands were forfeited to the superior lord, at that
time the Crown in right of the Duchy of Cornwall, there being no son to be
Duke during the reign of Edward VI. That opened the way for a long period
of domination by the Godolphin family and their successors by marriage,
the Osbornes. The Godolphins had an ancient family seat near Helston,
in West Cornwall, and by this time had acquired great wealth from tin
mining. Sir William Godolphin had been responsible for the defence of the
Isles of Scilly against the French under Edward VI,[10] and in 1571 Elizabeth

....

6   Rowley (note 2 above), at pp. 27–29.
7   Ibid., at pp.31–33.
8   Ibid., at p. 32–33.
9   Ibid., at p. 33.
10   Sir Francis Godolphin, in the *Calendar of State Papers*, as quoted in *The Fortunate Islands*

I granted a lease of the islands to William's son, Sir Francis Godolphin, which was successively extended by subsequent monarchs. The lessees were members of the Godolphin family until the male line ran out, but in 1740 Lady Mary Godolphin, one of the two co-heiresses to the estate (the other married the Duke of Newcastle) married Thomas Osborne, 4th Duke of Leeds, and the lease of the islands passed through her to their son, Francis Godolphin Osborne, 5th Duke of Leeds (Foreign Secretary under William Pitt the Younger from 1783 to 1791), but his son, the 6th Duke, who had taken a further lease for 31 years in 1800, declined to renew it in 1831.[11]

The Godolphin-Osdorne era can conveniently be considered in two parts. The first runs from 1571 to the end of the Civil War in 1651. During this time the interest of commentators centres on the activities in the islands of the Godolphins themselves. The original Sir Francis took on terms that he defended the islands, the primary threat being from Spain. On 23 June 1588 his report of the appearance of the Spanish Armada off Scilly reached the Council. After the defeat of the Armada Elizabeth supplied the sum of £400 (£67,500) for the erection of a fort overlooking the harbour on St Mary's.[12] Sir Francis supervised its erection, and funded the cost overrun of £558.11s. 2d (£94,227), most of which was not refunded by the Crown until after Elizabeth's death.[13] The fort was named Star Castle, a fine building still in occupation, now as a hotel.

The exertions and expenditure of the Godolphins in the defence of the islands continued under James I and Charles I. In the Civil War (1642–1651) they were loyal to the king, and the Isles of Scilly were under the control of the Royalists until the summer of 1646, when they were ousted by the Parliamentarians, who held them until 1648, when the garrison mutinied and declared for the king (by now Charles II, Charles I having already been executed). They remained in Cavalier hands, under Sir John Grenville, until finally recaptured in April 1651, at the very end of the Civil War.[14]

The legacy of the Civil War includes, on the one hand, two notable landmarks on Tresco, in the form of King Charles' Castle and Cromwell's

---

(note 2 above), at p. 42.

11   Rowley (note 2 above) at p. 34, and *Wikipedia* entries for the Godolphin and Osborne families.

12   Rowley (note 2 above), at pp. 34–38.

13   Ibid., at p. 38.

14   *British Civil Wars & Commonwealth* (David Plant, website): *1651: The Scilly Isles.*

Castle, and on the other our first authoritative picture of the inhabitants and their land holdings – the victorious Parliament, suspicious of the islanders' loyalty, commissioned "A Survey of those islands commonly called the Syllyes [or] the Sullyes, with the right numbers and appurtenances thereof".[15] Some of its findings will feature in the next chapter.

In the second part of the Godolphin-Osdorne period, from 1651 until 1831, their own activities largely disappear from view; they seem to have been absentee, and indeed neglectful, landlords, collecting their rents through a resident agent who was the local manifestation of their authority. That neglect left the islanders to their own devices, which were strained to the limit in the struggle to survive. Communication with the mainland was slow, haphazard and hazardous, so subsistence farming had to be the core activity for almost every household, but that did not provide money for the rent. Moreover cultivable land was in short supply, and in any event could not provide by any means all of even the barest necessities of life. There was therefore a constant need for some source of a supplemental cash income which would not be crippled by the problems and expense inherent in remoteness. The surrounding seas teemed with life, but there was no practicable means of getting fresh catches to mainland markets, so although almost everyone could and did fish, and although some ling was dried, salted and exported, fishing was for the most part just another subsistence activity; commercial fishing was largely left to visiting boats from mainland ports.

Although it is not usually mentioned when the activities are listed to which resort was had to earn money, the existence of a military garrison and the erection of fortifications must while they lasted have been a material support to the economy of the islands, but apart from some revival during the French wars of 1790 to 1815 that element did not feature to any significant extent after 1748.[16]

Such other cash "crops" as there were varied over the centuries. For example kelp-making was carried on from 1684 until 1835. There is a detailed account of the process by Robert Maybee (1810–1891), a ballad singer and poet who could not read or write but had a photographic memory, and at the age of 73 dictated his *Sixty-Eight Years' Experience of the Scilly Islands*. From March until August seaweed was gathered from the

....

15　Public Record Office, Scilly Islands Survey: E.317/Corn/39.
16　Rowley (note 2 above), at pp. 66, 67.

Kelp burning. © Gibsons of Scilly.

beach, dried and then burned in large open-air pits. "The women would burn most of the kilp and the children would bring the weed to them … they would light up between twelve and one o'clock and keep it burning till about eight or 9 o'clock in the evening, putting on the weed in handfuls … some days there would be as many as 100 kilns burning on the different islands. The smoke would come … as thick as it would from a steamer when new coals were put in …". The residue was "like so much hot lead", and after being "worked up" into large masses of about three hundredweights would be allowed to cool and broken up into manageable lumps. About 22 tons of seaweed produced about one of kelp, worth in good times some £4 (about £300 in 2014 money). The demand for kelp was as a source of potash, used in making glass and soap, and of iodine, and collapsed when by the 1830s cheaper sources of those chemicals emerged elsewhere.[17] It is not difficult

....

17   Ibid., at pp. 80, 81, 86.

to imagine what back-breaking work it was, or how offensive the smoke and smell of the kilns, and for such a meagre reward, but over something approaching 150 years it was a mainstay of the islands' economy.

Other sources of cash arose, flourished and declined, but they extended into, or arose during, the period when the Godolphin-Osbornes had been replaced, and are best considered after that change of governance has been described.

For nearly three years after the expiry of the Duke of Leeds' last lease in 1831 the Duchy of Cornwall administered the islands directly, but found that so daunting and unrewarding that they were soon seeking a new lessee. Rents were low, and even then often wildly in arrear, because of the poverty of the tenants.[18] By 1834 a new lessee had been found. His name was Augustus Smith, and he was to prove a dominant and, for the most part, benevolent force in the life of the islands for the remaining 38 years of his life and beyond.

In 1834 Augustus Smith was 30 years old, rich (the family money came from banking), well educated, energetic and intent on finding some outlet for his wealth, learning and energies. He was already interested in the working of the Poor Laws and had written in support of a system of national education,[19] and now sought an estate which would enable him to realise his beliefs about how an underclass could be encouraged, led or (if necessary) driven into rising out if its poverty and dependence into a state of self-sufficiency and comparative comfort. The Isles of Scilly proved ideal for that purpose. He heard about the withdrawal of the Duke of Leeds, made intensive enquiries during a visit to the islands, and entered into negotiations with the Duchy of Cornwall which led to a long lease of the islands to him.[20] The consideration was a premium of £20,000, a rent of

....

18   Rowley (note 2 above), at p.87.
19   William Prideaux Courtney in the *Dictionary of National Biography*.
20   The term is described in most sources as being 99 years, but *The Fortunate Islands* (note 2 above) has, more informatively, 99 years "or three lives" (p. 88), and Courtney (note 19 above) 99 years "contingent on three lives". Neither spells out the limitation verbatim, but there is a clue in that Augustus' nephew and successor, Algernon Dorrien-Smith, apparently obtained an extension of 31 years in 1884 (*The Fortunate Islands*, p.98). That suggests that, as was possible under the land law and conveyancing practice at the time, the lease was in reality one for 99 years, determinable on the death of the survivor of three named persons living at the date of the lease. Given the values of life expectancy at the time that was almost certain to be determined in the event well before the expiry of 99 years, even if young children were chosen as the "lives in being", and it is not therefore

£40 per annum, and covenants to pay the island clergy and to build a new church and a quay on St Mary's.[21]

Smith made the Scillies his life work. Although he already had estates in Hertfordshire and Buckinghamshire he made the islands his home, living on St Mary's until he had completed the construction of a large new house, the Abbey, on Tresco. Apart from some few additional statutory powers, in particular to appoint magistrates, his authority derived solely from his position as universal landlord, but in practice that gave him almost unfettered power over almost every detail of the islands' life, and he was widely described as "the Lord Proprietor" or more commonly, by the islanders

Augustus Smith. © Gibsons of Scilly.

themselves, as "the Governor" or, when his nephew had succeeded to that title, as "the old Governor".

One of his first steps was to deal with the fragmentation of land holdings, under the custom by which farms were divided, on a tenant's death, between all his sons,[22] which had led to the proliferation of tiny holdings, each hopelessly inadequate for the support of a family. Smith re-allocated the land into viable units and insisted that on death only the eldest son could succeed to a farm. He averted consequential hardship to the other sons, in the early days partly by providing work himself on his building projects, but more generally and enduringly by securing the

---

surprising that as early as 1884 either that had just happened or, more likely, the probability that it would happen well within the next 31 years made a fixed extension for that period an attractive bargain.

21   Rowley (note 2 above), at p. 88.

22   The position was similar under gavelkind, the system of freehold tenure which until 1926 operated in Kent, but that was a rule of law which applied on intestacy, whereas what happened in Scilly cannot have been a matter of law, otherwise Augustus Smith could not have reversed it; the practice must have been a non-binding, customary one, possibly as to the content of wills or, more likely, as to the landlord's willingness to give effect to family wishes on granting new tenancies following the death of a tenant.

availability of education and what would now be called vocational training for all and doing his best to ensure that every child took advantage of it. Notwithstanding his efforts at job creation, to which we shall return below, he recognised that the islands were overpopulated, and encouraged and helped many of the boys and girls he had educated and trained to obtain jobs on the mainland or at sea.

Even given his wide powers it is not entirely clear by what authority he laid down some of his rules, beneficent in intention as they no doubt were. It is said, for example, that he countered overcrowding by forbidding marriage until the couple had a house in which to live, and illiteracy by making parents pay a penny a week for each child sent to school, and two pence for each kept at home.[23] On the other hand, it was within his undoubted rights as landlord that he made what is perhaps his best-known and most dramatic decision, to evacuate the hitherto populated island of Samson in 1855. The census of 1841 had returned 29 inhabitants, but by 1855 there were apparently just two households, subsisting on limpets and potatoes.[24] Smith could see no prospect of continuing sustainable occupation of the island, and rehoused them elsewhere.

Another well-known, but very different, legacy of his was the Tresco Abbey Garden. His motive here was no doubt aesthetic rather than philanthropic, but it too has in the event contributed significantly to the economy of the islands. Although the weather there can be harsh the climate is mild, in the sense that frosts are rare, and extended hard frosts almost nonexistent. Sub-tropical plants can thrive, if protected from the wind and salt spray, which Smith ensured by careful choice of location and aspect and by planting extensive wind breaks. He obtained his plants chiefly through the network of contacts with seafarers worldwide to which the Isles of Scilly gave instant access. The garden became a major attraction to visitors, and now contains exotic plants from 80 countries, ranging from Brazil to New Zealand and Burma to South Africa.[25]

That brings us back to a consideration of the varied means by which Scillonians have, since the departure of the garrison and the collapse of the kelp industry, met the challenge of paying their way in a group of small

23 www.islesofscillyholidays.co.uk/history-and-archaeology/scillonian-history.html.
24 www.genuki.org.uk/big/eng/Cornwall/IslesofScilly/ and Wikipedia entry for Samson, Isles of Scilly.
25 Tresco Abbey Garden website.

Shipbuilding, John Edwards' yard at Porthcressa, St Mary's.
© Gibsons of Scilly.

islands, nearly 30 miles offshore. Some of them already existed before Augustus Smith arrived; some arose later. Some died out or declined; others are still significant. Some owed a great deal to Smith's initiative or support, others little or nothing. Most were legal, but one was not and another was sometimes doubtful. At least one is directly relevant to the story told in Chapter 1.

One of the earliest, and perhaps the most surprising, was shipbuilding – the surprise arising from the fact that virtually everything required had to be imported, and what countervailing advantage the location afforded is not clear. Despite that, ships were being built on St Mary's by 1770, and the trade continued to be active until 1880, by which time iron was beginning to replace wood and steam to drive out sail. The shipyards were on the beaches flanking Hugh Town on St Mary's (Town Beach and, more especially, Porthcressa) and the ships were mostly small (many of 59 tons in order to escape legislation applying to vessels of 60 tons or more), but with a range up to 528 tons. As many as 59 new vessels were registered in a year, so the total must have numbered several hundred.[26] Such an industry required ancillary trades, and we can see an example of that, and perhaps also of Augustus Smith's insistence on vocational training, in the fact that the Israel Hicks of Chapter 1, although clearly also a boatman and farmer, appears in successive census returns as an apprentice sailmaker of 17 (1881), a sailmaker (1891) and a sailmaker and farmer's son (1901).

In two ways the islands' situation did offer the possibility of some competitive advantage – their climate and their position at the mouth of the English Channel – and the influence of one or the other of them appears more clearly in the activities still to be mentioned.

The clearest example of an occupation based on location is pilotage. Local knowledge of seas in and around the islands,with their rocks, shoals and currents, must have enabled islanders to earn money in this way from the earliest days of regular coastal and oceanic trade. At first that would have been informal and unregulated, so its origins cannot be precisely dated, but by 1685 the St Agnes pilots were sufficiently recognisable as a body to be credited with raising the money to build the island's church, although that bounty came from the salvage of a wreck rather than from pilotage fees.[27] By the eighteenth century pilotage by Scillonians was regulated by the islands' "Court of Twelve", who required pilots in the off islands to make that their sole occupation, and in return provided for wives widowed by the dangers of such a life. By 1808, when the Act was passed under which Trinity House was to take control in 1810, there were 76 author-ised Scillonian pilots – 23 on St Mary's, 18 on Tresco, 7 on Bryher and 14 each on St Agnes and St Martin's. It is notable that although St Mary's had the most, they were nowhere nearly proportionate to its overwhelming preponderance of population – something like 60 per cent of the total. Pilotage was typically an off-island speciality. Trinity House wished to limit the number of licences to nine and to confine them to St Mary's, but that caused an outcry and in the end 37 were issued, including a reasonable

....

26   *The Scillonian and his Boat* (Alf Jenkins, 1982) at pp. 128–130 and *The Fortunate Islands* (note 2 above) at pp.94–96.

27   *Gigs and Cutters of the Isles of Scilly by* A.J. Jenkins (Integrated Packaging Group Ltd and the Isles of Scilly Gig Racing Committee, 1975), at p.6.

St Agnes Pilots, 1871. There is no definitive key, but the following list collates the best available evidence. Figures are of age (a.) and of dates of Trinity House licences (t). Numbers 4 and 18, and (if correctly identified) 5 and 6, were of course not pilots. Names read from left to right, facing the photograph.

Seated, front row: 1. Walter Hicks (a. 48, t. 1850-1881) 2. 'George' Hicks – said to be the father of Hugh (number 9), but other sources give the name of that Hugh's father as Hugh. 3. Humphrey Hicks (a. 55) 4. Augustus Smith – 'the Governor'

Seated, second row: 5. Possibly Augustus Smith's agent 6. Possibly 'young' Humphrey Hicks (a. 14) 7. Amor Hicks (a. 54) 8. Benjamin Hicks (t. 1844-1850)

At rear: 9. Hugh Hicks – father of Stephen (number 10) – (a. 68, t. 1830-1855) 10. Stephen Hicks – son of Hugh (number 9) and grandfather of the Stephen Lewis of our story – (a. 45, t.1857-1889) 11. Leonard Hicks 12. Abram Hicks – father of the Charlotte Ellen of our story (a. 33) 13. Israel Hicks – father of the Israel of our story (a. 36, t. 1856-1895) 14. Stephen Hicks (a.35) 15. Possibly Joseph Hicks (a. 39) 16. William Hicks (a. 27, t. 1866-1875) 17. William George Mortimer – the lifeboat coxswain in our story – (a. 24) 18. (partially out of frame) Rev Mr Cole.

© Gibsons of Scilly.

allocation to the off islands.[28] The jurisdiction of these Trinity House pilots was not purely local – they could and did take vessels up Channel and into London or any intermediate port.

When Augustus Smith arrived in 1834 he made support of pilotage one of his main interests. On the one hand his promotion of education in general included, specifically, a strong emphasis for boys on mathematics and navigation. On the other hand he fought Trinity House at all levels, up to and including Parliament, whenever the interests of Scillonian pilots were threatened by the activities or proposals of that authority. It seems clear that despite attempts by Trinity House to prevent unlicensed persons from acting as pilots a number did so with Smith's support, as appears from a well-known photograph in 1871 by John Gibson of Augustus with "his" St Agnes pilots, of whom there are in that photograph at least 14. The 1871 census discloses four more St Agnes men whose occupation is recorded as "pilot" (Thomas Albert Hicks, John Hicks, Isaac Legg and William Thomas Hicks) and there was also the Abraham James Hicks of our story, giving a total of 19, but only eight of them appear in the list of licences issued by Trinity House.

The extent to which pilotage could reduce the number of men actually on the islands at any particular time was substantial. The 1841 census record for St Agnes alone records fourteen as "cruising in pilot boats", the 1851 census eleven "not in houses" and the 1861 census seven "away piloting"

As a contribution to the economy of the islands pilotage had its heyday in the mid-nineteenth century. In 1854 201 vessels were returned as taking Scillonian pilots inward and 185 outward, paying total fees of £616 (£37,160 in 2014 money). The pilots themselves kept only a small part of that total, because, as we shall see in more detail in chapter 11, each pilot, or group of pilots required the support of a cutter and/or gig, each with its crew and owners, all entitled to their shares. By 1907 this sector was in sharp decline; in 1876 the number of Trinity House licences had been reduced to 15, and in 1900 it was only eight.[29]

Three pilots in particular feature prominently in our own story. As we have seen in chapter 1, it was William Thomas ("Billy Cook") Hicks who fatefully accepted the job offered by the *Lawson's* master. Abraham James

....

28   Jenkins (note 27 above), at pp. 13–14.
29   Ibid., at p. 4.

Hicks, who had declined it because of his duties as acting second coxswain of the lifeboat, became the longest-serving Trinity House Channel pilot, serving for 43 years.[30] Young John Horace (Jack) Hicks was then too young to hold a licence, but lived to become the last surviving St Agnes pilot.[31]

The islands' advantage in climate was that their mild winters, with their freedom from frosts, brought on some exceptionally early crops. In the work by Robert Maybee, *Sixty-Eight Years' Experience of the Scilly Islands,* already drawn upon for a description of kelp-making, there is a reference to a market for early potatoes "which brought high prices for a number of years".[32] That seems to relate to a period beginning about 1838, but for whatever reason potato-growing was by the mid-1860s no longer profitable. It was, however, about to be replaced by much the most important example of this kind, the flower industry.[33] The honour of despatching the first box is disputed, but there can be no doubt about the importance of the contribution made by Augustus Smith's nephew and successor, T.A. Dorrien-Smith, in research, education, the introduction of new species, and general promotion of the trade.

One effect of his efforts, and those of Augustus himself, was to transform the appearance of the islands, because by example and encouragement they promoted the planting as windbreaks for the flower-plots of veronica, escallonia, euonymus and, most profusely, pittosporum. Early photographs of the Isles of Scilly portray a bleak, almost treeless, landscape, and on the off-islands there are still wide stretches of granitic moorland, but the influence of flower-farming eventually (it is noteworthy that in places the appearance of treelessness persisted to a surprisingly late date) altered the picture presented by cultivable land beyond recognition into a patchwork of narrow fields, often well under an acre each in area, surrounded by high, dense evergreen hedges.

The importance of flower-growing to the economy of the islands was until recently immense. The trade was in species of the daffodil and narcissus families, most notably *Soleil d'Or* and *Paper White*, picked in bloom. From the first, experimental, box in 1865 or 1867 it grew (in tons of 200 boxes each) to 65 in 1885, 100 in 1887, 514 in 1896 and about 800

....

30 Ibid., at p. 15.
31 Ibid., at p. 71.
32 Rowley (note 2 above), at p. 85.
33 Ibid., at p. 104.

A Scillonian family bunching flowers. © Gibsons of Scilly.

by the date of our story, to peak later at some 1,200 tons before declining more recently in the face of competition from flowers grown nearer mass markets in artificial climates.[34]

The success of the flower industry, and of its successor as the islands' mainstay, tourism, which was only in its infancy at the date with which we are concerned, depended heavily on the speed, frequency and cost of transport. That was not just a matter of the sea link with Penzance; the accessibility of Penzance from the main urban centres of England was also important, and it was not until 1820 that mail coaches served the town regularly. A milestone was the arrival of the railway in 1859. Sailings to and from the islands were irregular and infrequent until a weekly service began early in the nineteenth century. From 1858 there was a more frequent

....

34   Rowley (note 2 above), at p. 104.

steamer, at first the *Little Western* three times a week, then from 1872 the *Lady of the Isles*, and from 1904 the *Lyonesse*, which we have already briefly met in chapter 1.[35]

The location of the islands led to another, murkier, activity: the trade in contraband goods. That took two distinct forms. There was plenty of outright smuggling – the planned running of uncustomed goods for profit. Everyone knew that that was a criminal activity, but there was also a great deal of incidental bartering of local goods or services, even pilotage, for tobacco, spirits and the like carried by visiting or passing vessels, which was probably regarded by those engaged in it as perfectly legitimate.

Commercial smuggling no doubt had a long history, but became notoriously widespread in the eighteenth century. Island gigs could, and did, cross the Channel – James Nance of St Martin, who also had a lawful occupation as a pilot, claimed to have done so 25 times, once riding out a gale for 30 hours in the process.[36] No prosecution was practicable unless the goods were actually in the boat when stopped, so at the sight of a revenue cutter kegs were dumped overboard, each tied to a shaped stone to hold it on the bottom, and cross-bearings taken of the position. But at the height of the trade bigger business interests and larger vessels seem to have been involved. It is more than once said in the literature, albeit without citation of authority, that at one time more customed goods were being shipped as contraband into the Isles of Scilly than were being landed legally in the port of London. Apparent respectability was no guarantee of innocence; the Rev. John Troutbeck, celebrated Chaplain and historian of the Isles, was forced to resign his living in disgrace in the 1790s because of his involvement.[37]

Successive attempts to deal with the situation were for many years unavailing. Harsher penalties were no deterrent because such small numbers, proportionately, of the smugglers were successfully prosecuted. Reducing the duty on a frequently run commodity, such as tea, was futile; the trade simply switched to those still highly taxed, such as tobacco and spirits. A basic weakness was the low pay, poor organisation, understaffing and consequent low morale of the enforcement agencies. The one partially redeeming feature of the Scillonian scene was that the area seems to have

....

35   Ibid., at pp. 157–8.
36   *The Scillonian and his Boat* (note 26 above) at p. 24.
37   *The Scillonian and his Boat* (note 26 above) at p. 21, and *Gigs and Cutters of the Isles of Scilly* (note 27 above, at pp. 16 & 23.

escaped the really serious violence which terrorised and scarred whole communities in Kent and other parts of South-East England.

In the nineteenth century the tide at last turned, for two main reasons. One was the improvement of the preventive services. In 1809 the Preventive Waterguard was established, with better pay and conditions, more co-ordination and a consequent rise in morale. After a setback when the end of the Napoleonic wars in 1815 released a tide of unemployed ex-soldiers and sailors as potential recruits to the smuggling gangs a further reorganisation produced the Coast Guard, which by 1831 had taken over all responsibility and was making real inroads. The other, and decisive, reason was the advent of Robert Peel's free trade policies in the 1840s, which cut customs duties across the board and thus slashed or eliminated the smugglers' profit margins.[38] Although small-scale smuggling persisted for some time in the Scillies it seems to have ceased to play any significant part in island life by the date of our story.

Not so the final activity of economic importance – salvage. Salvage was of two kinds, first assistance to a vessel in difficulties which saved it from becoming a loss, and secondly wrecking, the recovery of cargo from a vessel already lost. Its debt to location is obvious. Richard Larn, in *Shipwrecks of the Isles of Scilly*, lists 726 vessels, by name, known to have been total losses in the Isles of Scilly down to 1992, and given the incompleteness of evidence for earlier centuries that must fall well short of the true total.

The word 'wrecking' has designedly been introduced above, not only because it is correct technically and the one used by Scillonians themselves, but also in order to dispose at the outset of the persistent calumny, sometimes repeated tongue in cheek, but too often uttered or listened to in all seriousness, that the islanders lured vessels to their destruction for the sake of their cargoes. Not only is there no shred of credible evidence that that ever happened; it would also have been wholly inconsistent with the scores of well-authenticated instances in which islanders risked, and sometimes lost, their own lives in perilous attempts to rescue the crews of wrecked vessels. Saving life was always the first thought and the highest priority. Our own story is one example. It suffices, perhaps, to give just one other (perhaps the best known) of the many available, and this time from another island.

....

38   *Smugglers' Britain* (Richard Platt, 2006, www.smuggling.co.uk).

Early on 20 December 1871, during a west-north-west gale, the inhabitants of Bryher sighted a large steamer in distress, being driven into the Northern Rocks, which lie to the west of the island. She was the *Delaware*, 3,243 tons, bound from Liverpool for Calcutta with a general cargo and passengers. By noon, with the wind still rising, she was drifting between Seal Rock and Mincarlo, towards Bream Ledge. She was apparently without power, because the watchers saw her crew hoisting storm sails, only to have them blown out. Then her bridge structure was swept away by one huge wave, another swamped her open deck, and shortly after that she foundered. There had been fifty persons aboard the vessel and after she sank the islanders saw five clinging to wreckage or in the ship's boat. They believed that any survivors would fetch up on White Island, west of Samson, but there was no lifeboat station in the islands at that time and no gig could have lived in the sea that was running off that shore of Bryher, so they devised a different plan.

It involved launching the *Albion* gig on the south coast of Bryher, more sheltered and the nearest to Samson, but she was housed at Great Par (in modern maps Great Porth), on the west. The *Albion* was bigger and more heavily built than the standard pilot gig to be described in Chapter 11, which was an advantage for the job she had to do, but meant that a 30 foot, half ton, boat had to be manhandled across the island. There were of course no paved roads. They lashed her six oars across her and twelve men (presumably not including any of the crew who would have to man her) dragged her across the half mile distance and over the rise to Rushy Bay. There she was put in the water and set out southwards under oars, at first across the relatively exposed channel between Bryher and Samson and then, with a little easting, into the lee of Samson. Samson consists of a North Hill and a South Hill, joined by a narrow and low-lying neck of land. They passed North Hill and landed on the beach of East Par, or Porth, on the sheltered side of that neck, got ashore and, looking across to White Island to the west, saw the *Delaware's* boat strike the rocks there and two occupants scramble out.

The *Albion's* crew, already soaked and exhausted, next dragged her across the neck of Samson to West Par and, leaving one watchman on North Hill, re-launched her, this time into the full force of the storm, with only the partial shelter of tiny White Island itself, and that not squarely to windward until they had made some southing. Somehow they made the crossing and managed to get the gig ashore among the rocks without being holed, to find that the two men from the *Delaware,* half naked, had gathered stones to throw at the supposedly hostile natives. Persuaded otherwise, they were given some of their rescuers' own clothing, and the Bryher men then searched the rocky islet in vain for any other survivors before rowing back to Samson, this time with the gale over their quarter, which helped them on their way but had its own dangers. They were by now incapable of any further exertion, and some accounts have them spending the night on Samson, but what seem to be more reliable versions of the story have it that their watchman had already signalled for a second gig, the *March,* to come over from Bryher, so that with the help of its crew rescuers and rescued could make the journey back. The two survivors from the *Delaware* were her first and third mates. No-one involved received any recognition or reward from the shipowners or any government, but there was a grant of £15 from the Royal National Lifeboat Institution.[39]

There is a link between that story and wrecking, properly so called, because next day, the wind having dropped, every able-bodied man on the island was out, as always after a wreck, recovering salvageable cargo from the sea, the coast or the offshore rocks. When the wrecked vessel herself was stranded above water that would involve boarding her, itself not a risk-free activity, as witness the deaths of Charles Mumford of St Mary's and Charles Hicks of St Agnes in 1909, while below deck in the *Plympton,* which had struck on the Lethegus rocks off St Agnes and was apparently securely wedged, but fell off into deep water as the tide rose.

The law of salvage from wrecks is clear: all property recovered must be delivered to the Receiver of Wreck, but the salvor is entitled to a reward commensurate with the service rendered, taking into account the value of the property recovered and any risk undertaken, as well as the work done and time expended. To conceal or retain any such property is an offence. What actually happened, and still happens, in the islands (and probably in all maritime communities) is rather more varied, and the line between lawful and unlawful behaviour rather less clear-cut.

....

39 The story of the *Delaware* is told in many places, but this summary draws chiefly on *Shipwrecks of the Isles of Scilly* by Richard Larn (Thomas & Lochar, 1993), at pp. 80–81, *The Scillonian and his Boat* (note 26 above) at p.52–53, *Gigs and Cutters of the Isles of Scilly* (note 27 above) at p. 56 and *Ships, Shipwrecks and Maritime Incidents around the Isles of Scilly* (Isles of Scilly Museum Publication No. 3, 1999 revision).

The Castleford aground on Crebawethan, 1887, with one of its cargo of cattle in the fore-ground. © National Maritime Museum, Greenwich, London. Gibsons of Scilly shipwreck collection.

There is, in practice, a broad spectrum of situations. At one end lies cargo which is of value to its true owner but of no practical use to the salvor, or not realistically capable either of being turned to account or concealed. Legal duty and self-interest combine to ensure that it is dutifully delivered to the Receiver and the reward claimed. On two occasions vessels ran into rocks in calm weather carrying live cattle (the *Castleford* on Crebawethan in the Western Rocks in 1887 and the liner *Minnehaha*, 13,433 tons, on Scilly Rock, off Bryher, in 1910) and on both occasions gigs were used to tow cattle to the nearest uninhabited island carrying vegetation (Annet in the case of the *Castleford* and Samson in the case of the *Minnehaha*), where they could be collected later. For every head of cattle saved from the *Castleford* the salvage reward was £2, in those days an enormous sum by the standards of the islanders,[40] although when the same price was offered for cattle

....

40 *Shipwrecks of the Isles of Scilly* (note 39 above) at p. 34 and *Gigs and Cutters of the Isles of Scilly* (note 27 above) at p. 26. According to *The Scillonian and his Boat* (note 26 above), at p. 65, 400 head of cattle were salvaged in that way, making the total award £800 (£66,000 in 2014 money).

Cattle being towed ashore from the Minnehaha in 1910. © National Maritime Museum, Greenwich, London. Gibsons of Scilly shipwreck collection.

from the *Minnehaha* 23 years later there was "some indignation amongst the men, as ... last time [unspecified] they had £5".[41]

The second category, at the other extreme, consists of individual items so trivial in commercial value as not to be worth the expense of collection by the owners, or in a state in which they are no longer saleable, but of use to finders in the position of the islanders. Whatever the letter of the law the practical reality is that such items can safely be kept without need of concealment or fear of prosecution.

In between, thirdly, are goods which ought, no doubt, to be delivered to the Receiver, but which are of debatable net value to the owner and certainly worth more to the finder, if kept, than the reward which would be paid for their delivery up. There is, however, a continuous gradation

....

41 *The Islander* magazine, Spring 2010, p.27, quoting a copy letter from *The Isles of Scilly: their Story, their Folk and their Flowers* by Jessie Mothersole.

from those very close to the first category to those nearer the second, and arguably in it. There is also a considerable difference between the organised unloading of cargo from a stranded but stable vessel, which would normally be declared, and goods afloat, washed up on shore or rescued from the hull in more chaotic circumstances. Some salvors may be meticulously law-abiding, going to the Receiver whenever in doubt, but it seems clear that in the Isles of Scilly the widespread opinion, historically, was that most goods of the latter kind could justifiably be kept, although an appreciation that the Receiver might take a different view was sometimes betrayed by the lengths to which people occasionally went to conceal the booty until the hue and cry had died down, after which they were often very open in using and displaying it and acknowledging its origins

The other kind of salvage, the rescue or recovery of the vessel itself, with or without its cargo, if in danger of wreck, or if already damaged but not a total loss, was of course entirely legitimate and, although it capriciously yielded the occasional windfall to the particular persons involved rather than a steady income to the islanders in general, was a significant contrib-utor to the islands' economy. The erection of the St Agnes church by the use of salvage money received by the island's pilots has already been mentioned. That came from a vessel abandoned amongst the Western Rocks. One other example from the many instances recorded is the schooner *Boadicea*, which in 1864 lost her rudder in a gale. A St Agnes cutter provided her with steerage by being lashed to her stern and the cutter's crew brought her into Scilly, for which they received a salvage award of £530. Another is the three-masted American schooner *Marion G. Douglas*, sighted derelict off Bryher in 1919. The crews of the gigs *Czar* and *Sussex* (on that day almost every able-bodied man on the island) boarded her, set sail and brought her safely in, earning salvage of £3,000.[42]

So much by way of general introduction to the islands into the waters of which the *T.W. Lawson* had inadvertently sailed on the afternoon of Friday 13 December 1907. The next chapter turns to some specific facts about the islanders – the ebb and flow of their numbers over the years, and especially the composition of the population of the island most closely involved in our story, St Agnes, and the links between its members.

....

42   Jenkins (note 27 above), at pp. 29–30.

· 8 ·

The Islanders

U NTIL THE INSTITUTION of the decennial census in 1841 information about population numbers is scant. The story in chapter 7, told
in 1540, of the loss within recent memory of the loss by drowning of five
households, the entire population of St Agnes, suggests really tiny communities on the off islands and, if their relationship with numbers on St Mary's
was roughly similar to that when we have exact figures, possibly something like three hundred islanders altogether. In 1579 Francis Godolphin,
reporting on an inquiry he had been ordered to conduct into the state of
the islands, speaks of "not a hundred men, but more women and children",[1]
which would represent a total in the same region. Not dissimilar, estimated,
figures of 250 in 1551 and 300 in 1571, compiled from unstated sources,
are given in *The Fortunate Islands*.[2]

The earliest reliable count, although of households rather than individuals, is recorded in the Parliamentary Survey of 1652, commissioned by
the victors in the Civil War as part of the pacification of the last outpost of
Royalist resistance.[3] It found 113 households on St Mary's, 19 on Tresco,
8 on Agnes, 2 on St Martin's and 6 on Bryher, a total of 148. Extrapolating
from that to individuals is speculative, but the impression is of a rather

....

1   Calendar of State Papers (Eliz. I add: 1579), as quoted in *The Fortunate Islands* (R.L. Rowley,
    Rowley Publications, 8th ed. 1990), at p.36.
2   *The Fortunate Islands* by R.L. Rowley (Rowley Publications, 8th ed. 1990), at p.188; the
    figures in the text, above, are approximate, because those on pp. 188 and 189 differ.
3   *Scilly Islands: survey (67ff)* Public Record Office E.317/Corn./39.

larger population than that glimpsed in the sixteenth century snapshots, perhaps in the region of 500 to 600.

In 1715 individuals were counted, in a survey by Col. Christian Lilly, Chief Engineer to the West Indies, in a report on the military strength of Scilly and its fortifications. He found 822 inhabitants in all, of whom 477 were on St Mary's and 345 on the off islands.[4] That suggests somewhere around 70 on St Agnes. From then until the end of that century the best source is the Duchy rent rolls, but they revert to counting by households rather than individuals. Those for St Agnes are examined in more detail below, but for present purposes can be summarised as showing a slow increase over the first half of the century, quickening toward the end,[5] to give 35 households in 1799, as compare with 13 in 1710. It so happens that the figure for 1799 can be compared with those from other sources for three nearby dates, two of which also give individual numbers. Graeme Spence, in 1792, counts 37 houses.[6] John Troutbeck writes in 1794 that "there are "42 dwelling-houses upon this island, and about 200 inhabitants."[7] Alf Jenkins states that "by the turn of the [eighteenth] century St Agnes claimed 300 inhabitants living in some 63 houses"[8] but he is writing in 1982 and does not cite any sources, so the contemporary authors, who accord reasonably well with the rent rolls, seem more reliable, and suggest a population at the turn of the century of around Troutbeck's figure of 200.

There is then a gap until the first census in 1841. The full census returns for St Agnes are tabulated in Appendix 3, but the picture for the islands as a whole is of a fairly steady decline from about 2,700 in 1841 to about 2,100 in 1901.[9]

The story in Chapter 1 cannot be read without its becoming apparent that one surname dominates among the St Agnes men involved, and that will be even clearer when the full lists of the lifeboat and gig crews are given in later chapters, It is illuminating to examine how that came about.

It is not known when the first Hicks arrived in the Isles of Scilly. Like so

....

4   *The Story of Samson* (Z.T. Cowan, Englang Publishing, 1991), at p. 6.
5   Henry Spry, writing in 1800, refers to the building of "a great many houses" within the last 20 years.
6   *A Survey of the Scilly Isles* (Graeme Spence, 1792).
7   *A Survey of the Ancient and Present State of the Scilly Islands* (John Troutbeck, 1794).
8   *The Scillonian and his Boat* (1982), at p.22.
9   Rowley (note 2 above) at pp. 188, 189; the figures in the text, above, are approximate, because those on the two pages cited differ.

many old Scillonian names Hicks is not "Cornish", in the sense of coming from the Celtic group of languages, but Anglo-Saxon – a variant of Dixon or Dickson (i.e. Dick's son). It may therefore have been brought to the islands by a soldier in the garrison, but that is no more than a plausible speculation.

The 1652 survey already cited lists, on "Agnes Island", eleven "tenements", with eight named "occupiers", presumably heads of families.[10] Three of them are Hicks – Henry, Richard and Bernard, and it seems certain that since some unknown date before 1652 there has never been a time when there was no Hicks on St Agnes.

There is a mathematical theorem which proves that in a closed community in which surnames descend in the male line all but one will tend eventually to die out. The mathematics is beyond the scope of this book, but the basic idea behind it is very simple: there is always the possibility that in any particular generation all the men of any given name will either be childless or have only daughters, whereupon that name disappears, never to be recovered. For reasonably common names in a community of any substantial size that possibility has such a tiny probability that the process would take thousands of years to have any visible effect, and in an open community, with new names arriving from outside, the theorem does not in any event apply, but St Agnes was so small, and although never completely closed it was during the period which concerns us so nearly so (at least in terms of marriage), that the process can actually be seen at work.

After the 1652 survey the next source of information on this subject is the rent rolls from 1710 to 1799, mentioned above. In 1710 there were thirteen tenants on St Agnes, of whom three were Hicks. All the other 1652 names had disappeared, except Stevens (now Stephens) and Eady (now Eddy). By 1745 there are six Hicks tenants out of sixteen, and the name Eddy has gone. In 1763 there are eight Hicks tenants out of twenty, and by 1767 nine out of twenty. The surge in population towards the end of the century brought in some newcomers, but nevertheless, in 1799, out of 35 tenants, 18 are Hicks. The new names include Legg and Mortimer, which were to prove the only other survivors by the end of the new century about to begin, Stephens finally dying out between the 1871 and 1881 censuses.

From 1841 the census returns each ten years until 1911 give such a wealth of information that it is better to organise it in tables than attempt

....

10   Public Record Office (note 3 above).

to set it all out in narrative form. In the first two tables in Appendix 3 the total population is classified as "incomers", by category, and "islanders", by name. The next table gives some idea of the extent to which St Agnes approached a truly closed community, by giving the places of birth of the islanders as between St Agnes, the rest of the Isles of Scilly, and elsewhere. Finally there is a table expressing the salient information in percentages. In 1851 99.4 per cent of the islanders had been born in the Scillies and 89.2 per cent on St Agnes, and in 1911 those figures are still as high as 84.9 per cent and 76.7 per cent respectively, although there had been a sharp drop in the last ten years, spanning the date of our story. There is a steady growth of the three dominant names from 76.4 per cent of all islanders in 1841 to a peak of 86.2 per cent in 1901, falling off to 79.7 per cent in 1811, and within those three a trend of growth of Hicks from 58.1 per cent in 1841 to a peak of 69.2 per cent in 1891, falling off to 63.0 per cent in 1911.

It is to be expected that in such a small, close-knit, community there will be an intricate web of familial relationships, and indeed there was. Those among the members of the lifeboat and gig crews will be explored later, and this is not the place for an exhaustive study of others,[11] but some more general questions do call for brief answers.

The first is whether all the islanders, or at least all those with a shared name, were related to each other. So far as those called Hicks were concerned the answer is the perhaps surprising one that in 1907 there were at least two distinct family groups, with no common Hicks ancestors for as far back as surviving records of births (or baptisms), marriages and deaths (or burials) extend, that is to say since the early to mid 1700s. The only ascertainable Hicks link between them since then was the marriage in 1889 between the Israel who opens our story, from one branch, and his wife Charlotte Ellen, from the other.

That leads naturally to another question, which inevitably raises itself when such a small, nearly closed, community is studied. How can opportunities to find a spouse from outside it arise? Some were very occasional – at least one St Agnes woman married a man working on the final enlargement and strengthening of the Bishop Rock lighthouse between 1882 and

....

11   There is a fuller treatment by the present author in *The Hicks Family of St Agnes* (*The Scillonian*, Summer Issue 2008, p. 177, and Winter Issue 2009, p.154), drawn upon extensively in this chapter by kind permission of the editor, Mr Clive Mumford).

1887.[12] Others were more persistent – in earlier centuries, as we have seen, soldiers, and later a steady succession of schoolteachers, curates and Bible Christian ministers and, in rather larger numbers, lighthouse keepers and coastguards. Was there much intermarriage with them or their families? The birthplace percentages in Appendix 3 and the high proportion of Hickses who married their own namesakes during the eighteenth and most of the nineteenth century suggest that the answer then was negative (in some of those categories perhaps for social reasons), but the daughters of lighthouse keepers seem to have been something of an exception.

The converse question to that, and equally inevitable, is how often marriages occurred between close relatives. The perhaps unexpected answer seems to be rarely. Only three first-cousin marriages have been traced in a fairly full examination of the registers.

Much more of interest and, in other contexts, importance could be written about the islands which, at the end of Chapter 6, the *Lawson* was approaching, and their inhabitants, but this book is primarily about what happened there to the schooner, and to that we now return.

---

12 The workman was a labourer called Pearce, who married Rovena (or Rovina) Hicks and settled on the island, where their descendants still live.

· 9 ·

The Lifeboats

BOTH OF THE LIFEBOATS which attended the *T.W. Lawson* were provided by the Royal National Lifeboat Institution and operated under its auspices.

To the birth of that remarkable body, a charity privately governed and funded, and operating boats almost entirely crewed by volunteers, but nevertheless providing the only organised fleet operating throughout the British Isles and dedicated to the saving of life at sea or on the coast, we must shortly turn. It would not have occurred, however, had there nor been earlier, more dispersed, pioneering efforts, beginning with the conception and invention of lifeboats themselves.

An ordinary boat is unsafe in a rough sea because it is liable to fill with water and sink, or to capsize. To combat the first it needs more buoyancy and the means of discharging shipped water rapidly. To combat the second it needs more stability, and possibly also the capacity to self-right if capsized. These requirements are interconnected. The most obvious and common way of improving stability is to add weight low down in the form of a heavy keel or of ballast stowed in the bottom of the hull, but that increases the need for additional buoyancy. The "possibly" in the statement above reflects the fact that the capacity to self-right is itself bought at what some have thought to be too high a price in reduced initial stability.

The first person to address and satisfy those requirements was Lionel Lukin, a London coach-builder, who in 1785 patented, and twice realised, a design in which buoyancy was added, first, by projecting gunwales divided into compartments filled with either a light, water-repellent, material such as cork or with watertight air-chambers and, secondly, by packing suitable spaces in the interior with similarly filled compartments. Stability was provided by the addition of a heavy external metal keel.

If, however, a boat is not just to be safe for its occupants, but to be of use in rescuing others, there is a further requirement – it must be capable of carrying several more people than its own crew. Lukin was not originally concerned with that aspect, but in 1786 a coble with such a capacity was sent to him for conversion, and was then used for many years at Bamburgh for rescuing shipwrecked sailors. It was the first lifeboat. Lukin also seems to have been the originator, in 1807, of valved ducts as means of shedding water taken inboard. In the years which followed a number of boats based on his design were built, in particular for use around the coast of Norfolk and Suffolk.

Independently, on Tyneside, following a particularly distressing wreck, a committee of gentlemen offered in 1789 a prize for the best plan or model of a boat that would live in heavily broken water. William Wouldhave, a music teacher and house-painter, had already made and tested such a model, which he entered. It shared many of the characteristics of Lukin's boats, but unlike them was self-righting. The committee accepted that it was the best entry, but grudgingly awarded Wouldhalve only half of the prize. His design, apart from the self-righting capacity, was nevertheless the basis of the boat, the *Original*, which they commissioned and had built by Henry Greathead. It was launched in January 1790, was the first purpose-built lifeboat, the first in regular use in a constantly available lifeboat service, and the pattern for some 30 more built by Greathead over the next 14 years and used at various stations at home and abroad.

There were no mechanical means of propulsion, so all these boats had to be pulled by oars or sailed. It would seem from illustrations that Wouldhalve's design provided for propulsion by oars alone, whereas there are indications that Lukin's allowed for the use of sail also.

The invention of the lifeboat provided the necessary tool, but for some time its use was at best sporadic. A comprehensive service required a national organisation. The prime mover in its formation was Sir William Hillary, who was inspired by his own experiences in rescues and attempted rescues off the coast of the Isle of Man to publish in 1823 an *Appeal to the British Nation* on the subject. That elicited enough influential support to enable a preparatory public meeting to be held in London on 12 February 1824, which unanimously resolved that " ... a National Institution should be formed ... for the preservation of life in the case of shipwreck ... " and that "with a view to the formation of such an Institution, a general meeting of the Nobility, Gentry, Merchants, Traders and others be convened ...".

By the date of that general meeting, 4 March 1824, the promoters of the scheme had secured the patronage of King George IV, the support of several royal vice-patrons, and the agreement of the Prime Minister, Lord Liverpool, to be the President and that of the Archbishop of Canterbury to chair the inaugural meeting, Numerous other influential persons were willing to serve in various capacities. Not surprisingly the meeting unanimously passed several resolutions, the first and crucial one being that "an Institution be now formed for the Preservation of Life in cases of shipwreck on the Coasts of the United Kingdom, to be supported by donations and annual subscriptions; and to be called the 'National Institution for the preservation of Life from Shipwreck'."

The Institution thus started with a big bang, and in its first year it received donations of £9,706 (£620,000 in 2014 money) and arranged to establish fifteen lifeboat stations. But that first burst of enthusiasm rapidly dissipated; by 1838 income touched bottom at £254 and for several years the whole project was near collapse. It needed a major overhaul, and that began in 1850 and received a decisive impetus in 1851 from the appointment of the Duke of Northumberland to the long-vacant presidency. By 1854, when it was re-named the Royal National Lifeboat Institution, it had acquired all the essential characteristics which we shall see in evidence in the events of 14 December 1907 and which still obtain today.[1]

On the Isles of Scilly gigs had regularly been used in rescue attempts, but they could not live in the heaviest seas, and in 1837 the islands' Inspecting Commander of Coastguards formed a local branch of the National Institution, raised some money and applied to the national Committee of Management for the stationing of a lifeboat. That was done by transferring one formerly at Brighton, and St Mary's became a lifeboat station. The boat itself was broken up in 1839 and another transferred, this time from Plymouth, but "neither [was] a success",[2] and that first station was closed

....

1   This account of the origins of lifeboats and of the RNLI is summarised from the opening chapters of *Britain's Life-Boats* by A.J. Dawson (Hodder and Stoughton 1923).

2   *Cornwall's Lifeboat Heritage* by Nicholas Leach (Twelveheads Press 2000), p.39.

in 1855, there having been only one occasion, in 1841, when its lifeboat was launched in service.[3]

Shipwrecks continued, however, and there were two in particular, early in the 1870s, which revived local pressure for a station. One was that of the *Delaware*, described in chapter 7. The other involved the *Minnehaha*, a four-masted barque whose master had mistaken the St Agnes lighthouse for that on the Wolf Rock.[4] The RNLI was prevailed upon to reopen the station in 1874, and it has remained in active operation ever since, with a notable record of service, evidenced by the number of awards to its crew members, in particular to the members of the Lethbridge family, who supplied, in addition to many other positions, its coxswains for 71 successive years (James Thomas 1914–25, Matthew (senior) 1925–56 and Matthew (junior) 1956–85).[5] "Young Matt" achieved notoriety in 1967 when the St Mary's lifeboat was called to the wrecked 120,000 ton tanker *Torrey Canyon*, but that was not, by his standards, a dangerous outing and did not compare in real importance with countless other less newsworthy launches, some in really fearsome conditions, for example during the Fastnet race of 1979.

As to St Agnes, the RNLI's Station Record for "St Agnes (Scilly)" – there was, and still is, another lifeboat station at St Agnes on the mainland of Cornwall – has the following succinct entry: "Opening History. After SCHILLER wreck (7 May 1875) Inspector visited St. Agnes re possible new station. Men preferred to use their gigs. Apr. 1889 an Inspector again visited and men then wanted a lb."

That invites some unpacking. One of the reasons for the significance of the *Schiller* disaster was no doubt its sheer scale, she having been a passenger liner with a total complement, including crew, of 355, of whom only 43 survived, 27 in the only two of her own boats to get clear and just 16 others.[6] Another reason, however, was surely its location, on the Retarrier Ledges, far out in the Western Rocks, among which so many vessels came to grief; a pulling and sailing lifeboat based on St Mary's had to spend much costly time and energy in reaching and passing St Agnes before it could begin its passage into that danger area. It is noteworthy, next, that it is now the RNLI

....

3   Apart from the quotation (note 2) this paragraph is summarised from *The Story of the Isles of Scilly Lifeboats* by Jeff Morris (RNLI 1987), pp 1 and 2.
4   *Ibid.* at p. 2 where, however, both wrecks are dated 1870; the *Delaware* was in fact lost in 1871 and this *Minnehaha* (she had a namesake – see chapter 7) in 1874.
5   RNLI: Personnel Record for St Mary's (Scilly) station.
6   *Shipwrecks of the Isles of Scilly* by Richard Larn (Thomas & Lochar, 1993), at pp.22–23.

Digging a mass grave in Old Town churchyard, for victims of the Schiller. © Gibsons of Scilly.

itself which takes the initiative; it clearly has the resources and vigour to be seeking to extend its reach wherever it judges there may be need.

But, finally, those short sentences illustrate how utterly dependent the whole enterprise was upon local involvement, and how crucial to that involvement was faith in the craft which the RNLI could provide. The "men" whom the inspectors quote would be the volunteers needed as crew, but so far from being amateurs they were seasoned boatmen with an intimate knowledge of the waters in which they would have to operate. And the issue was not whether they would be concerned in seeking to save lives, but how. In 1875 they "preferred to use their gigs". But in 1889 they wanted a lifeboat. And that was that; in 1890 they got one.

That interrelationship between the RNLI, its committees and officers, on the one hand, and the lifeboat crews on the other, will be further explored when we examine the aftermath of the *Lawson* wreck in chapter 12, but at this point two illustrations from the RNLI regulations help to set the scene. By regulation 6 appointment of the officers of the boat and other arrangements for manning it are to rest with the committee, but they are to consult the crew in the selection of the coxswain and assistant coxswain,

Left: Launching the Henry Dundas, the St Mary's lifeboat 1899–1919; Right: Christening the Charles Deere James, the St Agnes lifeboat 1904–1909. © Gibsons of Scilly.

and by regulation 19 the coxswain and crew are to be fully consulted about any new boat (and as we shall see that happened, to decisive effect, at St Mary's and St Agnes). On the other hand the RNLI did not take the skills of even lifelong boatmen for granted; there were regular inspections, and regulation 16 required that the boat be "taken afloat for Exercise, fully manned, <u>in rough weather</u> once in every quarter" (added emphasis).

The boat supplied was for ten oars instead of the usual twelve, and that was probably because of the constraints imposed by the small population of St Agnes. The Station Record already quoted continues and ends as follows:

> *Launching Methods*
> By carriage over concrete slipway.
> *Houses*
> 1890 house and slip at Priglis Bay – £988.18.2.
> 1901 horses no longer available to launch lb.
> 1902–3 new house and long slipway (1068ft) with launching trolley– £4945. Subsequently many alterations and repairs. e.g [and several are listed].
> *Closure*
> 1920 closed in view of stationing a motor lb at St Marys, also difficulty in getting a crew at St Agnes and necessity for further extensive repairs to the slipway.

That also can be fleshed out a little. The reasons for choosing Periglis (as it is now spelt) are not given, but choice was strictly limited and it had the advantage of facing west, while not being unduly exposed, because of the shelter received from Annet. Its big disadvantage was that launching at anything below half tide was difficult because of the distance the water receded and its shallowness for some distance out – hence the inadequacy of the original slipway and the enormous length and cost of the new one (said to have been the longest in the United Kingdom).[7]

The officers of the boats are recorded in a plaque in St Agnes church as follows (although another source gives Abram Hicks as coxswain from the outset).[8]

Abram Hicks	Coxswain 1891–1901 Second coxswain 1890
William George Mortimer	Coxswain 1901–1912 Second coxswain 1891–1901
Osbert Hicks	Coxswain 1912–1920 Second coxswain 1911–1912 Bowman 1901–1911
Abraham James Hicks	Second coxswain 1901–1911 Bowman 1891–1901
Francis Grenfell Legg	Second coxswain 1912–1919 Bowman 1911–1912
Obadiah Hicks junior	Bowman 1912–1920
Stephen Hicks	Signalman 1890–1901
Isaac Legg	Signalman 1901–1920

That brief history sets the scene for the part which the lifeboats played in December 1907. The one then in service at St Mary's was the *Henry Dundas* (the fourth of that name), a 38 ft Watson class boat for twelve oars.[9] She will have weighed about six tons.[10] At St Agnes there was the *Charles Deere James,* also 38 ft long, but a lighter Liverpool class of just over four tons for ten oars.[11] She had been christened on 25 August 1904.

It is noteworthy that neither the *Henry Dundas* nor the *Charles Deere James* was a self-righter, although each station had earlier had a boat or boats which were.[12] The change must have reflected the preferences of the crews. The self-righters of that time required substantial buoyancy chambers placed very high at stem and stern, which caught the wind and hampered manoeuvrability. Their capacity to recover from a capsize had to

....

7   *The Fortunate Islands* by R.L. Rowley (Rowley Publications, 8th ed. 1990), at p.136.
8   *The Story of the Isles of Scilly Lifeboats* by Jeff Morris (RNLI 1987), at p. 5.
9   Ibid., at p. 6.
10   *Britain's Life-Boats* by A.J. Dawson (Hodder and Stoughton 1923), at p. 257.
11   RNLI specification.
12   Morris (note 8 above, at pp. 2–8).

be set against their reduced ability to resist one in the first place. A capsize, even if survived, was an appalling experience, and the Scillonian boatmen clearly preferred to back their ability to avoid one altogether if given the better odds afforded by the alternative design.

It is difficult to find any direct evidence of how many rescued "passengers" such a lifeboat was designed to take on board, perhaps because the number it could safely take depended on sea conditions. The record of the commissioning tests of the *Charles Deere James* includes the rather cryptic note: "34 'deadmen' on Gunwale to bring it awash, crew and gear in." If that means what it seems to say the safe limit, even in calm conditions, would be rather lower, and in a gale like that on the night of the wreck lower still, but probably not so low that the *Lawson's* crew of 18 could not have been accepted. The *Henry Dundas* would no doubt have had a slightly larger capacity.

The St Mary's coxswain at that time was Eustace Thomas and the second coxswain the James Thomas Lethbridge already mentioned.[13] The make-up of the St Agnes crew needs to be examined in more detail, because of its relevance to several aspects of the story. As we have seen, William George Mortimer was at that time the coxswain and Abraham James Hicks the second coxswain, and they were both on duty. The bowman, Osbert Hicks, however, was not, William Trenary serving as acting bowman. The full complement was as follows:[14]

Coxswain:	William George Mortimer
Second coxswain:	Abraham James Hicks
Acting bowman:	William Trenary:
Oars:	William Thomas (Billy Cook) Hicks
	Obadiah Hicks
	Frederick Charles (Freddy Cook) Hicks
	Frederick (Fred) Hicks
	James Thomas Hicks
	James Hicks
	Benjamin Hicks
	Stephen Lewis Hicks
	John Horace (Jack) Hicks
	William Francis Hicks.

....

13 RNLI (note 5 above).

14 The composition of the lifeboat crew is recorded in several sources and is not in doubt, although there are minor differences in the way some members are identified.

Two features of that list invite further examination. The first is the absences, and their implications. Osbert Hicks is the obvious absentee, since he had an official duty to be in the boat, if available, but there are at least two others. As we have seen in chapter 1, Israel Hicks was a sufficiently experienced and competent boatman to have obtained the Trinity House contract for lighthouse relief, and was in the crew of the *Slippen*, the rescue gig, next day, so he would clearly have been in the first-choice lifeboat crew. Francis Grenfell Legg was a qualified pilot, and he also was in the *Slippen's* crew and was later to become bowman and then second coxswain of the lifeboat, so the same is true of him. We know that Israel was relieving the Round Island light that day. He would clearly want some of the better boatmen in the island in his gig, so that is in all likelihood why Osbert and Grenfell Legg, as well as he, were not in the lifeboat.

Whether that also resulted in other absences we cannot be sure (although one possibility will emerge later), because we do not have Israel's crew list or know precisely who would have been the first-choice lifeboat oarsmen, but it seems likely. What we do have, moreover, are indications that there was some difficulty in assembling a fully qualified and experienced crew. One pointer in that direction is Jack's presence. There is not the slightest indication that he did not acquit himself to everyone's satisfaction, and in that time and place a 17-year old would have been much more mature than nowadays, but it nevertheless seems very unlikely that he would have been there if more seasoned oarsmen had been available. There is some support for that in his father's refusal, recounted in chapter 1, to let him take a place in the *Slippen*. There is a similar issue about William Francis. He was clearly not medically fit, and it appears that he was so inexperienced and unprepared as to get into the lifeboat without oilskins.[15]

Difficulty in making up a full crew would be unsurprising. We have noted the probability that the limitation to ten oars reflected the small population, and have seen that "difficulty in getting a crew" was to be given

....

15   Information received by Richard Gillis from crew member James Thomas Hicks, as recorded in *The Loss of the Thomas W. Lawson*, at p.337. (This article was published in at least two versions, the earlier in an unidentified publication of about 1951 and the later, not quite identical, in Gillis' *A Sea Miscellany of Cornwall and the Isles of Scilly* (1968). Our quotations are from the former, as containing an unedited, or less edited, record of what James Thomas actually said.). The same detail about William Francis' lack of oilskins was included in the story of the wreck as told to the author, when a teenager, by his father Charles (Israel's son), himself a boy of ten at the time of the wreck.

as one of the reasons for closure in 1920. Detailed consideration of the demography shows how tight the margins may have been. In the 1901 census there were 109 inhabitants, of whom 22 were "incomers", leaving 87 genuine islanders. Of those 48 were female, leaving 39 males. 21 of them were over 65 or under 18, leaving 18 between those ages. Figures in 1907 are likely to have been very similar (in the 1911 census the overall total was rather less). It is unlikely that William Francis was the only man within that age bracket not fully fit for lifeboat duty. It is true that the census does not include men at sea, but there were liable to be just as many away for that reason when the lifeboat was needed as when the census was taken. It is true also that some of the incomers (in particular coastguard boatmen) will have been qualified, and may have been willing, to serve, although we know that with one possible exception that did not happen on 13 December 1907. On any view, however, the island would have been only too likely to be overstretched if a gig's crew for lighthouse relief and a lifeboat crew had to be found on the same day.

The "Regulations of the Royal National Lifeboat Institution" current in 1907 provided for such a situation. General Regulation 4 provided that the crew was to consist of a coxswain (officially the "Coxswain-Superintendent"), a second coxswain (officially the "Assistant Coxswain", a bowman and "as many more as the boat pulls oars". That last phrase, however, clearly related only to the complement for any particular launch, because the regulation continued that whenever practicable double that number should be enrolled from the resident fishermen, boatmen or coastguardmen. Regulation 5 provided, in addition, for a signalman, who was not to be one of the crew. Under Regulation 8 the coxswain was, when there was a wreck or a vessel in distress, to assemble "his Crew" (meaning those actually manning the boat) and launch, but if not enough of "his Crew" (meaning all those enrolled) were present he was to select the best volunteers he could get to supply their places. There is every reason to believe that that was what William George Mortimer had had to do on this occasion.

The other feature of the crew list calling for further examination is the family relationships between its members. That is a topic which many readers will find easier to follow diagrammatically than in words, and there is accordingly a table at Appendix 4, but a brief narrative account can be given here. One person only, William Trenary, was unrelated to anyone else. His father was a fisherman from Sennen, near Land's End, who with his family had settled on St Agnes in the 1870s, so William, also a fisherman, now aged 29, had grown up there. As to the others there were, as explained in chapter 8, at least two distinct family groups of Hickses on the island, one related to Israel and the other to his wife Charlotte Ellen. Although Israel himself was not in the lifeboat it is convenient to trace the relationships of those who were from those two starting points. To avoid tedious repetition the surname Hicks will normally be omitted and any other surnames italicised. Occupations are from the 1901 census for those then old enough to have one.

Starting on Israel's side, Billy Cook, a pilot and farmer aged 50, and Obadiah, a farmer and pilot of 45, were his first cousins, being the sons of his mother Bathsheba's sister Mary Ann, but they had also become his brothers-in-law by marrying, respectively, his sisters Elizabeth Ann (Lizzie Ann) and Bathsheba Jane (Jane). Billy Cook's son Freddy Cook, a farmer of 26, was Israel's nephew, as Elizabeth Ann's son, and Stephen Lewis, a farmer's son of 24, his first cousin once removed, as the grandson of Bathsheba's brother Stephen. Finally, William George *Mortimer*, a pilot and farmer of 61, was related by marriage, Israel's similarly named father's sister Loveday having had a daughter, Jane Hicks *Jenkins*, whose husband William George was.

On Charlotte Ellen's side Abraham James, a pilot and farmer aged 60, was her uncle by marriage, being the husband of her mother Charlotte Elizabeth's sister Emily Paulina. James Thomas, a farmer's son of 34, Fred, a farmer's son of 23, and Jack, a farmer's son of 17, were Charlotte Ellen's first cousins, James Thomas as Emily Paulina's son and Fred and Jack as the sons of Charlotte Elizabeth's brother Osbert. Finally, William Francis, a farmer of 38, was more distantly related, Emily Paulina's daughter of the same name having married Augustus Frederick, whose brother William Francis was.

That leaves Benjamin and James. Benjamin is almost certainly the Benjamin William who was baptised on 27 April 1851 as the son of Benjamin William and Jane (probably née Ellis). In that event he was a farmer aged 50 from a long-established St Agnes family, and so must have been related to other members of the crew in some way, but the details of that link cannot be traced from the material available. James is more of a puzzle. He cannot be identified in any St Agnes census return or baptismal or marriage register, but there was a James Hicks, recorded as

St Agnes, with its 'towns'. © Gibsons of Scilly.

being from St Agnes, who obtained a Trinity House pilot's licence in 1873 at the age of 28,[16] and he would have been 62 in 1907 and seems the most likely candidate. If he had moved elsewhere and was visiting, which is one possible explanation of his absence from local records, he may have been an exception to the otherwise complete absence of any incomers, and also an addition to the list of those who would not normally have been in the crew. Another possible explanation, at least for his absence from census returns, is that although a resident he happened, as a pilot, to be off the island at the dates when the censuses were taken.

On such a small island the crew members were nearly all close neighbours as well as relations. There were five named localities: Higher Town, which is still a group of houses of that name, Palace, a group now called Middle Town, Lower Town, now a single farmhouse, but then including also a group of cottages, Downs, the name of which now survives in Downs Farm and Downs Cottage, and Troy Town, a little separated from the other settlements at the west end of the island, all as marked on the photograph

....

16 *Gigs and Cutters of the Isles of Scilly* by A.J. Jenkins (Integrated Packaging Group Ltd and the Isles of Scilly Gig Racing Committee, 1975), at p. 71.

above. Billy Cook, Freddy Cook, Abraham James, James Thomas, William Francis and Benjamin all lived in Higher Town, Obadiah, Fred and Jack in Palace, William Trenary in Lower Town, and Stephen Lewis and William George Mortimer in Downs.

At the beginning of this chapter lifeboat crews were referred to as volunteers and so, essentially, they were and (with a few exceptions)[17] still are, but their time on duty did not go wholly uncompensated, and it is as well to be clear about the terms under which the St Mary's and St Agnes boats set out that day. In the RNLI regulations already cited General Regulation 20 dealt with payments. The coxswain, second coxswain, bowman and signalman received what were called "salaries", but were in reality retainers. The basic rates were £8, £2, £1.10s and £1 respectively per annum, but since the *Charles Deere James* was fitted with two tanks for water ballast the St Agnes coxswain and second coxswain would have been entitled to an extra £1 and 10s (50p) respectively. The officers and the other crew members were also each allowed a payment for "going afloat in the Life-boats to save life": winter rates (50 per cent higher than in summer) were 15s (75p) for a day service (between sunrise and sunset), 30s (£1.50) for a night service, and 45s (£2.25) for a day and night service, with adjustments for "intermediate" services which began shortly before or ended shortly after day service hours.

The Charles Deere James on her slipway, with the lifeboat house and church behind. © Gibsons of Scilly.

The crew having been assembled the boat had to be launched. As we have seen from the station record horses were no longer available for that purpose, but a new long slipway had been provided for launches at the lower states of the tide. On 13 December 1907 low tide was due at 5.06 pm, so

---

17 Nowadays the crews at a few special stations, such as those on the river Thames, are a mixture of full-time professionals and volunteers.

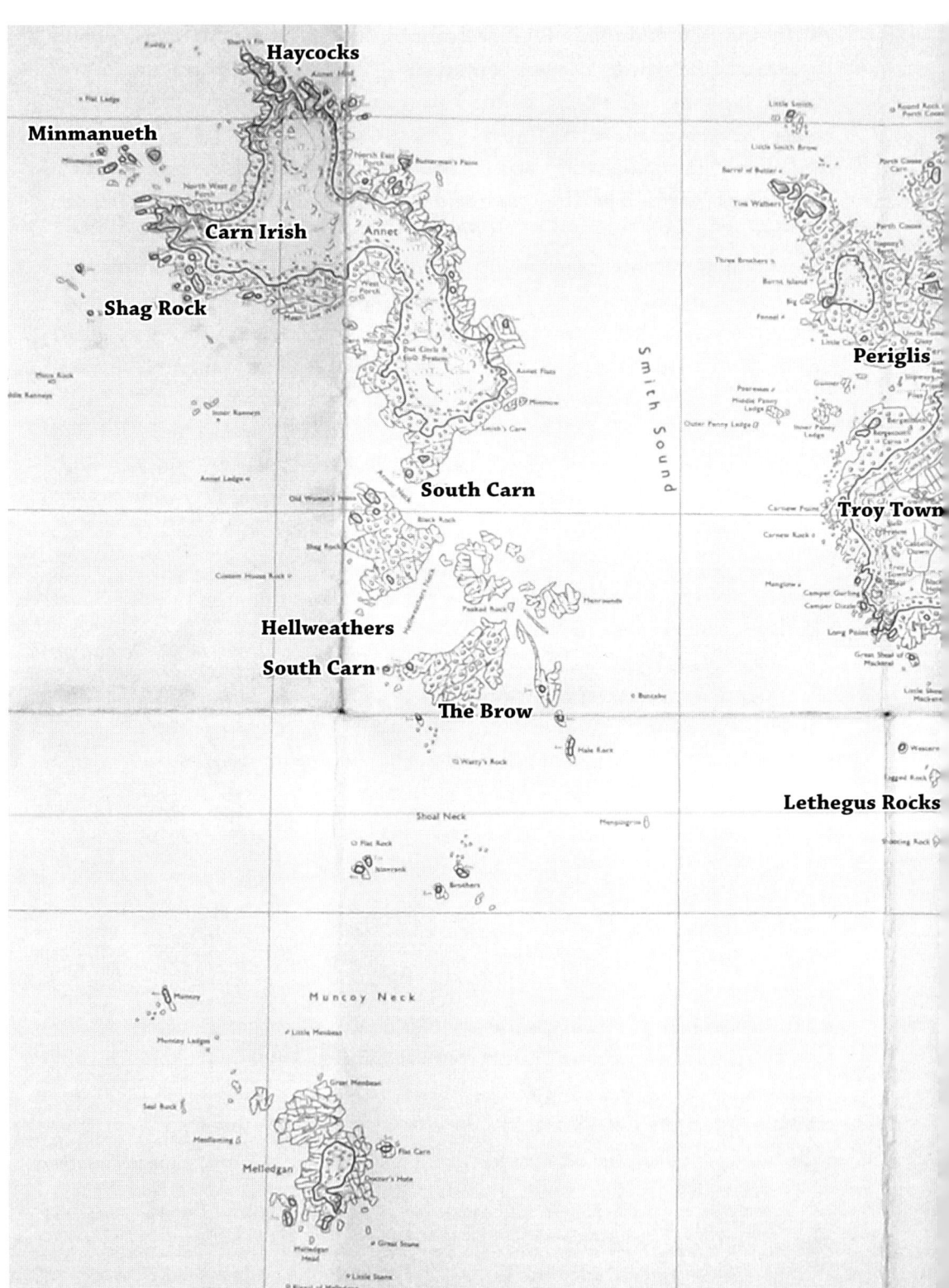

Haycocks

Minmanueth

Carn Irish

Shag Rock

Annet

Smith Sound

Periglis

South Carn

Troy Town

Hellweathers

South Carn

The Brow

Lethegus Rocks

Muncoy Neck

Melledgan

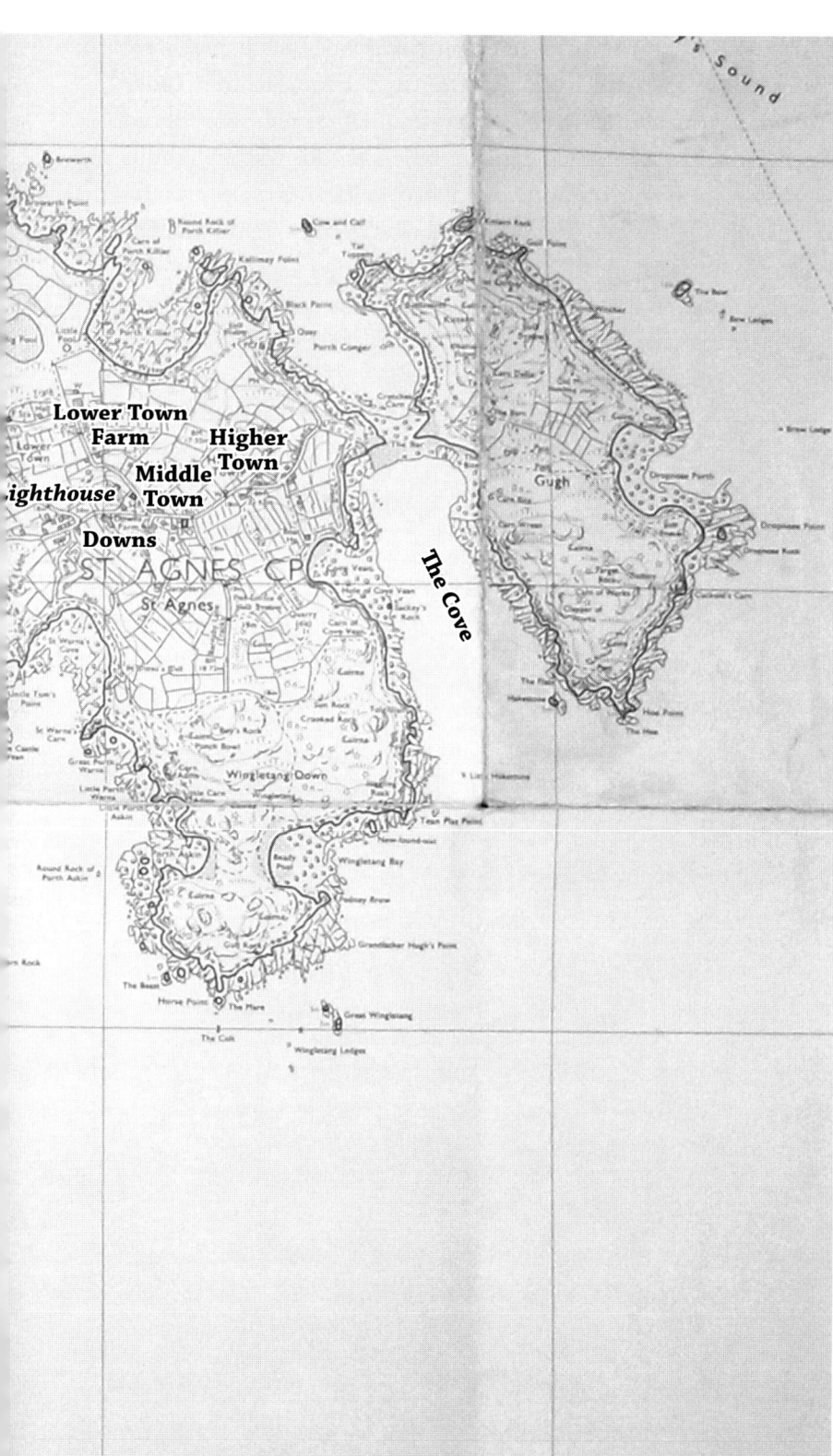

St Agnes, Annet and the Hellweathers © Crown copyright 2015 OS GV-156119

for a launch at about 4 pm, most of that slipway was needed. It had steel railway-style tracks for its full length, along which ran the launching trolley on which the lifeboat sat, as shown in the photograph. That greatly reduced the effort required from the "helpers" who provided the necessary labour (compare the accompanying photographs of the launch and recovery of the earlier St Agnes boat, the *James and Caroline*), and who, since virtually all the available able-bodied men were in the boat, must have been mostly women.

A summary of the journey out to the *Lawson* has been given in chapter 1 by reference to Jack's account of it. The distance (about 3¼ statute miles) and the course (north west to round Annet, and then almost due west) can be seen from the pull-out chart. As Jack's account makes clear, for most of the time they were proceeding under sail. The RNLI's official specification of the *Charles Deere James*, meticulously detailed in other respects, says against "Masts and Sails" only: "Special rig – foremast at 2nd thwart, Mizzen at after thwart (foreside)". In a boat of that size there can have

Preparing to launch the St.Agnes Lifeboat,
"James and Caroline", a 34ft. self-righter.
Photo by F.J.Mortimer, C.B.E.

Above: preparing to launch and right, recovering, the James and Caroline, the St Agnes Lifeboat 1890–1904. Photographs by Francis James Mortimer CBE.

Recovering the "James and Caroline", which
served at St.Agnes from 1890 to 1904.
Photo by F.J.Mortimer, C.B.E.

been only two masts, so what is called the foremast was in effect the main, and judging from its position and the comparable rig of a gig the mizzen was probably only a miniature mast, with a little triangular sail for balance and to help in steering and tacking rather than as a serious contributor to propulsion. What the "special rig" was is not explained, and no photograph of the *Charles Deere James* under sail has been found, so its nature remains a matter of speculation. A triangular sail on the foremast would have been simple and handy, but hardly "special". Gigs used a dipping lug, with which the crew would have been very familiar, so that is probably a stronger possibility, and it was perhaps "special" in the eyes of the RNLI as being specific to the Isles of Scilly. The lifeboat would not have been housed or launched masted, so the transition from pulling to sailing required, first, stepping the masts and hauling up the sails.

Jack's account gives a vivid impression of what the trip must have been like, but to remind ourselves of, or supply more precisely, some of the conditions in which it was made, sunset, at 4.24, would have occurred not long after they set out, possibly as they were rigging the boat for sail. The wind had been recorded on St Mary's at 2 pm as Force 5, SW. At 6 pm there are readings for St Mary's and St Agnes, both still Force 5, and the direction given at St Mary's was still SW, but at St Agnes it was WSW. The temperature – 49°F (9.5°C) at 2 pm and 51°F (10.5°C) at 6 pm – was mild for December. The apparent lack of change in wind speed must be assessed in the light of the facts, first, that Force 5 covers a range from 17 to 21 knots and, secondly, that at 8 am it had been Force 4 at both stations but by 9 pm there was a gale, so there would almost certainly have been some freshening in progress. The discrepancy in wind direction between the two stations at 6 pm is readily accounted for by normal variability from moment to moment, but the St Agnes reading suggests that any change was by way of veering rather than backing, which also would fit in with the longer-term trend, since at 8 am it had been S or SSW, whereas by the next morning it was NW or WNW. These wind changes were all in accord with the islanders' expectations, as reported in chapter 1.

On the arrival of the *Charles Deere James* alongside the *Thomas W. Lawson* there ensued the conversation between William George Mortimer and Captain Dow briefly summarised in chapter 1, which can now be examined more fully. The earliest account of it was given by William George himself at the inquest. There is no verbatim record, but according to what looks like quite a full report in the local daily press he told the coroner that in response to a question assistance was declined, that they then told the captain he was in a dangerous position and again asked if he wanted assistance, but his reply was "I am all right." They decided to go alongside, with the intention of trying to persuade the captain to "slip the ship" and go through Broad Sound. It was then that a rope was thrown down and the captain asked for a pilot.[18]

Jack's version is the fullest, and in direct speech. He has the captain coming to the side and saying to the coxswain:

> "Hallo"
>
> *"Do you realise where you are, Captain?"*
>
> "Yes, I am at the Scilly Isles"
>
> *"Yes, but do you realise the dangerous position you are in?"*
>
> "Oh, I'm alright"
>
> *"Well, you are not alright"*
>
> "I have got both my anchors down and I've ridden out worse storms than this on the American side. I've had boats on either side of me drag their anchors and go aground but mine have held – I'm alright"
>
> *"Beg your pardon, but you are not alright. You may have ridden out storms on the other side of the Atlantic Ocean, but not where you are now"*

The captain, Jack continues, was then asked to abandon ship, but he refused. He then asked whether there was a Trinity House pilot aboard the lifeboat, and when answered "Yes" asked him to come aboard.[19]

The only other surviving account by anyone present which has been traced is a brief reference in the story told by James Thomas Hicks to Richard Gillis, apparently in about 1951. As reported, he said simply that the captain's reply to their offer of help was "I guess I'm alright where I am", although it was pointed out to him that he was in a most dangerous position. James Thomas seems to put the request for a pilot somewhat later, after a reference to the increasing wind.[20]

What is common to all those is the offer by the lifeboat crew of "assistance" and its rejection by the master, so there can be no doubt that that

....

18 *The Western Morning News*, 17 December 1907.

19 *From Rock and Tempest*, in *Portfolio*, 5 June 1974. This account was published as part of the 150th anniversary celebrations of the RNLI. That was after Jack's death in 1972, and its date is therefore no guide to when he told the story. It is stated to have been "abridged from the copy of the file kindly supplied by the Science Museum", but unfortunately that file no longer contains such a document, so its date remains unknown.

20 *The Loss of the Thomas W. Lawson* by Richard Gillis (note 15 above), at p. 337.

happened. Just one eye-witness account (Jack's) adds that at the end he was asked to abandon ship, and refused that too. In some secondary sources that is indeed given as the only offer made, and the RNLI's *Lifeboat Gallantry* states at page 223 that the lifeboats were launched "but the schooner's Master refused to leave". It does, therefore, seem very likely that the subject was mooted, but for lack of confirmation in the primary sources that is not as certain as the offer and refusal of assistance.

In the context, the assistance offered and refused was clearly help in getting the schooner into a safer place. In the absence of a secure harbour with sufficient depth of water, which for a vessel of the *Lawson's* laden draught the islands did not afford, the next best resort for an ocean-going craft would normally be the open sea, and with a south-west to west-south-west wind the schooner was facing in the right direction for such a move, which may be what William George Mortimer meant by "trying to persuade the captain to 'slip the ship' and go through Broad Sound". The remaining possibility, presumably, was to try to get the *Lawson* downwind into the rather more sheltered (although not wholly secure) waters between St Mary's and Tresco, but whether the lifeboat crew envisaged that, or yet another, course does not appear from the contemporaneous evidence, and this is not the place for later views on what might have been done, which will be considered in chapter 13.

The distinction between the two courses of action mentioned – accepting assistance to move the schooner and abandoning her – is significant, both from the point of view of the master and from those of the lifeboat crew and the RNLI. Any acceptance of assistance by the master, other than of pilotage, would in the circumstances have amounted to an admission that his vessel was in difficulties and have exposed his owners to a potentially substantial salvage claim. In such circumstances a master has always to weigh the cost to his owners of acceptance against the risk of the loss of his ship on refusal, but in this instance that seems unlikely to have been a significant motive, because Captain Dow was willing to incur the probably greater cost of tugs. Probably a more important factor was his view that any assistance the lifeboat crew could give would in any event be ineffective.

Abandonment would, in intention, have been temporary and could have been without adverse consequences, but a master contemplating it would have to weigh the risk that either the vessel would while unmanned be lost in circumstances in which it would be said against him that a crew on board might have saved her, or on the other hand that it would survive unharmed but be boarded by someone else before the crew's return, yet again involving the owners in a salvage claim. The latter risk, but not the former, could be averted by leaving someone, who morally would have to be the master himself, on board.

For the lifeboat crew and the RNLI the distinction was at least as sharp. The RNLI was insistent that its purpose was solely, as its full title proclaims, "the preservation of Life from Shipwreck", and did not include the salvage of property, and that it would not itself accept salvage money. Regulation 13 provided as follows:

> 13. On boarding wrecks, the Preservation of Life to be the Coxswain's *sole consideration*, and he is on no account to take in goods or merchandise which might endanger the safety of his Boat, and the lives of those entrusted to his charge. Should this regulation be infringed, contrary to his remonstrance, he is fully authorised to throw the goods overboard.

On the other hand it recognised that its lifeboats might often be in a position to help save a vessel in difficulties, and thereby indirectly succour those on board. Had the crew of the *Lawson* abandoned ship, because of the danger of its situation, and been taken ashore in the *Charles Deere James* or the *Henry Dundas* that would clearly have been life-saving service by the lifeboat and its crew, and that service would have been at the charge of the RNLI under the regulations summarised above. But had the master accepted the coxswain's offer of assistance it would have been afforded under a quite different régime. Regulation 24 provided as follows:

> 24. When a Life-boat has been launched for the purpose of saving life, and it is found on arriving at the vessel in danger that the master … wishes to engage the services of the Life-boat's Crew to endeavour to save the vessel, the Life-boat's Crew are at liberty to accept an engagement with such master …and to make use of the Life-boat under the following conditions:—

> (a.) That all reasonable care be taken of the Life-boat and its gear.

> (b.) That it be clearly understood that the position of the Life-boat's Crew towards the Institution is changed from a Life-boat Crew endeavouring to save life, and entitled to be paid for such endeavours by the Institution, to

a party of salvors who have borrowed the Life-boat for property salvage purposes, for the remuneration of which services they are to look to the person in charge of the vessel who has engaged them. Should the Boat be damaged while rendering such services the cost of repair to be met by the Salvors.

(c) Should the attempts of the Life-boat's Crew to salve the vessel be successful, but the amount of salvage money paid them be less than the amount the crew, helpers, etc., would have been entitled to for an endeavour to save life, the difference will be made good by the Institution. Should, however, they be unsuccessful in salving the vessel they will be paid by the Institution as though they had launched for the purpose of saving life.

As we have seen, Captain Dow neither abandoned ship nor accepted assistance to move, but did ask for a pilot. Both Jack Hicks' story and George Mortimer's evidence at the inquest place that request towards the end of the opening exchanges, or very shortly afterwards. James Thomas Hicks, in the account mentioned above, has it possibly a little later, some half an hour before the arrival of the St Mary's lifeboat. Richard Gillis impliedly puts it after that arrival,[21] and Richard Lethbridge does so explicitly and circumstantially.[22] Of these sources the last two are wholly unpersuasive; Gillis contradicts his own informant, James Thomas, while Lethbridge, among other implausibilities, has his grandfather, then only the second coxswain at St Mary's, taking command of the situation, conducting the conversation with Captain Dow and telling the pilots in both lifeboat crews not to respond. By contrast Mortimer's is the only contemporary account and Jack's the only other by an eye-witness. They and James Thomas are not so far apart as to be outside the ordinary variations to be expected among reliable witnesses. Moreover it is telling that only the St Agnes pilots are ever mentioned as being potentially available.

Of the crew of the *Charles Deere James* William George Mortimer, Abraham James Hicks, Billy Cook Hicks, Obadiah Hicks and (if our assumption about his identity is correct) James Hicks were licensed Trinity House pilots.[23] A pilot's fees for such a commission would have been a significant

....

21 Gillis (note 15 above), at p. 314.
22 *Behind the Eyebrows* by Richard Lethbridge (Arden Craig Publications, 1994), at p. 39.
23 Jenkins (note 16 above), at p. 71.

Billy Cook at the wheel. Photograph from author's family collection.

addition to the meagre cash income of any of them, but the days when cutters and their attendant gigs routinely raced for such work were by now a distant memory, and in any event "first alongside gets the job" would never have applied to their situation, so they worked to a rota, which gave Abraham James first refusal, but as we saw in chapter 1 he declined the tempting offer on the ground that he was on life-saving service (and in the event, although that was not his motive, by that decision he saved his own). It does not seem that his reason for refusal was taken as involving any criticism of Billy Cook, who accepted; Abraham James, being the second coxswain, was in a special position as a retained officer of the boat, and William George Mortimer would even more clearly have had to rule himself out had it been his turn.

Captain Dow's reasons have always been a puzzle. His evidence at the inquest was kept to the minimum, because of his injuries, and he was not asked that question. His report to his owners has never reached the public domain. He never wrote or spoke about the wreck in later life. Had he contemplated the possibility of leaving his anchorage, but without assistance, thus avoiding a salvage claim, he would have needed a pilot and that possibility, at first sight unlikely, is given some colour, first, by the doubt which his later call for tugs casts on his professed certainty that he was "alright" and, secondly, by Gillis' statement, just after he has told us that Billy Cook went aboard, that the "Captain, pilot and lifeboatmen all agreed that nothing could be done", which implies that "doing something" involving the pilot was discussed.[24] Another possible explanation, perhaps, although still difficult to comprehend, is that he was sufficiently confident of riding out the storm in good shape as to contemplate resuming his voyage in the morning. The days when ocean-going vessels might take on a Scillies pilot for the whole passage into a Channel port, or even London, had long since passed, but he would have been very much in need of one to get safely out to the open sea. The problem is that one would expect such a decision to be implemented when the need arose rather than when preparing for a night riding out a major storm at anchor.

The way in which the St Agnes boat and its crew disposed themselves to stand by after Billy Cook had gone aboard has been described in chapter 1. The next occurrence of note was the arrival of the St Mary's lifeboat. At the inquest William George Mortimer put that at about an hour after his own, which would give a time soon after 6 pm and accord with the recorded launch at 4.24. That she was dismasted under the *Lawson's* counter, that Captain Dow requested her to wire for tugs, and that she returned to St Mary's, all as described in chapter 1, are not in doubt, but the relationship of those events, chronologically and causally, is difficult to disentangle and of some significance, in particular to an understanding of Captain Dow's beliefs, motives and actions.

At the inquest William George Mortimer is simply reported as saying, immediately after he had spoken of the St Mary's boat's arrival, that "[s]omeone aboard the vessel told St Mary's lifeboat to return and wire to Falmouth for tugs."[25] The report goes on to refer to the dismasting of the lifeboat as if that were a subsequent and unrelated event, and to the same effect Thomas Frederick Bradley, the divisional officer of coastguard, told the coroner's jury that about 7.30 the St Mary's lifeboat came in and the coxswain told him that he had been asked to return to wire for tugs.

24   Gillis (note 15 above), at p. 337.
25   *The Western Morning News* (note 18 above).

133

He makes no mention of the dismasting in that context.[26] His timing would also be consistent with a very short stay alongside by the St Mary's crew, given that she had had to return under oars. Jack Hicks does not refer to this episode but James Thomas Hicks, in the account he gave to Richard Gillis, does. He does not mention the dismasting, but says that the St Mary's boat remained for about an hour and then returned to send a message to Falmouth for tugs.[27] Had there indeed been a delay of an hour that would suggest that Captain Dow was slow to accept that such help might be needed, but the weight of the contemporary evidence against any such delay is telling.

That evidence is, however, unanimous in one respect, it makes the call for tugs the only reason for the return. It is true that there are early press references to the dismasting as another reason, or even the primary reason,[28] and that the minutes of the RNLI committee meeting of 9 January 1908 read, at this point in the District Inspector's report: "St Mary's Lifeboat carried away her mast and returned ashore". These may be the origin of frequent statements to the same effect in the secondary literature.[29] However, the evidence to the contrary, rehearsed above, should prevail. It is from three independent witnesses, it is contemporaneous or first-hand or both, and it has the weight of inherent probability in its favour, because dismasting alone was, or should have been, at best a doubtfully adequate reason. The only attraction would have been that if the boat left, refitted and returned, and subsequently had to take the *Lawson's* crew on board it would be able to use sail on the laden voyage back. But it was going to have to make one returning trip under oars in any event, and to add the labour of an extra "there and back" journey and the risk that the *Lawson* would need help during the many hours the lifeboat would inevitably be off station seems a wholly disproportionate price to pay for any advantage gained.

The position is therefore that Captain Dow, despite his repeated protestations to the St Agnes cox that he was "alright", not only asked at once for a pilot but, almost as soon as a second lifeboat appeared, sent it back to

....

26 *The Western Morning News* (note 18 above).
27 Gillis (notes (15) and (20) above).
28 *The Western Morning News*, 16 December 1907. (*The Cornishman*, 19 December 1907, gives both reasons, each as if the only one, at separate places.)
29 For example by Gillis (note 15 above), at p. 314.

call for tugs. That must be taken into account later in assessing the part he played in the tragedy.

The next event needing attention was the collapse of William Francis Hicks, although moving directly to it should not make us forget that by then the St Agnes crew had endured getting on for four hours of "standing by", or overlook the ever-worsening conditions in which they had done so. The basic narrative has been given in chapter 1, and the (probably) special circumstances of William Francis' position discussed earlier in this chapter; what concern us here are how the decision to return to land with him was reached, and what everyone concerned said or thought about the consequences.

At the inquest William George Mortimer was asked by the coroner "What made you leave the ship?" and replied:

> "Because one of our men was dying. We thought it was absolutely neces-
> sary to save his life to go ashore. We talked it over, and if he had died we
> should have been at fault. It was to save his life that we came ashore. We
> told the pilot we were leaving because William Francis Hicks was very ill.
> We also told him to show a light if he wanted assistance and he replied 'All
> right; keep a good look-out'."[30]

That speaks of a decision already made by the lifeboat crew and simply communicated to Billy Cook. When asked by a juror whether he did not think it was his duty to call the attention of the pilot to the rising wind and call upon him to leave with them he replied: "He was aboard the vessel, and could see as well as we could how bad the wind was", although he added that had it not been for the man that was ill they would have stayed on until the last minute.

Jack Hicks' account is rather different. After the unsuccessful attempt to revive William Francis described in chapter 1 he has the lifeboat crew asking each other: "What are we going to do? We can't stay here like this. The man may die or be dead. Shout up to the pilot.", and continues:

> "It was blowing hard, about force 11 or 12 now. We shouted and shouted:
> 'Tell the pilot we want to speak to him please'.
> The pilot came to the stern and we told him that William Francis was lying
> unconscious and we could do nothing by him. 'What about it?', we asked.

....

30   Ibid.

'You cannot get up alongside — you'll smash your side in. The only thing to do is to take him ashore. That's the only answer'.

'Will you come along with us: come down over the warp and ask the Captain and crew to come as well because if we leave go from you now to take this sick man ashore it'll be impossible to get back again. It is blowing a hurricane now'.

'Hold on a minute. I'll have a word with the Captain'.

Presently he came shouting again. 'Alright. You go ashore. I'm remaining here. The Captain guarantees his chain and anchors. Take William Francis ashore, but after you're ashore and get him right, keep an eye on me all night for my riding light and if we get into trouble whatsoever I'll fire rockets. Good night'. With that we let go ...".[31]

Some of the differences are more apparent than real; although Jack puts the final "You go ashore" into the mouth of Billy Cook it is clear from his "We can't stay here like this" that the decision to return had in reality already been made.

The remaining discrepancies are more difficult to resolve. William George Mortimer was the responsible officer and was giving evidence on oath within less than 48 hours of the event. Moreover his failure to assert any attempt to persuade the pilot or schooner's crew to leave was apparently against his own interest or reputation, as the juror's question clearly implied. All that would tend to support his credibility. On the other hand we shall see that there was at least one other quite significant statement in his evidence which it does not seem possible to accept, and there is a strong inherent improbability in the scenario of the lifeboat crew's leaving the schooner in what they had already advised was a dangerous situation without some final attempt to persuade its crew and pilot (their neighbour and kin) to go too, or at least an offer to take them.

Jack, for his part, was telling the story some unknown period after the event, and his dialogue cannot be verbatim either. His wind level of force 11 or 12 is an exaggeration, the consensus is that it was at most 9 or 10 at this hour. Moreover the arrangement to "show a light" or "fire rockets", on which he and Mortimer (and every other source) agree, at first sight sits awkwardly with an openly acknowledged "it'll be impossible to get back again". Nevertheless it would, as already suggested, be surprising if the core of what he gives as passing between Mortimer and Billy Cook (the offer and

....

31   *From Rock and Tempest* (note 19 above).

rejection of a passage to land) did not take place, and there is the ring of truth in his detail that Billy Cook conferred with the master before giving his final word; having accepted engagement as a pilot, he could not desert his post except as part of a general abandonment of the vessel. There is also significant confirmation of Captain Dow's involvement in the consultation and refusal to abandon ship in what the RNLI committee were told by their inspector, presumably as a result of questioning the cox: " ... the illness of one of the crew caused the Coxswain to return ashore, the Captain having refused to leave his Ship."[32]

It is not an easy judgment to make, but on balance the evidence that there was an offer, not accepted, to take the pilot and crew into the lifeboat seems more reliable than the coxswain's denial at the inquest.

Perhaps the most intriguing feature of Jack's dialogue has not, it would seem, ever before attracted attention. It lies in Billy Cook's opening word's: "You cannot get up alongside — you'll smash your side in." They assume that the first resource to be thought of was the *Lawson* herself, and once that has been mentioned it seems an obvious course to consider. The schooner was warm and well found. Although it did not have a doctor (but then neither did St Agnes) it must surely have had some sort of first-aid equipment and someone able to use it. Attention and treatment could immediately have been given to William Francis, rather than having to await a long, cold and wet passage back to shore. The lifeboat would not have had to leave her station. But there is just that one dismissive hint; we simply do not know whether the possibility was ever seriously weighed.

What both accounts of the conversation concur in, perhaps unexpectedly, is that there was no reference on either side to the possibility that the lifeboat might return as soon as it could, rather than awaiting a signal sent in what would necessarily be critical, and probably even rougher, conditions. The truth is probably that, although not blurted out in the way Jack describes, or indeed voiced at all, "it'll be impossible to get back again" was the reality tacitly accepted by the two seasoned boatmen who agreed that the lifeboat must leave, and that the reference to a call for assistance by light or rocket was a necessary but forlorn tribute to appearances.

So the lifeboat took William Francis ashore in the journey described in chapter 1. Dr Brushfield (described in the report as "Thomas Brushfield,

....

32   Committee minutes, 9 January 1908.

surgeon at St Mary's") told the inquest that he was taken to St Agnes by the St Mary's lifeboat on Saturday. That was in evidence about the rescued survivor George Allen, and so cannot have been before early afternoon. RNLI records show that the lifeboat crew were paid for that journey at daytime rates, so they must have returned before nightfall. Unless he crossed earlier in another boat, which is very unlikely if conditions were still such by Saturday afternoon that the lifeboat was needed, that seems to be the only occasion on which he could have attended William Francis, as a number of sources agree he did; indeed Jack Hicks told a reporter in Penzance on the following Monday that "the doctor stated that if [William Francis] had not been brought ashore he would have died".[33] But by the afternoon of Saturday William Francis must have been well on the way to full recovery without, it would seem, any earlier professional medical care.

The St Mary's crew were not informed that the St Agnes boat was off station, and indeed it would not seem that they could at that stage have re-launched; it was apparently not until about midnight that their boat was again seaworthy.[34] On St Agnes Israel and his gig crew had by now had plenty of time to rest and recuperate after their lighthouse relief, so the lifeboat crew could have been reconstituted at full strength and with several fresh and able members but, just as the possibility of an immediate return does not seem to have featured in the discussions out by the *Lawson*, so equally none of the many references to a debate ashore on the subject of re-launch places it at this stage; they all do so much later, when the schooner was adrift. William George Mortimer, at the inquest, is reported as saying simply that they did not return to the ship. Asked by the coroner why not he replied "Because we could not get out".[35]

The waiting and watching from the lighthouse on St Agnes, and the ominous disappearance of the *Lawson's* riding lights, have been described in chapter 1. There had been a lighthouse there since 1680, making it one of the oldest sites in the country, and at the time it was still lit, although it was to close in 1911 and has since served simply as a daymark.

When the riding lights disappeared the question whether the St Agnes lifeboat should be launched again did, everyone agrees, arise, despite the

....

33 *The Cornishman*, 19 December 1907.

34 *The Cornishman*, 19 December, 1907, and *Behind the Eyebrows* by Richard Lethbridge (Arden Craig Publications, 1994), at p. 41.

35 *The Western Morning News* (note 18 above).

absence of any distress signal. Not so on St Mary's. There the chief coast-guard officer was called at 3.15 am, when the lights of the schooner had not been seen since 2.50, but he told the inquest that he thought the captain had slipped his cables and proceeded to westward.[36] The implication is that he did not, therefore, think it necessary to inform the lifeboat officers. Had he done so it is almost certain that nothing would have happened; conditions were altogether too severe, the schooner's position was unknown, they were over two miles (another hour or so in those circumstances) further away than St Agnes and there were no special ties which might have made any one of them question the obvious conclusion.

On St Agnes, however, there were; several of the lifeboat crew were related to Billy Cook, and in particular Freddy Cook was his son. There seems to be no doubt that he was the principal, if not the only, advocate of a re-launch. The primary evidence for that is contemporaneous press reports that he "pleaded for an endeavour to launch the lifeboat when the lights of the ship disappeared".[37] Secondary sources, to the same effect, give necessarily imagined, and sometimes fanciful, verbatim dialogue, but more solid verification is available; Freddy Cook himself, in later life, persisted in maintaining that the lifeboat could and should have set out again, and could have rescued the *Lawson*'s crew and pilot.[38]

Whether anyone else supported him does not appear, but the decision was ultimately for the coxswain, and if William George Mortimer had been clear on their return that they "could not get out" he must have been even more certain now that it was an impossible task. It seems likely that that was a view shared by most of his crew. Jack, in the account already drawn on several times, reflected that it might have been "an act of Providence that our man came unconscious",[39] since otherwise they, as well as the *Lawson*, would have been lost. That being his view of the position had they stayed on station he, and very likely others, would have seen even greater certainty of failure and useless sacrifice if the further peril of finding and reaching the schooner in the first place had to be added.

....

36 Ibid.
37 *The Western Morning News*, 16 December 1907 and *Lake's Falmouth Packet*, 20 December 1907 (probably from the same correspondent, since the wording is identical).
38 E.g. in conversations with his son and grandchildren, (oral communications to the author from his son Joe Hicks and granddaughter Amanda Pearce).
39 *From Rock and* Tempest, in *Portfolio*, 5 June 1974 (note 19 above). This passage is quoted more fully, and discussed, in chapter 13.

Jack and Freddy Cook together. Picture sourced from the Scillonian *magazine, 1958.*

Such a sharp, continuing, division of opinion on what was quite literally a matter of life and death might easily have disrupted a small, isolated, community. It is a tribute to the quality of relationships on St Agnes that it did not. There is striking testimony to that in the adjoining photograph, showing Freddy Cook and Jack together in maturity. Every detail of their facial expressions and body language speaks eloquently of two men fully at peace with the world and each other.

The St Agnes lifeboat was not further involved. RNLI records show that St Mary's *Henry Dundas*, after the original call to the *Lawson* and the journey on Saturday afternoon with Dr Brushfield already described, took him again that day to St Agnes and "searched rocks". That was late enough to entitle the crew to night rates and must therefore have been for the doctor's first attendance on the *Lawson*'s master and engineer as well, probably, as for a second on George Allen. Finally, she was out again on Sunday for a "further search of rocks & islands".

It is fitting to end the lifeboats' part in this tale with the full entry in the RNLI record for the St Agnes boat, *Charles James Deere*:

Date of wreck	1907 Dec 13
Site of wreck	NW corner Annet
Direction and Force of Wind	WNW 9–10. Whole gale
State of Sea and Weather	Heavy to very heavy
Nature of Service	No service
Lives saved.	–
Vessels saved	–
Expenses of Service	13 men @ 30/- 19-10-0
	12 helpers @ 6/- 3-12-0
	Signalman 6-0
	Messenger 7-0
	23-15-0

Grant to fund for widow etc of L-Btmen W T Hicks who boarded vessel as a pilot & lost his life.

· 10 ·

The Wreck

AT THE END OF CHAPTER SIX we left the weatherbeaten *Thomas W Lawson* sailing, as her navigators thought, into the English Channel, some distance south of the Isles of Scilly, but in fact so far north of her supposed position that in leaving well to starboard what they thought was a ship's light they were in fact steering over two miles inside the Bishop Rock lighthouse. Their exact course is not known, but a vessel entering the English Channel would have been heading generally east or a little north of east. The wind, in the south-west, would on that heading have been over the starboard quarter, so there would have been no need to tack or gybe, and by the time Captain Dow had realised what was happening and dropped his anchors between Gunners and Nundeeps (see pull-out chart) he must, with the tide not much over an hour short of a predicted 5.06 pm low water, already have passed perilously close to at least one group of half-tide rocks, probably most nearly the Crim Rocks, with outliers at Zentman's Rock and Tearing Ledge.

The reason given in several sources for anchoring rather than turning out to sea, which is assumed to have been what the master would have done had he been able, is that the schooner was, in one version, "too close in to wear, and with not sufficient sail to tack"[1] or, in Rowe's words at the inquest, "with no room to stay or wear ship".[2] It may well be doubted,

....

1   *The Loss of the Thomas W. Lawson* (Richard Gillis, 1951 – see note 15 to chapter 9), at p.314.
2   *The Western Morning News*, 17 December 1907. To similar effect is *The Cornishman*, 19 December 1907.

however, whether even with a well-found and handy vessel it would have been prudent for a navigator without local knowledge and experience to attempt such a manoeuvre in those hazard-strewn waters. And conversely, had a local pilot been on board the *Lawson* herself at that very moment, it seems unlikely that he would have done so either; in her condition a better option would have been to run on before the wind through Broad Sound into a sheltered anchorage in St Mary's Road. But without a pilot immediate anchorage was clearly the only course.

Everyone agrees that Captain Dow laid out both his port and his starboard anchor, and all sources except two have both holding until disaster struck in the small hours. One of the two exceptions is Rowe, who in one of his stories has both anchors dragging throughout, or in another, from about 10 pm, but that can be discounted both because of his general unreliability, already explored in our examination of the voyage, and more specifically by the contradiction in those two versions and between both and a third in which he has the *Lawson* letting go the anchors with a "towering cliff ...[not] more than a mile dead ahead" and "[slowing] to a stop, practically under the precipitous cliffs of Annet Island".[3] In reality the masts of the Lawson would have towered over Annet, which has a maximum height of 16 metres (52 feet). Moreover all these rather preposterous assertions come long after the event and contradict the much more credible evidence on the subject which he gave at the inquest, and to which we shall come later.

The other exception is more troubling. William George Mortimer, in his evidence at the inquest, is reported as saying, at the point where he is describing his arrival alongside the *Lawson* and conversation with Captain Dow: "She had two cables out, but only one was holding."[4] That, however, is frankly beyond belief, and serves only, as we have seen, to undermine his credibility elsewhere. Not only is it contrary to every other account (even Rowe's); Captain Dow has been criticised for his judgment, but he was an experienced master, nor has anyone ever suggested that on that night he was drunk or out of his mind, and no sane and sober ship's captain would repeatedly have professed and acted on a belief in the ability of his ground tackle to ride out an impending storm had one of his two anchors already failed.

The *Lawson's* tackle was indeed formidable. In the very brief summary of

....

3   *The Luck of the Lawsons* (Alton H. Blackington, in *Yankee Yarns*, Dodd, Mead, 1954, at p.24.
4   *The Western Morning News*, 17 December 1907.

Captain Dow's evidence given in public at the inquest (which the press had at second hand from the coroner, because no-one except the coroner and three of the jurors went into his bedroom) he said that it was, he thought, such as to hold her anywhere; "her anchors weighed five tons each". William George Mortimer had a little earlier given evidence of being told by the master that he had 150 fathoms (900 feet or 274 metres) of cable out, and "made fast the bare ends", implying that that was the entire length of anchor chain available.[5]

The next chapter of the story belongs to the lifeboats, and has been told. After their departure the wind continued to rise, but for some hours the anchors held. High tide was due at 11.27 pm, and in the summary of Captain Dow's evidence already cited he is reported as saying that "After the tide turned he thought they were quite safe." In another press report of the same evidence (probably a fuller version of the same reporter's copy) he adds that he and the pilot were "both of the same mind" and that he would not have felt justified in making signals of distress.[6] That is important and calls for some examination. The "turn" of a tide normally means the change from flood to ebb or vice versa at the turning points of high and low tide, but at anchor it is the direction and strength of the tide stream or current which matter, and changes in them do not necessarily coincide with those turning points.

Other references to the subject are tantalisingly sparse and confusing. The senior coastguard officer told the inquest that he wondered at the schooner's remaining as long as she did, "as with the ebb tide the sea increased in force",[7] but he was in St Mary's and tidal currents off the islands vary sharply from point to point. A 1953 article, giving no attributions, states that when the *Lawson* found herself in the Scillies "A strong east-going tide added to her troubles", but that does not accord with the official information considered below and in any event says nothing about conditions later in the night.[8]

The Admiralty chart for the Isles of Scilly (see pull-out) provides the most objective evidence. Its diagrams of tidal streams are to such a small

....

5   *The Western Morning News* (note 4 above).
6   *The Western Weekly News,* 21 December 1907.
7   *The Western Morning News* (note 4 above).
8   *The fate of the world's largest schooner* (Capt R. Barry O'Brien, September 1953 edition of unidentified journal), at p. 26.

scale that precise conclusions are difficult to draw, but they appear to show that about two hours before high tide the site of the *Lawson's* anchorage would have been near the eastern edge of, but still within, a strongish (nearly one knot) tidal current heading about north by east (bearing 11° 15'), that between then and high tide that current would have veered round to north-east by north (33°45') and its edge have moved westward, so that at about an hour before high tide it shifted clear of the anchorage, giving way to a very light current heading east (90°), which would thereafter have strengthened a little and continued to veer until at about an hour after high tide it was heading south-east (135°).

Remembering that winds are conventionally described by the direction <u>from</u> which they blow, but currents by the direction <u>towards</u> which they flow, a current approaching one knot flowing between north by east and north-east by north would, although not directly in line with a generally westerly to north-westerly wind, appreciably have increased the drag on the anchors, and its virtual disappearance at about 10.30 pm could well have been sufficiently noticeable to seamen as experienced as Captain Dow and Billy Cook Hicks to make them think they were now "quite safe".

Sadly, as by hindsight we know, they were not, and the failure of the riding lights to reappear after a particularly heavy squall has been recounted. The basic fact is common ground, and its timing not greatly in doubt. Israel Hicks told the inquest that he saw the lights at 2.15, but later missed them. We have noted in chapter 9 the chief coastguard's evidence of the report to him that the light had not been seen since 2.50. William George Mortimer's was that it disappeared at 2.30.[9] Before the inquest an unnamed correspondent had given the *Western Morning News* of 16 December the same timing of 2.30.

Most accounts have assumed that until then the *Lawson* had remained safely at her anchorage, but in truth there is no reason why the mere failure of one anchor should have caused the riding lights to go out. Mortimer tacitly accepted that, because when asked by a juror for his conclusions on the cause he said they had thought that the vessel's lights had been blown out. No-one else gave that explanation, it required the simultaneous dowsing of more than one independent lamp, and by that fact and by dissociating the disappearance of the lights from any direct connection

....

9   *The Western Morning News* (note 4 above).

with the loss of the schooner it imposes a great strain on the long arm of coincidence.

There are two hints of another possibility. One is that before telling the inquest of the lights' disappearance Mortimer himself had said that they were "drawing to the southward". The other is that on the same occasion Rowe said that the port anchor parted at about 1.15 and the other dragged for about an hour before the vessel struck.[10] Both of those pieces of evidence are consistent with the lights' having been extinguished, as one would expect, by the shock of the impact rather than the earlier failure of one anchor. Neither, however, is without its own difficulty. Rowe's is affected by his general unreliability. As to Mortimer's, the *Lawson* dragged on a bearing of 115° (about east-south-east) from her anchorage to where she sank, almost directly towards an observer near the St Agnes lighthouse, rather than to the south, although maybe it would be a mistake to take his "southward" too literally, given the difficulty in such conditions of observing anything more precise than that the motion was from right to left in his field of view.

The difficulties surrounding both explanations leave us without any certainty whether the loss of the light at about 2.30 marked the beginning or the end of the *Lawson's* unwilling journey from her anchorage to her last resting place, although the latter seems the more probable.

Other features of that journey are clearer. Despite the assertion at various points in the literature of several other destinations (for example Annet itself, Minmanueth, some 400 yards too far north, the Hellweathers, stretching away to the east of Annet and even the Tinks, on the inshore side of Great Crebawethan, about 1¼ miles away to the south-west)[11] there is no doubt that the schooner struck on Shag Rock, which manifests itself as a tiny projection above the surface (see photograph overleaf, map on p.124 and pull-out chart), some 200 to 250 yards (depending on the state of the tide) west of the shore of the western headland of Annet, below Carn Irish, and rising out of about 5 fathoms (30 feet) of water. The certainty arises both out of the firmness of the family tradition among the current descendants of the islanders who were witnesses of the wrecked vessel herself before she was finally submerged and out of subsequent diving

....

10   *The Western Morning News* (note 4 above).
11   The location at Minmanueth has even been picked up and repeated in the memorial plaque
    in St Agnes church.

Shag Rock (the nearest to the right), with St Agnes and its lighthouse rising behind Annet and its outlying rocks. The camera is pointing east by south, a little to the left of the Lawson's *probable direction of approach. Photograph: the author.*

activity on her remains.

That gives, as already noted, a direction of travel bearing 115°, about east-south-east, which if wholly determined by the wind would have required one blowing a touch north of west-north-west. There was by that time, however, according to the Admiralty chart, a tidal current of about half a knot setting roughly to the south-west, so to offset that the wind would actually need to have been coming from a little nearer west, perhaps dead on west-north-west (292° 30'). That is rather back of the north-westerly which the islanders had forecast and of the north-north-west gusts of which at least one source speaks, but it may well have reached the latter sort of direction at an earlier stage and then started backing again, as the 1953 article already quoted states.[12] It is a measure of how much turned on details which could so easily have been different that had the wind not

....

12   O'Brien (note 8 above).

backed as much, or had the anchor failed earlier, there was a narrow arc of bearings, about 27° south of the one along which the *Lawson* was driven, which would have taken her clear of any rocks and through the Gorregan Neck to the open sea.

The speed of the gust of wind which delivered the death blow is not quite as easy to establish as its direction, because there was no recorded meteorological reading. Some of the figures given must be exaggerations. Rowe, for example, put the maximum at 112 mph, but that was 50 years after the event[13] and he is at best an erratic witness. Richard Larn, in a very comprehensive study of Scillonian wrecks,[14] put it at 90 mph, but unfortunately his source seems to have been Rowe himself, so that is not independent evidence. Jack Hicks, as we have seen, had the speed as high as force 11 to 12 (say 74 mph) even before the St Agnes lifeboat returned, but in that he is not supported by others. What was said at the inquest was more restrained. William George Mortimer told the court that it rose from force 9 (47 to 54 mph) on their return to force 10 (55 to 63 mph).[15] The chief coastguard's evidence was to similar effect, but they were both on shore and the latter, in particular, in a less exposed situation than the schooner, so it seems entirely possible that out on the *Lawson* the fiercest gust did reach at least somewhere in the lower part of force 11 (say 64 to 70 mph).

The only accounts of what the crew did after the anchor failed, and of what happened to them when the *Lawson* struck Shag Rock, are those of Edward Rowe and one reported remark of George Allen that he had seen the captain, mate and pilot lashed in the rigging.[16] We have noted that when dealing with other aspects of our story Rowe has often been unreliable, and as to this phase too it will be seen that there are implausibilities and variations in what at various times he said, but apart from some very limited cross-checking by reference to what divers have since discovered they are all we have. Whatever their inaccuracies they paint a vivid picture of the experience he underwent and in any event something like what he describes must have happened, although not necessarily in the order he first recalled.

....

13   *The Sinking of the Thomas W. Lawson* (Edward Rowe Snow, in the *Boston Herald,* 9 January 1972), from p.31.
14   *Shipwrecks of the Isles of Scilly* by Richard Larn (Thomas & Lochar, 1993), at p. 56.
15   *The Western Morning News* (note 4 above).
16   *Lloyd's List*, 14 December 1907.

It is likely that he told his story initially to one or more newspaper correspondents on Sunday, the day after his rescue; one report of it appears in the *Western Morning News* of Monday 16 December and although another, in the *Cornishman*, did not appear until Thursday the 19th that was a weekly and this part of its feature appears before its narrative has reached the inquest.

The relevant passage in the *Western Morning News* reads:

> "She laid there with both anchors out. We did all we possibly could, and could not prevent the ship from going ashore between two and three o'clock in the morning. The captain, mate, second engineer, pilot and myself were in the spanker rigging, and the rest were scattered round in the rigging and on the forecastle head. One of the anchors broke and the other dragged, and then she struck sideways against the rocks, and smashed in her starboard side. That snagged the rigging, and the masts began to sway with the motion of a boat as she was battered by the sea. Before she struck I asked the pilot: Have we any chance of getting ashore? and he said, No. The second time she struck the stern was cut right off, and then I jumped overboard with a lifebelt on, and was washed around amongst the rocks, and in the sickening sea of oil. It nearly suffocated and blinded me. Twice I gave myself up. Once, when I was entangled in the rigging and almost was gone, I got off one of my boots, but could not get the other off. I was banged around and about those reefs I should think up to quarter-past four, and then I crawled up on a reef. I stayed there for about twelve hours. I was paralysed in the limbs by exposure. I could hardly stand on my feet. I don't know how the captain managed to got there, but I presume he got there just about the same way as I did. I helped him to get up on the rock. He was battered about badly. My own legs and hands are knocked about."

The words "One of the anchors broke and the other dragged" might appear at first sight simply to have been misplaced by the reporter, but the *Cornishman's* version suggests that the confusion was Rowe's who, unlikely as it may seem, but probably still disoriented from his ordeal, really was giving the impression that the desperate measure of resorting to the rigging occurred while both anchors were still holding:

> "As the evening wore on the captain, mate, second engineer, pilot and myself took refuge in the rigging. The ship was then lifting sharply

The western shore of Annet and its outlying rocks, where George Allen and others may have been washed up, looking from the direction of Shag Rock. Photograph: the author.

under the restraint of her cables, and it seemed only a question of time before we should strike. The wind blew with terrific velocity and showed little signs of abating. One of the anchors parted and that was the beginning of the end. The other could not sustain the weight and we began to drift towards the rocks. The pilot held out no hope of getting ashore and then we struck. Our stern was torn away like matchwood and it did not seem to me the ship could hold together another minute, her masts threatening to go by the board. I sprang overboard with a lifebelt on and had a tremendous struggle for life. I was tossed about like a cork, and dashed against rocks, which I vainly endeavoured to grasp. Then I should be torn back again until I was almost suffocated and blinded in a sickening sea of oil. The masts must have given way almost at the same time as I was swept away, for in my struggles I became entangled in the rigging which was under water. Try as I would I could not free myself, being held by the legs. I succeeded in getting off one boot and then I despaired of ever getting away. With a supreme effort I forced myself to the surface more dead than alive, to begin my struggles over again.

Rocks battered me unmercifully and after what seemed an eternity I was thrown against a log of wood which I grasped. The tide swept me away rapidly, and swimming in the distance I noticed another man. He came and laid hold of the same piece of wood and so we were carried along. Feeling another piece of timber rising underneath me I wound my legs round it and waited. We were hurried towards two large rocks with an opening between, and as we neared them I trusted to the piece of wood between my legs. It was fortunate I did so, for I was flung upon a rock, while the other man was swept away and has not been seen since. I managed to crawl to a place of comparative safety where I remained twelve hours. How the captain came there I know not, but I helped him to get up on the rock. I was almost paralysed with the cold and could hardly stand."

His evidence at the inquest on the following day, Monday, is similar, although shorter, as to his experiences in the water, but very different as to the sequence and content of what went before, and altogether more credible. We have had recourse to one aspect of it already. The *Western Morning News* of 17 December has it in recorded speech as follows, picking up at the point when they anchored:

It was not then blowing very hard, and there was only a short chop of sea. He thought they were about a mile and half from the rocks to leeward and ahead.

And then, after referring to taking a pilot:

The sea increased in force, and was breaking heavily over her, but she was not then riding very heavily. About a quarter past one on Saturday morning she parted her port anchor, and then she started to drag slowly on the starboard anchor for about an hour, and struck the ledge of rocks. ... when she struck he was in No. 7 rigging with the captain, pilot, mate, and steward. When she struck a second time, she broke in two between No.6 and 7 rigging within fifteen minutes. He left the ship just before with a lifebelt on, and got hold of a piece of timber. All the crew had lifebelts on. He saw one man in the water, and was dashed onto a ledge of rocks. The other man he believed was struck, and he did not see him again. About an hour and a half afterwards he saw the captain on the same ledge, but he did not see anything of the pilot."

The later accounts by Rowe referred to in chapter 6 add nothing of any weight on this part of the story, and are in many respects clearly fanciful (as in the reference, already cited, to coming to rest under the "precipitous cliffs of Annet Island"), His stories of how he and Captain Dow came across each other, so as to be found on the same rock, vary wildly; in one account, particularly full of palpable errors, he was on one rock, saw a "huddled form" on another, "[s]ome distance away", swam across and found it was Captain Dow.[17] In truth it would not be surprising if, in the condition he must have been in by then, he could later remember nothing very clearly about it.

How, indeed, did Allen, Rowe and Dow, quite apart from the injuries and battering they had received in the water, survive, soaking wet, the exposure and wind-chill of a stormy December night plus, in the case of Rowe and Dow, most or all of the following day? Desperate as their plight was, there were some mitigating factors. In the first place Dow for one was, we know, a very heavily built man, and in such circumstances that helps. Secondly the tide was falling from high water at 11.27 pm to low at 5.42 am, so it was not until well into daylight, when they could see the layout of the rocks, that there would have been any need to consider dragging themselves higher. Thirdly, cold as they must have felt, temperatures were rather mild for the season: on St Mary's air temperature was 51°F (10.5°C) at 6 pm on 13 December, still as high as 49°F (9.5°C) at 8 am the next day and back to 50°F (10°C) at 2 pm. The nearest station recording sea temperature was the Seven Stones lightship, between Land's End and Scilly, where it was 51.5°F (11°C) that night.

The *Lawson* did not immediately disappear wholly from sight; there is a photograph (overleaf), taken from Annet, of a length of her side showing above the water – stationary and sad, like a beached whale. But within a few days even that slid under the waves. Diving on the wreck has confirmed that she did break into two parts against Shag Rock, and that the split occurred near the aft end of the hull, although whether just where Rowe said, between masts 6 and 7, is not clear;[18] another account has it between 5 and 6.[19] Wrecks lying in less than 50 feet of water become progressively

....

17 Blackington (note 3 above), at p. 28.
18 Thomas Hall, in *The T.W. Lawson: the fate of the world's only seven-masted schooner* (Orchid Hill Publishing, St John, U.S.V.I., 2002) at p.102.
19 *Lloyd's List* (note (16) above).

The wrecked hull of the Lawson, while still visible at low water. © National Maritime Museum, Greenwich

broken up by the swell, and that has happened to the remains of the *Lawson*, but in addition to the plates of the hull itself several other objects have been identified, including two donkey engines, and some trophies have been brought ashore.

· 11 ·

The Gig

I N CHAPTER NINE we left the watchers on St Agnes at the point at which the *Lawson's* lights had disappeared and the decision against an immediate launch of the lifeboat had been made. The report of Israel Hicks' evidence on that at the inquest continues that "afterwards a strong smell of oil pervaded the air. They concluded the ship had been wrecked." He went on to describe the manning of the *Slippen* in the morning, but in order to understand why a gig was chosen rather than the lifeboat, and indeed the part played by gigs in stories told in earlier chapters and in the life of the islands generally, it will be helpful to have some account of their origins, history and characteristics.

Scillonians must always, since the islands were first settled, have been boatmen, but the first hint of the need for a specialised kind of small boat, combining speed with seaworthiness, comes with the advent of pilotage as a specialised occupation. As we have seen in chapter 7 it was sufficiently established on St Agnes by 1685 for the pilots there to be able as a body to be able to pay for the erection of the island's church. That tells us nothing about what boats they used, but by 1756 William Borlase was writing:

> These Pilots have something singular and daring in their manner of getting on board the Ships as they come in; they go off ten or twelve together, and from their little Boats steering up along side, the Pilot jumps into the Ship; the Boat then goes away to another Ship, drops another Man there, then to a third, and so on, till they have but two Men left in the Boat, which then returns, and is rowed to the first Shore they can best get at.

> We were in pain for the little Boats in such rough Seas, but as all Ships take a Pilot, this encourages them to venture, (oftentimes for so small a reward as five shillings) and custom makes them so dextrous that few accidents happen.[1]

There the "little boats" still have no special name and indeed, given the "ten or twelve" on board, on the one hand, and the "rowed to the first Shore" on the other, it may be that Borlase is describing something between what we know as gigs and what later became a distinct class of pilot cutters. Nevertheless there must, in the nature of things, have been some progressive specialisation of form, and while cutters developed as sailing vessels up to 70 feet long, well able to stay at sea for a week or so at a time and cruise up to 100 miles out in the Atlantic, they could not over a short distance, except in the most favourable wind conditions, match the performance of a smaller boat under oars, built for speed. Nor could they usually compete with such a boat when the vessel to be reached was sighted from the shore while they were at their moorings, so there were niches for both in a situation in which the first pilot to reach a vessel in need of one usually got the job.

Little seems to be known, however, about what may be called the prehistory of a specialised boat of the latter kind. Moreover, although the mode of pilotage described by Borlase was so characteristic of the Isles of Scilly, it is a singular feature of the history of the pilot gig that both the name (apart from one passing reference in 1666) and, in all essentials, its design, materials and construction methods seem from all accounts to have sprung into existence, fully formed, and over a very short period, in a single boatyard on mainland Cornwall. In 1790 William Peters set up business in a converted salt store at Polwarth, near St Mawes and received his first order for a six-oared gig. By 1838 his yard had built, among many others, the *Treffry*, still in use, whose overall dimensions and scantlings (the dimensions and materials of component parts) were so perfectly adapted to its function that they were to be used in 1987 to set the standards to which all racing gigs built since have to conform.[2]

....

1   *Observations on the Ancient and Present State of the Islands of Scilly* (William Borlase, Oxford, 1756, 1966 edition published by Frank Graham, Newcastle upon Tyne) at p. 41.
2   The general history and descriptions of gigs and cutters, and the histories of particular craft, in this and the following paragraphs are taken with gratitude, at points too numerous for separate annotation, from two indispensable works: *Gigs and Cutters of the Isles of Scilly* by A.J. Jenkins (Integrated Packaging Group Ltd and the Isles of Scilly Gig Racing Committee, 1975) and *Azook!* by Keith Harris (Dyllansow Truran, Redruth, 1994).

There is surprisingly little in the literature about the working relationship between gigs and cutters. For the reasons already rehearsed it seems unlikely that a cutter and a lone gig would often have been in direct competition for the same vessel. For inshore work, as we have seen, gigs would be used, but was that their only involvement? Two current references to the subject seem to imply that it was,[3] but they are anonymous statements on the websites of mainland clubs and cite no sources. Given the advantage of intercepting incoming shipping as early as possible, that would surely have sharply limited their usefulness for the very purpose

William Peters, the father of the Cornish pilot gig. Photo courtesy of Keith Harris

which gave them their name of pilot gigs and shaped their development. It would make much more sense for one or more cutters and one or more gigs to be operated in concert. Is there evidence that that happened?

What we know, for a start, is that both gigs and cutters were, in the Isles of Scilly, commonly owned in shares by syndicates, most members of which seem likely, from what we know of them, to have been also the men who crewed them. In the small off islands, at least, there would inevitably be an extensive overlap, if not identity, between the gig and cutter owners, and therefore crews, and in the nearest instance to a direct comparison available that is borne out by specific names.[4] Connections between gigs and cutters are evident in the histories of individual gigs, several of which are stated or believed to have "worked with", or are recorded as being "owned by the pilots of" a named cutter each,[5] and even more of which are known

3   *GigRower* and *Working Sail* websites as at 17 February 2014.

4   This point is developed below by reference to the ownership lists for the St Agnes cutters and the gig *Slippen*.

5   *Gigs and Cutters of the Isles of Scilly*, as in 2 above.

Jack (bow), George Mortimer (2) and Osbert (3) at the oars of the Elaine, *approaching Bishop Rock on lighthouse relief, probably on 8 January 1911. Photo: Francis James Mortimer.*

each to have been owned by the pilots of a named off island, who must also have had one or more cutters at their disposal. So common ownership and working together seem firmly established.[6]

Just how a gig and cutter "worked with" each other, however, is frustratingly not developed in these records, but perhaps the most obvious way of doing so would have been for a cruising cutter to carry or tow a gig out with it. Just two assertions have been found that that actually happened, and both are made without reference to sources, but each has

....

6   According to the works cited in note 2 above there were the following such pairings (gig's name first):

   Albion with *Rapid* and *AZ*
   Bee, *Boot* and *Bull* with *Bull*
   Bonnet with *Queen*
   Cetewayo with *Agnes*
   Dolly Varden with *Presto*
   St Vincent and *Sultan* with *Atlantic*
   Shah with *Gem*
   Swift with *Swift*.

Jack (bow), George Mortimer (2), Osbert (3) and Israel (4), at the oars of a gig. The gig and the occasion are unidentified, but this photograph seems close in time to the last, and is included by way of comparison with it, since it enables us to see Israel (there out of shot, presumably coxing the Elaine*) and shows Jack, at bow, rowing right-handed, on the port side of the boat, which seems to be customary in six-oared gigs, whereas in the five-oared* Elaine *he is on the other side, so that stroke's position can be unchanged. Photograph in author's collection, believed to have been taken by Francis James Mortimer.*

the weight of an author who, and who's family, had been steeped in, and played their part in making or recording, Scillonian lore for generations. Alf Jenkins writes:

> To beat the Falmouth men the island cutters, during the summer months, would often tow a gig or carry her on deck until she was well out. In light winds the pilots would board their gig from the cutter and operating this way could beat the Falmouth cutters to the job.[7]

....

7   *The Scillonian and his Boat* by Alf Jenkins (Penwell Ltd, Callington, 1982). Alf Jenkins was

To the same effect is Frank Gibson:

> The gigs were used to take off pilots when ships were leaving the islands [and] take pilots out when the sailing cutters were laid up in winter ... Some gigs were used in conjunction with the pilot cutters, who would tow them while they went about their business in the Western Approaches several miles from the islands. The gigs were useful if the wind was against the pilot cutter making a quick passage to a ship, the pilot would transfer to a gig and be rowed to a vessel.[8]

Since cutters had to be registered there is a complete record of their dimensions, tonnage and ownership, and from 1786 to 1974 it has been published. In some instances that enables us, with greater or less confidence, to deduce the succession of the vessels owned by what seems to be an evolving but continuing syndicate. Specifically there seem to have been two such lines on St Agnes. The first comprises the *Cyclops* from 1815 until sold in 1837, the *Active* from 1837 until sold in 1857, the *Gem (I)* from 1857 until blown from her moorings in 1874 and the *Gem (II)* from 1875 until sold in 1883. The second, not quite so continuous in dates, but firmly based on owners' names carried over, includes the *Happy Return (I)* from 1787 until seized for smuggling in 1790, the *Happy Return (II)* from 1790 (no end date recorded), the *Fly* from 1815 until sold in 1836 and the *Agnes* from 1841 until sold in 1883. By 1883, as we have seen in chapter 7, pilotage was in sharp decline and there is no record of any cutter owned by St Agnes pilots after that date.

Gigs lasted much longer, probably for two main reasons. One was that they always had been used for more diverse purposes than just pilotage. By now smuggling was insignificant and lifesaving largely taken over by the lifeboats, but there were still salvage, lighthouse relief and the simple carriage of goods and passengers. The other reason was that they not only involved a substantially smaller capital investment but, even more significantly, were very much cheaper to maintain, both because of their smaller size and less complex layout and equipment and also because they were

---

himself a boatman and a member of the ancient Bryher family of that name.

8   *Visitors companion to the Isles of Scilly* by F. Gibson (Beric Tempest & Co Ltd, St Ives) – undated, but from internal evidence probably early 1990s. Frank Gibson was a member of the Gibson family, who had lived in the Isles of Scilly for some 300 years and had been the islands' photographers of record since 1860.

kept in dry gig-houses when not in use instead of having to be moored at the mercy of the elements. Their owners were therefore able to survive lean times without having to incur too heavy a drain for upkeep.

Since they were not registered there is no public record of ownership, so direct contemporaneous comparisons between owners' lists for gigs and cutters is not possible, but at St Agnes the surviving log books of the *Slippen* from 1885 onwards[9] contain two lists of owners, the first in 1898. The names will be examined in detail later for their relevance to the events of 14 December 1907, but their interest here is the connections with the 1883 cutter lists. In 1898 there are some entrants from a new generation, so matching is not complete, but there are enough identities and known family relationships to see that the *Gem (II)* and *Agnes* owners are pretty equally represented. It looks as if the island could now support just one pilotage syndicate and that what were formerly two groups had merged.

Although not standardised until 1987 the dimensions and layout of most gigs varied little from the beginning of the Peters era onwards. The oft-told tale that they had only six oars because an eight-oared gig could outrun a Revenue cutter, and so was forbidden, sounds on first acquaintance too good to be true, but that there was such a restriction is in fact well-authenticated. It seems to have been imposed by H.M. Customs under their draconian delegated powers, and once to have been even more restrictive, because in 1829 the owners of a number of gigs joined to petition the Commissioners of Customs for the repeal of a regulation limiting crews to four men.[10] That restriction, and the need to combine rowing speed with seaworthiness, resulted in overall dimensions clustering around a length of 30 feet (9.14m) and beam of 5 feet (1.64m), although the *Treffry* herself was even finer at 32 feet (9.75m) by 4 feet 10 inches (1.47m). Gigs built primarily for carrying rather than pilotage, such as the *Campernell* and the *Queen*, had broader beams – 6 feet 6 inches and 7 feet respectively. Moreover the *Campernell*, still on St Agnes, can be seen to have been built or adapted to row seven oars, as famously (although in her case for speed) was also the *Czar*. These two examples imply that the restriction on oars was, strictly, "not as many as eight" rather than the "not more than six" generally assumed and quoted. In the other direction one gig, the *Elaine*,

....

9   Now in the possession of Mike Hicks, grandson of the Jack and great-grandson of the
      Osbert already familiar.
10   *Azook!* by Keith Harris (Dyllansow Truran, Redruth, 1994), at p.14.

built for the Israel Hicks first met at the beginning of chapter 1 for use in lighthouse relief, had places for only five oars, presumably as an economy, chiefly in terms of manning.

The *Elaine* features in one of the rare surviving descriptions of a direct contest between gigs for a job It is out of the ordinary as coming long after the heyday of pilotage was over and concerning a pilot needed in unusual circumstances – the grounding of the *Roche Castle* on Penninis in 1911:

> Gigs from several islands had attempted to be the first to find the trawler but the prize went to the *Elaine*, Isaac [a mistake for Israel] Hicks' privately owned five-oared gig which was used for doing the Round Island and Bishop Rock Lighthouse reliefs. The *Elaine* outmanoeuvred the *Dolly Varden* from St Mary's to reach the *Roche Castle* first. Pilot Osbert Hicks had to be hauled on board as his gig shot past the trawler, as the need for speed and the desire to win precluded a gentler approach to the vessel.[11]

The *Golden Eagle*, *Czar* and *Sussex* had also been in contention, and that story ends with an impromptu race back to Bryher between the *Czar* and the *Sussex*. A *Czar* man had goaded the *Sussex* with the taunt that only under tow could she arrive home at the same time, which provoked the *Sussex* crew to pull their hearts out and win by a hundred yards.

The hull planking consisted of strakes of small-leaf Cornish elm, the logs buried in mud for five years after felling, sawn to provide a ¼-inch finish and then stacked to dry for twelve months before finishing. They were so flexible and resilient that when the *Slippen*, already over 120 years old, was rebuilt in the 1950s, one of her original strakes was bent into a circle, with ends touching, and when released sprang back into its original shape, all without cracking. Gigs were clinker-laid (that is to say adjoining strakes overlapped rather than abutting edge-to-edge). Lines, keel, ribbing, thwarts, thwart-posts, tholes, rudder and all other fittings were carefully detailed and differ little from one gig to another.

There were eight thwarts, one in the stern for the cox, six for oarsmen and one in the bow for a pilot, a bailer, a spare oarsman or a passenger. Although no earlier mention of the point has been found it seems clear from the photographic record that a distinctive feature of gigs, in comparison

....

11   *The Islander* magazine, Spring/Summer 2012, at p.60.

A gig rigged for sailing. © Gibsons of Scilly.

with other rowing boats, such as those raced on inland waters, is that gigs are generally "bow rigged", with stroke (the aftermost oar) rowing left-handed, and therefore on the starboard side of the boat, whereas in other boats the usual (but not universal) rig is the reverse – they are normally "stroke rigged".

A gig typically weighed not more than 7 hundredweight (784 pounds or 356kg), so that it could be carried by its own crew.

Although gigs were, in terms of design and performance, primarily rowing boats no crew, unless racing (whether to take a pilot to a job, or for recreation), wanted to pull if they could sail, and gigs were capable of that. A main mast could be stepped through a ring fitted to number three oar's thwart to carry a dipping lug sail, and there was a short stick of a mizzen carrying, usually, a small leg of mutton sail. When in sailing mode a gig would need to load, if it could, some ballast for increased stability. There

The Slippen, a photo included for its intrinsic beauty, but it is undated and the gig is not in the livery she wore in 1907. Photograph © Adam White Photography

are records of sailing races (one of them involving the *Elaine*[12]) in the days when gigs were working boats, but nearly all modern racing is under oars.

Although speed and seaworthiness were the aims exact measures of what was achieved in either respect are difficult to find. Racing was widespread, even when gigs were primarily working boats – indeed the late Ralph Bird, a noted gig builder and historian, believed that in the 1840s "there were more gigs built to go racing than ever went piloting"[13] – but it was racing to beat the opposition rather than the clock. At the dawn of the modern revival of interest in the craft, purely for racing as a sport, a Newquay club crew in the *Dove* was timed in 1928 at 6 minutes 15 seconds over the measured mile, an average speed of 9.6 mph or 8.4 knots. Modern crews, in full training and with the best new gigs to the *Treffry* specification, may well be able to do better, especially in sheltered conditions, but no published figures have been found, perhaps because currents and other factors make any attempt at exact comparisons futile. In working conditions a pilot gig was out in the open sea and carrying its stowed masts and sails and a pilot, so it is doubtful whether it could quite match such a performance, although

....

12 *Gigs and Cutters of the Isles of Scilly* by A.J. Jenkins (Integrated Packaging Group Ltd and the Isles of Scilly Gig Racing Committee, 1975), at p.64.

13 *The Islander* magazine, Spring/Summer 2010, at p.52.

The Shah. Photograph credit: Kevin Pyne

the abilities of a crew whose daily exercise and livelihood this was, and whose spur was what was by their standards a lucrative contract, should not be underestimated.

Seaworthiness is even more difficult to quantify. A gig was not unsinkable, and sadly and fatally one was from time to time swamped, but it is significant that the stories of such events are few in number, that often the boat was under sail or the crew in festive mood, and that each is recorded and re-told as a matter of moment. Something of a feel for their capabilities has already been made available in chapter 7 in the account of their cross-channel use in smuggling and in the story of the *Albion's* role in the rescue of survivors from the *Delaware*. There is another illustration in our own narrative: on the morning of 14 December 1907, when *Slippen* was launched, there was not only the after-swell of the night's gale but a wind recorded as force 7, and although in the morning she had some shelter from Annet, in the afternoon, when she was out on the seaward side of the Hellweathers, the wind was still force 6. In giving the 1969 annual lecture of the Society for Nautical Research R.H.C. Gillis recounted two much more recent (1954 and 1956) occasions when a gig (in each case the *Golden Eagle*) demonstrated its capacity to weather high winds and heavy seas, but although they are described in graphic terms no figures are given for wind speed or wave height.

This combination of qualities can fairly be described as unique. Modern Olympics-style racing eights and fours are of course faster, but they are featherweight shells (200 pounds or 91kg for an eight), carrying only their crew and designed for nothing but all-out maximum speed on a dead flat millpond. On the other side there may well be other working inshore rowing-boat types with good sea-handling qualities, but none to match a pilot gig's speed.

The gig with which we are directly concerned in the *Lawson* story was even older than the *Treffry*, having been built by Peters in 1830 as the *Bernice* for the pilots of St Martin's and renamed *Slippen* when purchased by the pilots of St Agnes in 1869. It is perhaps a reflection of her early date that she was a little shorter and broader than what later became the norm, being only 28 feet (8.5 metres) long and having a beam of 5 feet 4 inches (1.6 metres). Although the change of name is unquestioned her two surviving log books, the first opened in 1885 and the second in 1912, still bear the name of *Bernice*. They paint what looks like a graphic picture of decline in pilotage as a significant contributor to the island economy.

The first accounting period, from mid-1885 to mid-1887, shows income of £40-14s-4d and expenditure of £9-7s-11d (about £3,340 and £770 in 2014 money). Several of the items of income, including the largest, have no explanation, but five substantial ones stand against ship's names. The payments are all particularised by payee or purpose, several being for the sort of expense one would expect – paint, oil, leather and a new sail (made by Israel Hicks for 14s 7d) – but delightfully there is one reading "Dinner for 6 at 9p: 4s 6d". During that period a dividend was paid each July to the owners – £14-7s-6d (about £1,200) in 1886 and £17-5s-0d (about £1,380) in 1887.

After that turnover drops sharply, but for some years there is some net income, enabling the payment of dividends of £1-8s-5d in 1892, £3-19s-5½d in 1898, £2-15s-4½d in 1901 and £4-15s-5d in 1902. In 1905, however, there are no receipts at all, and £2-6s-9d has to be collected from the owners to meet expenses, and until the entries relating to the *Lawson* a total of only 13s 8d in 1906 and 1907.

We can, therefore, return to the log book after considering the events of 14 December 1907.

Chapter 1 noted briefly that as the men of St Agnes considered how best to attempt a rescue of any survivors there might be of the *Lawson* a gig was preferred to the lifeboat because it was lighter and handier and drew less water. That can now be expanded a little. As to weight we have seen in chapter 9 that the *Charles Deere James* weighed over four tons (4,064 kg). A gig, at under seven hundredweight (356 kg), was less than one tenth of that. With six oars against the lifeboat's ten that still left the gig's crew with far more control as well as far less hard work, in conditions in which sailing would be out of the question because of the need to thread a course through inshore rocks. That of itself made it handier, but as we shall see in the next chapter the lifeboat crew also had specific complaints to make about the performance of the lifeboat the night before, which no doubt added to their reluctance to use it again in the morning. Another advantage was, quite simply, that fewer men were needed. Against that had to be set the plain fact that the sea was still rough enough to be at or near the edge of a gig's capability of surviving. There seems, however, to have been no hesitation in making the choice.

It is noteworthy that in relation to that choice, as in the case of the earlier debate whether to launch the lifeboat when the Lawson's lights were lost, there is no mention of the involvement of anyone other than the islanders themselves. According to the Regulations of the RNLI the coxswain was where possible to act under the directions of the local committee (Reg. 8), but there is no suggestion that on this occasion the honorary secretary was consulted.

Before leaving this aspect of the story it should be recorded that some accounts do assert that it was the St Agnes lifeboat which was launched again that morning and used in the rescue,[14] but that must be mistaken; not only was there Israel's explicit and uncontradicted evidence at the inquest of manning and launching the gig, and a mass of circumstantial detail from various sources about her activities and such matters as the identity of the crew, but the RNLI station records show, as we have seen,

....

14 *Ships that made history* No. 172 by Frank C. Bowen in *Shipbuilding and Shipping Record*, February 19, 1953, *Merchant Sail* by William Armstrong Fairburn, 1955, and *Wrecks in the Isles of Scilly* by Juliet du Boulay in an unidentified collection at p. 102, but re-published separately by its author in 1960 as *Wrecks of the Isles of Scilly*.

that the *Charles James Deere* was not used again that weekend, while the *Slippen's* log book shows that she was, and why. Moreover the RNLI's committee minute of the awards to Freddy Cook and others involved refer to them as having manned a "shoreboat". Cyrill Noall and Graham Farr, in *Wreck and Rescue round the Cornish Coast, Part II*, at p. 85 have both lifeboats going out "at dawn", and at some point "other boats" as well, including the *Slippen*, but as we have seen in chapter 9 the only involvement of the St Mary's lifeboat was much later in the day, and there is no evidence that any other boat except the *Slippen* ventured out to the search area.

Having decided to use a gig, why did the St Agnes men choose the *Slippen*? That is also not mentioned, and indeed many later tellers of the story may have assumed that she was the only one to hand, but that cannot be so. The *Shah* had been built by Peters in 1873 for the pilots of St Ives, but not taken up, and had been bought instead by the owners of the *Gem*, which as we have seen was a St Agnes cutter. She remained on St Agnes until sold to Newquay in the 1950s, but returned in 1961, at first on loan, but later permanently, and still races for the island's men. The *Campernell*, another Peters gig, had been built for St Agnes pilots in 1895, and is still in a gig house on the island. More doubtfully the *Cetewayo*, reputedly the fastest ever, also by Peters, had worked with the St Agnes cutter *Agnes*, but it is not clear whether she still existed in December 1907, since the notable occasion of her being patched up for a final winning race and immediate subsequent disintegration is variously dated between 1902 and 1908. Whether there were any others is not known, and in particular there is a question about gigs used for lighthouse relief. The five-oared *Elaine*, already mentioned as bought for the job, was not built until 1909, and there is an oral tradition emanating from Grenfell Legg, and spoken to by his grand-daughter Dorothy Barker, that it was the *Slippen* herself which Israel had used the day before, but her logbook does not reflect that and other gigs, in particular the *Klondyke*, now in the St Mary's museum, and the *O. and M.*, had been, and may still have been, available for that purpose.

Of the gigs available the *Campernell*, being a carrier, was no doubt rejected as too clumsy. The *Cetewayo*, if still around, was almost certainly in no fit state for such an enterprise. We do not know whether the *Klondyke* or the *O. and M.* was available. There is, however, no obvious reason why the *Shah* should not have been, but the possibility is not mentioned. It may be that she had been laid up for the winter, or it may be that the *Slippen* was for some unspecified reason judged fitter for this particular task, or was housed more accessibly to the chosen launch site (the *Shah* was kept in the Cove and the *Slippen* was probably launched from Periglis).

There is, however, also the possibility that the choice of gig was connected with who was prepared to volunteer to be the crew. Had the lifeboat been used its enrolled crew would been under a duty to man her. In the case of a gig, however, although for pilotage or other commercial use a gig's crew would come from her owners, for lifesaving the position may not have been so clear-cut. The owners would have to consent to her use, and no doubt had a right to be included, but how far there was any sort of expectation that they would form a crew is not clear. What is clear is that on this occasion there was a striking overlap between the two.

We know that because it so happens that we can see exactly who were the owners of the *Slippen* on 14 December 1907, and can compare their names with those of the crew. We know who were the owners because there is a list of them, with their shares, in the log book as at January 1898, and again in about 1912, and so far as working members are concerned the two lists coincide apart from the forced replacement of the lost Billy Cook Hicks by his son Freddy Cook and one query.

Four shares were owned in 1898 by J. Eynon Hooper, who was not a St Agnes man (according to the *Islander* of Autumn/Winter 2009, page 53, he was a Lloyds agent on St Mary's and the name, although possibly not this very person, also appears in records connected with Lelant and Penzance on mainland Cornwall). He must clearly have been a sleeping partner or passive investor. In 1912 those four shares were held jointly by Hooper and a Mr Banfield, of the leading St Mary's family. The other fourteen shares were (with one possible exception) held throughout, one each, by:

> William Francis Hicks
> Abraham James Hicks
> Grenfell Legg
> Osbert Hicks
> William George Mortimer senior
> William George Mortimer junior
> Isaac Legg
> Abram Hicks (with a query against 1912)
> Stephen Hicks
> Israel Hicks junior

> William Trenary
> Obadiah Hicks junior
> William Thomas Hicks [Billy Cook] (or in 1912 Freddy Cook)
> Albert Hicks.

That may be compared with the crew list on the morning of 14 December 1907, which is generally agreed as having been:

> Osbert Hicks, as cox
> Grenfell Legg
> George Mortimer
> Israel Hicks
> William Trenary
> Obadiah Hicks
> Freddy Cook Hicks
> Fred Hicks.

Of that crew only Fred was not an owner, or about to become an owner, and he was Osbert's son. Of the two William George Mortimers among the owners the "George Mortimer" in the gig was fairly certainly the junior; "George" is what he was commonly called, to distinguish him from his father, and at the inquest it was "William George Mortimer", as coxswain, who gave evidence of the lifeboat's involvement, but "George Mortimer" who was called separately to speak of the rescue of the survivors.

What that concurrence between owners and crew does not tell us is which came first – whether the gig was chosen and the owners were then expected to form a crew, or whether the crew first volunteered (as may be suggested by Israel's evidence that "after a little difficulty" they got a crew together) and then chose the gig. In either event ownership will have mattered less if there was by 1907 just one pilotage syndicate on the island, as suggested above, and as the neglected state into which the peerless *Cetewayo* had fallen perhaps also supports.

If the names are compared with those who had been in the lifeboat the night before Obadiah, Freddy Cook, Fred and William Trenary are common to both lists. The newcomers are Osbert, Israel, Grenfell Legg and George Mortimer. We have seen that, almost certainly, Osbert, Israel and Grenfell Legg had been absent from the lifeboat only because they were engaged in lighthouse relief, and the same may well have been true of George Mortimer also, since as the lifeboat coxswain's son he was quite likely to have been in its enrolled crew.

The relationships of those in the lifeboat have been explored in chapter 9. Of the others, Israel featured there as a point of reference for several of that crew. He was at this date a farmer's son aged 44 but was also a sailmaker by training, and as we have seen is recorded in the *Slippen's* log as having been paid for making a new sail for her in 1891. Osbert, as already noted, was the uncle of Israel's wife Charlotte Ellen, and the father of Fred and Jack. He was a farmer aged 54. Grenfell Legg, a farmer and pilot aged about 50, was more distantly related. His wife Abigail Jane was a sister of Abraham James who, as we have seen in chapter 9, was Charlotte Ellen's uncle by marriage. Finally George Mortimer, a farmer's son aged 38, was the son of William George Mortimer, the coxswain, whose relationship with Israel was set out in chapter 9, but he had himself acquired an additional relationship, this time on Charlotte Ellen's side, by marrying Martha Rowena Hicks, sister of William Francis and the Augustus Frederick mentioned in chapter 9.

The abodes of the lifeboatmen have been given in chapter 9. Of the others Osbert and Grenfell Legg lived in Palace, Israel in Lower Town and George Mortimer in Troy Town.

In chapter 1 it was briefly noted that Osbert was "by common consent made cox, as the master boatman of the island". It may seem surprising that he was not therefore the lifeboat coxswain, but there were probably at least two reasons for that. One was that, as the list of officers displayed in the church and copied in in chapter 9 demonstrates, progression through the lifeboat hierarchy went strictly by seniority, and Osbert's turn did not come until 1912. The other was that he was inclined, throughout his life, toward a rather relaxed attitude to, if not disregard of, authority. It is still recalled on St Agnes with relish that on one occasion, when coxswain, he took a routine RNLI inspection, including a launch and training trip, so casually that the inspector made a report casting doubt on his ability to cope with adverse conditions and the Institution ordered another, special, inspection by a senior inspector, whereupon Osbert, having primed his crew in advance, took the lifeboat at top speed through a hair-raising series of manoeuvres among the rocks which left the RNLI official so shaken that in order to escape he cut the inspection short and wrote a report giving the St Agnes station the highest of accolades.

It is implicit in the account already given of their collecting a lifejacket and rope for their final trip that the gig's crew had no lifejackets earlier, and there is an explicit statement to that effect in one source.[15] That is not as surprising as it may at first seem; the islanders were constantly out in boats and there had simply never been any practice of taking such precautions until it was required by the RNLI of lifeboat crews on duty, and that seems to have been accepted as a necessary but anomalous exception. It may be that there can here be seen just one aspect of a generally fatalistic attitude to the dangers of the water; it was, for example, not usual to be able to swim – the author's father, a boy of ten at the time, did not learn until required to do so by the Royal Navy on joining up ten years later.

The essentials of the *Slippen*'s three trips that day have been set out in chapter 1. They have been compiled from a number of sources, not entirely consistent in every detail, and in selecting a few of them here to add immediacy to the bare narrative some of those discrepancies will emerge. That is to be expected and for the most part need not be pursued but (surprisingly, for such an oft-told story) there are two major queries to be addressed.

There is nothing of any particular moment to add to the story of the first trip, but it is worth setting out in full the earliest account of it, as contained in the press report of Israel Hicks' evidence at the inquest. He said that they "left St Agnes shortly after seven o'clock, and just after landing on Annet found the dead body of a man who was evidently out of the wrecked schooner. A quantity of wreckage was strewn about. They divided into parties to search the island. Some of them heard shouting and thought it came from others of the crew, but they found the man Allen sheltering beneath the rock. He was calling for help. They assisted him to the boat, and a further search resulted in the finding of two more bodies. They brought Allen to St Agnes and he was conscious, though in great pain."[16]

No timing is given there, or elsewhere, for the return, but the second trip did not begin until 2.30 pm, and it is unlikely that time was wasted. High tide was due at 10.51 am, so the tidal rocks will have been covered for most of the first time out.

The second outing must have been much shorter, because otherwise there would not have been time for the third to be completed before

....

15 *The Loss of the Thomas W. Lawson* (Richard Gillis), 1951 – see note 15 to chapter 9), at
    p.315.
16 *The Western Morning News*, 17 December 1907.

darkness fell. The likelihood must be, therefore, that on this occasion the *Slippen* was rowed straight through Hellweathers Neck into what was, effectively, the open sea outside – a route which would have brought them almost directly to the South Carn. At that state of the tide little, if any, of the flatter part of the Brow would have been above the wave tops, and the South Carn itself and its twin rock at the west extremity of the Brow would have stood out prominently, rising sheer from the breaking swell. The wind was now force 5 (19–24 mph) from the south-west.

The only evidence of this trip at the inquest came in passing from Rowe, who said that a boat from the island "came and rescued him, and they had a difficult job in getting him off, as there were a lot of breakers. They threw him a line, and he jumped overboard."[17] Some colour is added by an account which seems to have come some years later from William Trenary.[18] It recounts that the gig had pulled out to the Hellweather rocks, where Israel Hicks "spotted two men". A rope was thrown, and after many attempts Rowe (as he proved to be) managed to grab it. He tied it to his body, and after some time and great persuasion jumped into the sea and was pulled aboard the *Slippen*, uttering groans and cries which William Trenary just could not forget.

The coroner, returning from Captain Dow's sickroom to report his brief evidence, ended by saying that he "spoke in the highest terms of the men who saved him". Perhaps prompted by that remark the Governor asked George Mortimer to speak, with the result that there was evidence at the inquest of the third and final mission of the *Slippen*. Mortimer said that "when they went to get the captain they could not then land." He "related the difficulties they had to contend with in effecting a landing. When they did land they found a gulf ten to twelve fathoms wide, with seas like a boiling cauldron between them and the captain. [Freddy Cook] volunteered to attempt to reach the captain, and they gave him one of the lifeboat jackets. Fastening a rope round himself he jumped in, and was tossed about like a cork, but eventually reached the rock where the captain was, and roping the captain got him down over the rocks. They had great difficulty in getting him through the sea. Then young Hicks jumped into the sea and they dragged him back".

....

17   Ibid.
18   Gillis (note 15 above), at p. 315.

The first of the two queries referred to above concerns the site of that rescue, the most dramatic and frequently recounted incident of the day. The rock involved was not identified in Mortimer's evidence and is not named in most published accounts, but it has always been understood locally to have been the South Carn. There are, however, two South Carns in that part of the islands, one in the Hellweathers, just west of The Brow, and one at the south-west corner of Annet. The account in chapter 1 places Rowe and Captain Dow on the former, but it would be wrong to leave the impression that that location is unchallenged. There is an important witness to the contrary. During a visit on him by the author the late Matt Lethbridge junior, the famous coxswain of the St Mary's lifeboat mentioned in chapter 9, said that Freddy Cook Hicks had told him that the rock could be reached by walking across a submerged bar, so that no swimming was needed. Matt concluded that the rock must have been South Carn, Annet, where in his view that would have been true, rather than the other, where it would not.

That has to be taken seriously. It apparently comes from Freddy Cook himself, the person at the heart of the event, by way of Matt Lethbridge, a man with an encyclopaedic knowledge of the waters around the islands. It is very difficult to understand how one or other of them can have been mistaken, or how Matt can have misunderstood what Freddy Cook said.

In the end, however, it is even more difficult to understand how Matt's conclusion can be correct, or how the site of the rescue can have been anywhere but the South Carn off The Brow. As we have seen William Trenary explicitly named the Hellweathers as the location of the sighting and rescue of Rowe, as had one of the earliest press reports.[19] Had Rowe and Dow been on Annet they would surely have been discovered during the intensive morning search of the island. It is central to the narrative that when Rowe was discovered he could be rescued only by catching a rope and jumping into the water and that it was plainly impossible at that stage to make any attempt to reach the master. That was true off the Hellweathers – as we have seen, at that state of the tide only the South Carn itself and the equally inaccessible pinnacle facing it at the western tip of The Brow would have been standing clear of the water – whereas on Annet at that time some effort to reach Captain Dow would surely have at least been contemplated. George Mortimer's evidence at the inquest (the earliest

....

19   *Luke's Falmouth Packet,* 20 Decxember 1907.

reliable account of what happened) is clearly compatible only with a swim across a "gulf". It must have been given in the presence of other members of the crew. The official citation to the RNLI award of a silver medal to Freddy Cook states that the schooner's "Master and Engineer had been washed on to Hellweather Rocks" and that Freddy Cook "swam into a deep gulley". Freddy Cook's son Joe and Osbert's grandson Osbert junior ("Ob") had each heard the story many times from their forebears and were clear in conversations with the author that the site was the South Carn in the Hellweathers. Ob, moreover, on a calm summer's day, took the author on foot across The Brow from his grandfather's probable landfall to the point opposite the South Carn and back at, as nearly as could be judged, the same state of the tide as had obtained when Freddy Cook and his companions made the same journey in very different conditions.

Quite recently, apparently for the first time, an account given by Freddy Cook himself to his nephew Vernon in 1964 has been published.[20]

'I expect you read T Moyle's account in the magazine. This was fairly true but it read as if he was there. I am the only one left of the gig's crew that took off the two men from the rocks, although J Hicks [Jack] was in the lifeboat when we went to the ship.

The following morning the Coxswain said it was impossible to go out in the lifeboat, so a party manned the gig and went to Annett [sic] and brought back a badly injured man, who died later. In the afternoon, we went again and, on the way over, someone spotted these two on Hellweathers. So we went down there and waved to them to jump in the sea, as the boat could not get near the rock. The youngest man did so and he was huddled aboard and he said the other was the Captain of the ship and was in a bad way. Well it was decided to get this one to St Agnes (what the Captain thought when he saw us going away, doesn't bear thinking about) but anyway, the engineer was landed and we went back again as the tide was lower and hoped to land on the inside of the brow and walk out to the outer side, like going over White Island brow. When we got out there we found a channel between us and the rock where the captain was. Several tried heaving a line over but it was too far and I said I think I could get over and I went on the end of the line, nearly got drowned in their hurry

....
20   *The Islander* magazine, Autumn/Winter 2009, p.56, quoted with the kind permission of
     Mrs Angela Jenkins.

Top left: Shag Rock (the nearest to the left), with the southern tail of Annet behind it and the Hellweathers stretching out to the right – first the Old Woman's House and then the Brow, terminating in an unnamed pinnacle, and facing it the South Carn, where Captain Dow and Edward Rowe were found. The camera is pointing south-east by south.

Middle left: The west end of the Brow at half tide terminating in an unnamed pinnacle, and facing it the South Carn (essentially the same view as in the preceding photograph, but approaching much more closely). Between the two is the gap across which Freddy Cook swam and returned with Captain Dow

Bottom left: The same gap as the previous photograph, from a shorter distance and in the opposite direction, with Annet behind.

Above: The 'level' part of the brow, which Freddy Cook and his companions crossed to reach the South Carn and return with Captain Dow. The camera is pointing east, with St Agnes in the background. Author's own photographs.

Above: Freddy Cook, in life-jacket and sou'wester. Photograph from author's family collection.

> to pull me over but the biggest job was getting the Captain over the brow to the boat but with four or five men (George Mortimer and W. Treneary [sic] in particular) it was done and he was soon in Lower Town house, where he was for several weeks."

Under that compelling weight of evidence the conclusion must be that, despite its apparent authority, Matt Lethbridge's siting must somehow have been mistaken, and that Captain Dow was indeed rescued from South Carn, Hellweathers, after Freddy Cook had swum an impassable channel to reach him.

The second query concerns the composition of the crew of the *Slippen* on its final trip. That it was as stated above in the morning has never been in doubt or dispute. The earliest newspaper reports, probably both from the same correspondent, explicitly state that "the same crew" went out at 2.30, and that again has not been challenged. As to the final trip, however, Richard Gillis, in the account already cited several times, and a little after telling us that Rowe was "helped ashore by Israel Hicks and Fred Hicks, and then to the cottage of the former", states that the *Slippen* "put out again with Isaac Legg and Albert Hicks making up the crew in place of those who had gone to the aid of the engineer" (sc. Israel and Fred).[21]

Against that there are indications that the crew remained the same throughout, although they are not by any means as specific. The newspaper reports cited in the last paragraph in relation to the crew for the second trip simply go on, after describing it, to say: "They took him [Rowe] ashore and went back to rescue the captain." The natural sense of that is that the "they" who "went back" were the same persons as those who "took him ashore". As recorded in chapter 1 the citation for the U.S. gold watch and medals refers to the rescue of "the <u>captain</u> and two men" (added emphasis), and the presentation of those awards was made to the original crew, including Israel and Fred and excluding Isaac Legg and Albert. (Photograph at p. 192).

The resolution of this query is not as clear-cut as that of the first. The quotation from Gillis follows not long after a passage in which he cites William Trenary as his source, and may be part of the same material. It gains colour from the fact that there must undoubtedly have been some

....

21 *The Loss of the Thomas W. Lawson* (Richard Gillis) 1951, at p.315. *Leviathan's Master* by David M. Quinn (iUniverse, Inc., Bloomington, NY) 2009, at p. 64, is to the same effect, but that does not purport to be a factual account and is plainly derivative.

urgency about the turn-round, and getting Rowe to Lower Town Farmhouse would have taken time. Despite its lateness, therefore, it cannot be lightly dismissed. The contemporaneous indications to the contrary are sparse and implicit, although their very paucity and lack of explicitness may tell, on reflection, in their favour. The rescues were so dramatic and must have been so much discussed that surely, had there been a change of crew, some mention of it at the time would have emerged. Most tellingly, how could such a momentous process as the recommendation, award and presentation of the Congressional watch and medals have unfolded without any mention of which eight (or should it have been ten?) men were rightly the recipients, had there been any question about that? Nor is the "urgency" point, on examination, persuasive. The whole island must have been alive with involvement in the rescue attempt, and many willing hands would have taken over the care of Rowe the moment he was ashore – indeed, in a day when the roles of the sexes were still sharply segregated, that was clearly "women's work".

Although, as already acknowledged, the resolution of this query is more nearly in the balance than that of the first the better view is that there was no change of crew.

As a tailpiece to the discussion of that query it should be mentioned that there is a much-published photograph of the *Slippen* on Periglis beach, with her crew, usually printed in association with an account of the rescues on 14 December 1907, and often with at least the implication, and sometimes the assertion, that it portrays the crew on that date and the gig about to be launched. It plainly does not. It is taken in full daylight, the sea is a flat calm and the crew, which is named, is not just different in several respects from that of the rescue (on either version) but actually includes a visitor. The most likely date for it is the following day, when as recorded in chapter 1 the wind had dropped to Force 1 and many boats were out searching for bodies. Two other photographs of the *Slippen's* crew, by C.J. King, have recently been published,[22] one of which probably was taken on 14 December, because the men in it are in full oilskins and sou'westers, but they are not named and cannot now with any assurance be identified from their appearance. Nor is there any certainty to which trip it relates – the caption simply reads "at the time of the *Thomas W Lawson*".

....

22   *The Islander* (note 11 above) at p. 58.

Above: the crew of the Slippen in oilskins. Undated, but entitled "The crew of the Slippen at the time of the Thomas W. Lawson", and the most likely candidate for a contemporaneous photograph of the crew as constituted and dressed on 14 December 1907 Photograph: C. J. King, courtesy of Judy Douglas.

Facing page, top: The much published photograph of the Slippen, *with a crew sometimes assumed to be that of 14 December 1907, but most likely taken on the following day, when many boats searched for bodies. The crew are, from left to right, William Trenary, Albert Hicks, a visitor named Cummings, Benjamin Hicks, Jack Hicks, Israel Hicks. Richard Grenfell Legg, 'A' (probably Abram) Hicks and (in the water) Osbert Hicks. Photograph by Francis Mortimer.*
Bottom: The Slippen's log book, entries for 1907 and 1908. Photographer: Alasdair Moore. Image previously published in the Islander magazine, Autumn/Winter 2009.

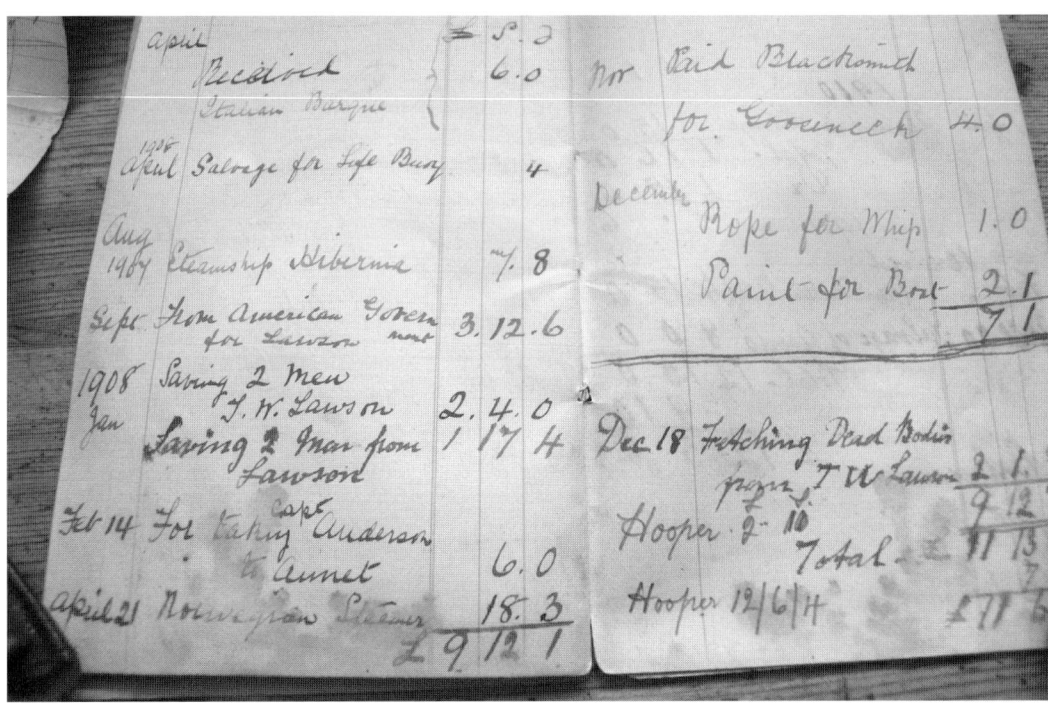

We broke off our summary of the *Slippen's* log book in order to recount her part in the rescue of the survivors from the *Lawson*. It can now be resumed.

In what reads as if it were September 1907 (but the date must be mistaken) there is a receipt of £3.12.6d "From American Government for Lawson", in January 1908 sums of £2.4.0d and £1.17.4d for "Saving 2 men from Lawson.", on 14 February 6s "For taking Capt Anderson [he was a salvage company surveyor] to Annet." And finally, on the facing page, which would normally record expenses, is another receipt, dated 18 December, which must be 1907, reading "Fetching dead bodies from T W Lawson £2.1.7d" That was not money for the crew as such, but in principle for shareholders generally, although the log book seems to record that it was for some unexplained reason all paid, less expenses, to Mr Hooper, the off-island shareholder. We shall see in the next chapter, however, that the crew did receive some recompense from another source.

The years 1907 to 1917, indeed, do seem to have been more prosperous for the *Slippen's* owners than those which had immediately preceded them, but that had virtually nothing to do with pilotage; nearly all the money arose from wrecks – the *Lawson* in 1907, the *Plympton* in 1910, the *Minnehaha* in 1911 and an "Italian wreck" in 1917. After that there are very few receipts and in 1920 18s is collected from the owners for expenses, in 1925 a further £2-2s-0d and in 1933 a further £1-8s-0d. A final entry in 1934 shows a balance of 6s-11d "taken for payment owing to J.H. [Jack] Hicks".

So far as the log books are concerned that is the end of the *Slippen's* story, but the revival of gig racing as a sport coupled with interest in this gig herself, because of her involvement with the wreck of the *Lawson*, has ensured that she has neither been broken up, left to rot nor forgotten.[23] In 1953 she was purchased by the Newquay Rowing Club and underwent complete renovation there at a cost of £60, during which the episode already recounted occurred in which it was found that one of her original strakes could be bent into a circle. At the end of the 1970s she was re-purchased by a Scillonian syndicate and returned to the Isles of Scilly, where she remains. After some twenty years of use as a training boat and to raise funds for the RNLI she underwent further extensive renovation in 2001, the subject of

....

23   Most of what follows is taken from *The Islander* magazine, Spring 2010, pp. 48–49.

a public appeal for funds,[24] which enabled her to be shipped in 2002 to the U.S.A., in a venture in which Tom Hall was a prime mover, to feature as one of the major attractions in an exhibition devoted to the wreck of the *T.W. Lawson* at the Scituate Maritime and Mossing Museum,[25] near the site of Tom Lawson's Dreamwold estate, described in chapter 3. Since her return she has has been rowed regularly in competition.

....

24 *Isles of Scilly News*, 9 August 2001, p. 18.
25 The *T.W. Lawson* by Thomas Hall (Orchid Hill Publishing, St John, U.S.V.I.) 2003, at p.109.

· 12 ·

The Aftermath

T HERE WAS PERHAPS some forlorn hope on Sunday 15 December that other survivors might be found, but everyone involved in the large-scale searches that day knew that realistically all they could expect to recover were bodies or, even more tragically, body parts. In the event, in addition to George Allen, those produced at the inquest were identified there as Mark Sansom of Brooklyn, described by Captain Dow as his steward (but, as we have seen in chapter 5, enrolled as the cabin boy under the name of Mark Sanson or Lamson), Victor Hansel, a Swede (who must be the fireman named as V. Olansen when enrolled), an unnamed Scandinavian (of whom we have seen in chapter 5 that there were four in addition to Olansen), and an unidentifiable torso. It was directed at the end of the inquest that any further bodies recovered were to be buried without inquest.[1] Another press report gives the same names for those of the bodies recovered by then, except that it identifies "Mark Samson" as the cabin boy, but it adds George Bolinke, a German (doubtless the man named as Gustav Bohnke when enrolled).[2]

The only report traced of later recoveries is of a search on Annet on Wednesday 18 December by [George] Mortimer, Obadiah Hicks, Osbert Hicks and William Trenary, in which two more bodies were found in the southern part of the island, one with a tattoo "J.A.P." (who may, therefore, have been the man enrolled as the Dane, A. Petersen) and one

....

1   *The Western Morning News*, 17 December 1907.
2   *The Cornishman*, 19 December 1907.

unidentifiable.[3] As to burials, there is in the St Agnes churchyard an undressed stone reputed locally to mark the grave of as many as 14 bodies ultimately found after the wreck, including that of Billy Cook. The number must, however, be mistaken. Not only does 14 look implausibly high as a total (with Dow, Rowe and Allen it would account for 17 of the 19 persons on board, a much higher proportion than one would expect) but, more specifically, the *Western Weekly News* of 21 December 1907 gives fully circumstantial accounts of two separate funeral services on Tuesday 17 December, one in the morning on St Mary's of five victims and the other in the afternoon on St Agnes of three. That accords with the fact that, as will appear below, there is evidence that the American consul paid for eight coffins in all. There is a family tradition that the discovery of Billy Cook's badly disfigured remains was never openly acknowledged, in case his widow, Lizzie Ann, demanded to see him.

Much of the evidence at the inquest held on Monday 16 December has already been drawn upon. It is a remarkable tribute to the capabilities and commitment of everyone involved that in what would be regarded by many nowadays as, technologically speaking, the Dark Ages, a full coroner's court could be assembled on such a small and remote island in mid-December, hear all the relevant witnesses and complete its inquiry on the first working day after the disaster. As already mentioned the court had to sit in Israel Hicks' home, Lower Town farmhouse, because Dow and Rowe were being looked after there and Dow, at least, could not even leave his bed. The inquest was presided over by the coroner for the islands, Mr W.M. Gluyas. There was a jury, who will have numbered at least seven. They are not named in full in the press reports, but included a Mr McFarland as foreman[4] and a Charles Hicks, who asked witnesses a number of questions. It seems likely that the jurors (at that time all men) will have come from St Mary's; the men of St Agnes would all have been either participants themselves or closely linked with those who were, and drawing on other off islands would have been a needless complication.

In attendance were T.A. Dorrien-Smith, the Governor, E.J. Bluett, the (local) hon. secretary of the RNLI, T. Bradley, the divisional coastguard

....

3   *The Western Morning News*, 19 December 1907.

4   *The Cornishman*, 19 December 1907, names Obadiah Hicks as the foreman, but that must be a mistake: Obadiah had been in both the lifeboat and the *Slippen*, and neither he nor his father or son of the same name could have been considered for service on that jury.

officer and Harold Sandrey, representing the American Consul.[5] The Governor, in particular, seems to have played an active part, and it is indeed likely that his accustomed dominance in island life meant that even on such occasions as these, when he should have had no official standing (the coroner being, as the title implies, for these purposes the representative of the crown), he felt entitled to intervene quite freely. As his invitation to George Mortimer to describe the *Slippen's* third trip illustrates, that may well be one of the reasons why the proceedings widened, to the great benefit of subsequent research, well beyond the inquiry into identities and causes of death which was strictly the limit of the business of the court.

The jury returned a finding of "Accidental Death" and recommended that the two lifeboat stations should work together "in a greater measure than at present".[6] That looks like a record of the formal verdict. A more discursive account of the foreman's closing remarks has him stating that the jury were satisfied that the lifeboats did exceedingly good work, but thought there should be a better understanding between the St Agnes and St Mary's boats. He had been asked, he said, to express the jury's admiration for the men who had saved the captain and engineer. It was exceedingly brave work, and the jury thought they deserved the highest praise, more especially Frederick Charles Hicks. The coroner concurred.[7]

The presence of Harold Sandrey at the inquest is a reminder of the interest of the American consul in the wreck and the rescue attempts. We have seen that the *Slippen's* logbook shows that at least one of the payments received for her work came "From American Government for Lawson", doubtless via the consul. A note has survived, of unknown provenance, reading:

> The American Consular Agent – coffins for bodies from the T.W. Lawson 7 masted schooner wrecked off Annet
> 16th Dec – Coffins to St Agnes for Victor Hansell – Fireman/Swedish seaman
> 17th Dec – 3 coffins to St Agnes
> 18th Dec – 3 " " " " .

It was presumably also the consul who initiated the proposal, which then went up through the many layers of the U.S. foreign service to the summit of government, that the crew of the *Slippen* should be honoured by the

---

5   *The Western Morning News* (note 1 above).
6   *The Cornishman* (note 2 above).
7   *Luke's Falmouth Packet,* 20 December 1907.

President and Congress.

One American with an intense personal interest in the schooner was Thomas W. Lawson himself. His superstitions have been mentioned in chapter 3. His son Douglas begins his account of the wreck in the *Boston Sunday Globe* of 12 November 1955 as follows:

> On Friday, Dec. 13, 1907, I had just come home for Christmas vacation from St Paul's school and, as was our custom, father and I talked late into the night. I remember so well his closing words, 'Well, this Friday the 13th went off without anything going wrong.' A few hours later, clad in our bathrobes, father stood beside me while I took the call over the telephone in the early hours of Saturday morning. ... The *Lawson* had broken her moorings and was presumably a wreck off Annet Head on the shores of the Scilly Isles.

Although Douglas does not comment on it, the fact is that because of the difference in time zones it was still Friday in Boston when the *Lawson* struck Shag Rock in the small hours of Saturday, Greenwich Mean Time, and she was already lost when Lawson spoke his words of relief.

To round off the American connection, as remarkable technologically and logistically as the Monday inquest is the fact that the wreck was fully reported in the *Boston Sunday Post* of 15 December 1907, as was, by a coincidence harking back to the *Lawson's* genesis, a lecture to a packed audience of Bostonians, on conditions in the Philippines, reported under the headline "Filipinos not ready for self-government".

There were also inquiries by the RNLI. The local committee met on Wednesday 18 December, with the Governor presiding and the RNLI's district inspecting officer in attendance. The press report states that the case was fully gone into, special attention being given to the evidence of the two coxswains "of the St Agnes lifeboat" (meaning, presumably, the coxswain William George Mortimer and the second coxswain Abraham James Hicks). The abandonment of the schooner when one of the lifeboat crew was seriously ill was "closely inquired into" and the committee "unanimously came to the conclusion that everything that could be done was done by the two lifeboats." The report continues that the omission to acquaint the St Mary's lifeboat that they had left also received their attention, and that they had "taken precautions to remedy any such omission in future." They also made recommendations about awards.[8]

The matter then went to the national committee, and there we have the relevant minute of the meeting on 9 January 1908 (the date is yet another testimony to the speed with which business was despatched in those days). It begins: "Reported that the District Inspector had enquired into the loss of the 7 masted schooner Thomas W Lawson". What follows interweaves several strands, which it is clearer to keep separate.

One concerned communication between the two lifeboat stations, the subject of the jury's rider and of the local committee's attention. Having recounted the facts of the arrival alongside the schooner and successive departures of the lifeboats the minute notes that the St Agnes coxswain "omitted to inform the St Mary's station what he had done." For that the committee decided to admonish him "to be more careful in future to keep St Mary's station informed by telephone etc. of his movements, and the requirements of the Service generally, in the interests of saving life". Although that was more critical of him than the local committee had been the national committee did not confine itself to allocating blame, and did not leave the responsibility for improvement to the coxswain alone. It also decided that "a reliable Telephone messenger should be appointed at both stations at helpers rate of pay".

Another matter for consideration was the performance of the boat herself, which is not mentioned in the press report of the local committee's proceedings, but which must have been addressed there, because the minute of the national committee records that complaint was made "of the behaviour of the St Agnes Lifeboat and the Local Committee and Crew asked either for a new Lifeboat or for such structural alterations in the present one to make her more satisfactory". That is unspecific about the nature of the complaint and of what alterations were required "to make her more satisfactory", but the committee was clearly told more than appears from that entry, because at the end of the minute it resolved, "subject to the approval of the Coxswain and Crew" to add a weight "not exceeding 30 cwts" (1.5 tons) to the keel. Given that as built the *Charles Deere James* weighed only a little over four tons the amount of the addition gives a measure of how sharp the criticism must have been and how seriously the committee took it. Such a modification would have made the boat significantly heavier to pull under

....
8   *The Western Morning News* (note 1 above).

oars, and the fact that the crew thought it a price worth paying for the additional stability it would give under sail shows how alarmed they must have been by how the boat had behaved in that rig in storm conditions.

There is striking vindication of the crew's judgment in a comparison of the original specification for their boat with that for her successor, the *Charles Deere James II*, which replaced her on 23 July 1909. The latter was also a 10-oar boat of generally similar design and dimensions, but the weight of iron in the fixed keel had risen by a factor of over 13 from 3 cwt to over 39 cwt 2 qr 10 lb, an increase of 36 cwt 2 qr 10 lb (1.83 tons). There was also an increase in the weight of the steel in the sliding keels, bringing the overall increase in keel weight to over 1.9 tons. The weight of the boat complete, without gear had risen from 4 tons, 3 cwt to 6 tons 4 cwt to 6 tons 4 cwt 1 qr 14 lb, an increase of 2 tons I cwt 1 qr 14 lb (2.07 tons), nearly all, therefore, in the keel. The price paid in the work load under oars came not just from that but also from the resulting increase of some 50 per cent in draught.

The committee also dealt with questions of awards and financial recognition and relief, but it was not the only or first body to address the last of those issues. *The Illustrated Western Weekly News* of 28 December 1907 had reported that a public meeting had been held at the Town Hall, St Mary's, "on Saturday" (sc. 21 December), presided over by the Governor, at which a committee was formed to collect subscriptions for Billy Cook's widow and younger children. As part of the same item was a letter from the Governor giving more details. Billy Cook, he wrote, had left "a widow and family of nine", of whom the four youngest, aged 16, 15, 12 and 7, were, with her, dependent on his earnings for their support. Those four can be identified from family records as William Hughes, Elizabeth Ann, Dorrien and Augusta. The RNLI committee voted £200 (£14,650 in 2014 money) to that fund "with an expression of deep sympathy", and in all enough was raised to enable Lizzie Ann and the children to emigrate and establish themselves in Australia, where many of their descendants still live and maintain contact with their relatives in St Agnes.

Billy Cook was, strictly speaking, not on lifeboat service when he died, having accepted a commission as a pilot, but it had been because of his service in the lifeboat that he had been where he was, and he is referred to in the minute as "a life-boatman", so that grant is understandable. What is rather more noteworthy is that another sum of money granted

Presentation copy of the R.N.L.I. resolution awarding its silver medal to Freddy Cook Hicks. Author's own photograph.

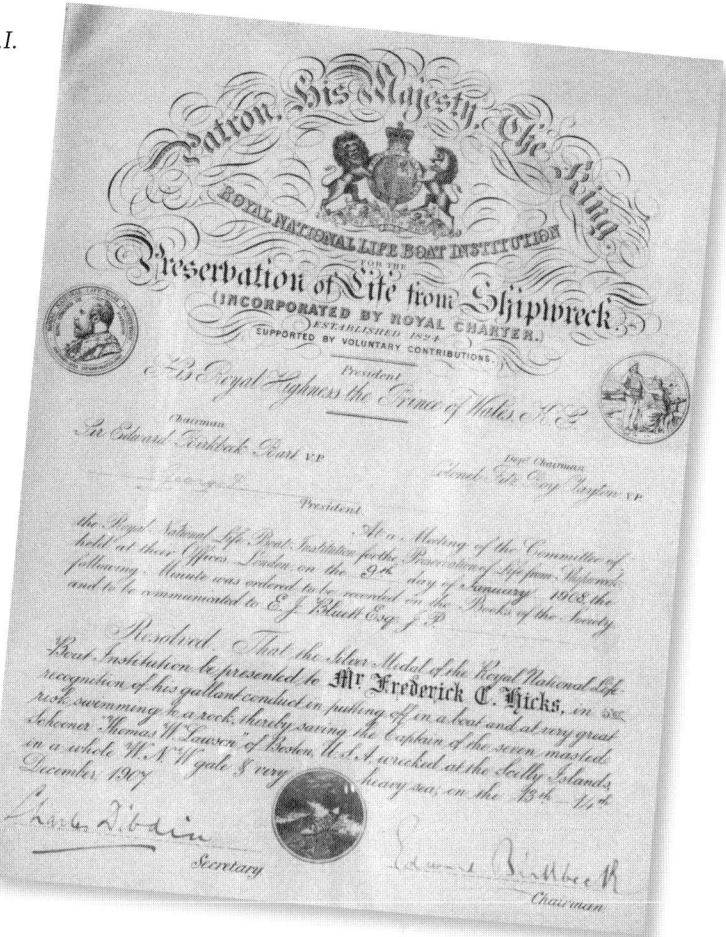

by the RNLI committee was £12 to the crew of the *Slippen*. and that that was associated in the minutes with the award of the Institution's silver medal to Freddy Cook, for saving Captain Dow "at imminent risk to his own life". Nothing of what they had done had, officially, anything to do with lifeboat service, although it was probably the case that they were all members of the enrolled St Agnes lifeboat crew, and it was in any event, as we have seen in the story of the *Delaware* in chapter 7, not unknown for the RNLI to grant awards for work done in what they termed "shoreboats".

Freddy Cook's silver medal was not, however, the only or best known of the awards bestowed in recognition of the *Slippen's* efforts. The gold watch for him and gold medals for the rest of the crew from the U.S.A.

Presentation of gold watch and medals. Reading from left to right: Israel Hicks, Obadiah Hicks, George Mortimer, Freddy Cook Hicks, Osbert Hicks, Grenfell Legg, Fred Hicks, William Trenary, Lt. T. A. Dorrien-Smith ('the Governor'). © Gibsons of Scilly

government have been mentioned in chapter 1 and the inscription on the medals quoted. They were presented by the U.S. ambassador or his representative in the presence of the Governor and there is a well-known photograph (above) of the crew and Governor on that occasion in front of the Town Hall at St Mary's, Freddy Cook holding his watch and the others wearing their medals.

The watch and medals have naturally been treasured by the recipients and their families, and in most cases their present locations can be identified. Freddy Cook's watch passed to his son Joe, and from him to his daughter Deborah Carter-Clout. Osbert's medal went to his son Jack, then to Jack's son Donald, and now to Donald's daughter Marigold Barbanchon. Israel's passed to his son Charles, and from him to his son, the present

Front cover of Freddy Cook's watch. Author's own photograph.

Face of Freddy Cook's watch. Author's own photograph.

Inscription inside cover of Freddy Cook's watch. Author's own photograph.

Compass on chain of Freddy Cook's watch. Author's own photograph.

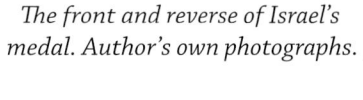

The front and reverse of Israel's medal. Author's own photographs.

author. Obadiah's went by way of his daughter Marian Camp and grand-daughter Kathleen Stephenson to his great-granddaughter Hilary Nicholas and William Trenary's via his daughter Lillian Willey to his grandson Gerald Willey. Grenfell Legg's passed to his grandson Herbert and from him to his widow Sheila and then to their son Christopher (Kit). George Mortimer's medal disappeared from view for many years, but has recently been purchased by the Isles of Scilly Museum, and is on display there. That leaves only Fred's, which passed to his son, Frederick John, but sadly when he died in 2007 it could not be found, despite a careful search by his family.

Initial investigation of the wreck site was prompt. *The Illustrated Western Weekly News* of 21 December reports that "Captain Robertson, one of Lloyd's special surveyors, on Sunday morning [15 December] went from Penzance to the Isles of Scilly on the Western Marine Salvage's boat Lady of the Isles, with Captain Anderson, the well-known wreck salver, to inspect the position of the vessel. They visited the scene and found at high water that it was not visible." We have seen from the *Slippen's* logbook the entry dated 14 February 1908 "For taking Capt Anderson to Annet", but the logbook entries record dates of receipt rather than when the work was done, and it seems rather more likely that this was payment for the December visit than evidence of a second, apparently pointless, one in the New Year.

Lloyd's List for 17 December 1907 quotes the reporting telegram of 16 December to the Salvage Association from "their special officer" verbatim: "Vessel … broke in two between fifth and sixth masts, afterpart sinking deep water, forepart capsizing, masts shorewards. Now lying on port beam ends submerged at high water, wood spars still attached. Position exposed, only approachable small boat finest weather. Vessel and cargo total loss."

It is apparent that what Capts Robertson and Anderson saw convinced them that no useful salvage of the schooner herself was practicable, and the nature of the cargo had from the outset put any recovery of that out of the question; the stench of floating oil was around the islands for two or three days. There is no mention in the telegram of environmental damage, and only one has been found elsewhere – partly, no doubt, because it was not in those days a matter of such concern as it is now, but also because the comparatively light petroleum fractions in this oil really did evaporate away quite quickly, without the persistent and destructive residue which the crude oil of recent highly publicised disasters has left. The one exception

A lifeboat (probably the Charles Deere James) approaching the Arden Craig, wrecked on the Gunners Ledge, photographed from the Elaine as she returned from relieving the Bishop Rock Lighthouse on 8 January 1911. Photograph by Francis James Mortimer.

is an assertion by Trevellick Moyle in the *Scillonian* of Autumn 1960 that "many gulls were found dead all around the shores".

Although the *The Illustrated Western Weekly News* reads as if the surveyors were on site at a time when the wreck was wholly submerged a substantial stretch of the *Lawson's* side did remain visible at other states of the tide for long enough to enable photographs to be taken (book cover and p. 154). However, apart from an important dive in the following summer, which needs detailed examination in the next chapter, their visit or visits constituted the only recorded formal inspection of the wreck site or anchorage and, since 1907 was long before the days of widespread recreational diving, the only investigation of any kind for many years. More recently, and especially since snorkelling and diving have become widely popular sports activities, there has been much interest in the remains of the schooner and much exploration of the site, in particular by Mark Groves, a leading St Mary's diver.

One story of more personal interest can be picked up from chapter 1, which recorded that Edward Rowe gave his hostess and nurse Agnes Hicks,

Israel's sister-in-law, a gold ring. The ring has two initials engraved. They are much degraded and not clearly decipherable , but what is beyond doubt is that they are neither "ER" nor "AH". Rowe was at the time unmarried, but he had reputedly left a sweetheart behind in America, so it may be that it was "her" ring which he gave away, in which case it must be hoped that his providential return to her from the jaws of death was sufficient extenuation.

Agnes herself was at the time unmarried. She did later marry, but too late to have children, so she left the ring to her niece, also Agnes Hicks, Israel's daughter and the author's aunt. That Agnes also married too late to have children, so she left the ring to her niece Joyce Hicks, the author's sister. Joyce, in her turn, also married too late to have children, so she gave the ring (she is, happily, still alive) to her niece Elizabeth, the author's daughter. Elizabeth, however is married and herself has a daughter but no niece, so although the ring can still descend in the female line that particular rule of succession will be broken.

The longer-term aftermath of the wreck and rescue on island life is difficult to assess. On the one hand almost every household had been affected in one way or another, and the tragedy of Billy Cook's death and the drama of the *Slippen's* final trip cannot but have made a deep impression. On the other hand it is easy for outsiders to exaggerate the long-term impact of events which were not, in truth, all that exceptional to the islanders themselves. To take only the best known of many examples, some of the men most closely involved in our story (certainly William George Mortimer and Billy Cook Hicks and probably Osbert Hicks and Grenfell Legg) had 32 years earlier been in the gig *O & M* in its rescue of survivors from the *Schiller*. And it was less than three years after the loss of the *Lawson* that, as already recounted, the *Plympton*, having struck close inshore off St Agnes itself, claimed the lives of two young men, one (Charles Hicks) a son of the same Osbert and brother of Fred and Jack, and the other (Charles Mumford) a relative from St Mary's, when she fell off the Lethegus rocks. Within months of that Israel's *Elaine*, on a routine trip to relieve the Bishop Rock lighthouse, came across the foundering *Arden Craig*, and was, with the St Agnes lifeboat, involved in rescuing the crew.

We have already noted that, happily, what might easily have been a very malign legacy – a festering division over the issue whether the lifeboat should have been re-launched – does not seem to have occurred. St

A gig and other boats alongside The Plympton, 14 Aug 1909. © National Maritime Museum, Greenwich, London. Gibsons of Scilly shipwreck collection.

Agnes remained a remarkably united island for an isolated community of that size. Not everyone was best of friends with everyone else, but really damaging feuds seem to have been wholly absent.

Much of this book has to be concerned with the rather mundane task of trying to disentangle the true facts on matters of detail from conflicting or confusing evidence. There is, however, room for one story in a quite different genre. The author owes it to Osbert's grandson of the same name. It relates that when the Governor, Dorrien Smith, (who had the only telephone on Tresco) met his boatman on the morning of Saturday 14 December and told him of the loss of the Lawson, with Billy Cook Hicks on board, the boatman replied that that was impossible because he had seen Billy Cook at 2 am that night in his (the boatman's) own kitchen, standing in a pool of water from his wet oilskins and asking for a light for his pipe.

· 13 ·

Questions

THE NARRATIVE SO FAR leaves a number of questions in the air,
and they must now be faced. Many of them concern decisions made
by Captain Dow, as master of the *T.W. Lawson*, or by William George
Mortimer, as coxswain of the St Agnes lifeboat. For the most part they will
be addressed in the order in which they arose, but there is one exception.
Dow's insistence on remaining at anchor, fully manned, was so crucial, has
been so much criticised, and consideration of it needs to take into account
the conclusions on so many ancillary issues, that it is best left to the end.

In contrast with the debate about that, what one might naturally suppose
to be the very first questions seem to have received no attention. They
concern how far Captain Dow and his officers were at fault, as navigators,
in being so far off course as to run into the Scillies or, as to the watch-
keeper, in mistaking the light of the Bishop for a ship's light. Accounts of
the wreck tend to start with those as given facts, without raising the sorts
of issues so vigorously discussed in relation to later events.

On the navigation question a critic can point to the simple fact that the
mouth of the English Channel is a huge target. "From Ushant to Scilly is
thirty-five leagues" (105 nautical miles), as the old sea song goes. Aim for
the middle, it might be said, and there is then ample room for a margin of
error wide enough to be sure of not running into land.

Whatever the theoretical advantage of aiming for the centre of the
Channel, however, it is likely that in 1907 accepted "best practice" for a
London-bound vessel started from the concept of a safe offshore land-
fall on the English side, and then built in whatever was judged to be the

required margin of error in the light of the navigator's confidence in or distrust of his plotted position. Rowe indeed said that Captain Dow's plan was to make his landfall 10 miles south of the Bishop.[1] On that basis the extenuating circumstances here were (i) the length of time since the last opportunity to plot the vessel's position accurately by a "fix" on the sun or a star, (ii) the difficulty of dead reckoning during the storm conditions which had prevailed for much of that period, and (iii), possibly, the unforeseen, because intermittent and little understood, effect of the Rennell current, described at the end of chapter 6. As to (i), there can have been no sightings since the *Lawson* encountered gale winds on or about 4 December. When there had last been clear weather before that is more difficult to establish, but making what at best can be only an educated guess by plotting the schooner's possible daily position on the weather charts it may have been on 29 November, 14 days before she arrived in the Scillies.

It can be said in reply that, as to (i) and (ii), those difficulties were well known to the navigators themselves, and should have been given greater weight in the form of a further shift of course to the south. But against that, finally, the sheer number, over the centuries, of incoming vessels wrecked in the Scillies invites the reflection that many of them, surely, must have been in the hands of competent, conscientious, navigators, in which case avoiding this particular peril was, before the day of electronic satellite navigation, probably more difficult than it seems to a modern outsider. The fairest conclusion is that Captain Dow and his officers cannot wholly escape blame for the navigation error, but that there is much to be said in mitigation of that failing.

If the absence of criticism on that score is therefore in some measure understandable it is more difficult to see why the misidentification of the light has also escaped censure. Here we are concerned with the individual responsibilities of the officer on watch, and of any lookout posted in the bow (as, given the *Lawson's* length, someone probably was). We do not know who they were or whether, if not on watch himself, Captain Dow was also on deck, as he may well have been, given the significance of entry into the English Channel.

The light of the Bishop Rock lighthouse emanated from 44 m (144 ft) or more above sea level and was extremely intense, with a range in 1907 of

....

1   *Boston Herald*, 9 January 1972.

18 nautical miles, very little short of its current 20 nautical miles. It had a distinctive "character", or pattern, of two four-second flashes, separated by five seconds of darkness and repeated every 60 seconds. (The current character has a similar overall "shape", but the cycle now repeats every 15 seconds and the paired flashes are each much shorter (0.1 second) and a little closer together (2.2 seconds).) It was, to state the obvious, stationary. In contrast a ship's masthead white light (even if no green or red could be seen below) would have been much fainter, and swaying, but continuous, any momentary disappearances from the ship's motion or for other reason being random. Even in conditions murky enough for the Bishop's light to have been turned on by about 3.30 pm its intrinsic brightness was such that it must first have been visible from a distance that would have allowed plenty of time to observe its flash pattern, and the other characteristics which distinguished it from a ship's light, well before the *Lawson* was irretrievably committed to passing on one side or the other. With the wind in the south-west the *T.W. Lawson* would have been on a broad starboard reach, with no obstruction from the sails to a clear view to starboard, where the Bishop must have lain, given a course far enough to the north to bring the schooner to its known anchorage. If, on the other hand, it be supposed that by some mischance it was not spotted until much closer there would have been the added considerations that it would have been much too bright and at much too high an elevation to be defensibly mistaken for a ship's light.

There seem to be only two possible explanations. One is that no proper lookout was being maintained at all, so that the *Lawson* was already inside the Bishop before its light was noticed, and the story of mistaking it for a ship's light was an invention. The other is that it was seen earlier, but the watch-keeper was so convinced that he was on a safe course, well to the south of the islands, that he paid no attention to the nature of the light, but just assumed, until it was too late, that it was from a ship. On either basis it was a culpable error.

What if those errors had not been made? Had a course been laid even as little as five miles further south the schooner would have escaped scot-free. Had the course been unaltered but the light correctly identified in time she would have turned sharply to starboard – preferably due south for a while – a simple manoeuvre requiring only the use of the rudder and some drawing in of the sheets, without any need to tack or gybe, and unless already nearly level with the Bishop would again have been in no danger. Only if that had happened at the very last moment would there have been some risk, still probably slight, of striking an outlying hazard, in particular the Crim Rocks, and even that, although a major disaster for the vessel, would have been unlikely to have resulted in any loss of life; the lifeboats would have had a rather (1.5 miles) longer journey than the one to the anchorage which they successfully made, but not a more difficult one, and could have taken off the crew.

The next potential issue is whether Captain Dow was right to anchor. That also has never been questioned, but in this instance rightly so. It is true that once safely clear of Gunners to starboard and Nundeeps to port, as by chance Dow was, a navigator completely familiar with those waters could have found a safe line north of Jeffrey Rock into the approach from Broad Sound to St Mary's Road, where there was good holding ground and sufficient depth, even for a vessel of the *Lawson's* great draught, far enough north to enable an anchored craft to obtain some shelter from Samson and Bryher against the expected westerly to north-westerly gale. But Dow was a stranger to the islands, almost certainly without any chart of them, and even if he had any sailing directions was not on any of the recognised approach courses for which they provide. It was the alternative of turning back and out to the open sea which he apparently considered, but for the reasons given in the second paragraph of chapter 10 he was right to reject it. To anchor was the only responsible course.

When the lifeboatmen arrived he rejected their advice. Whether he was right to do so will, as already indicated, be left to the end, but there are important questions, little addressed in the literature, as to what would have happened had he accepted it.

The main thrust of the advice was apparently that he should move, and that must be dealt with, but it is convenient to dispose first of the alternative suggestion, reported by Jack Hicks, that he was asked to abandon ship. Had he acceded to such a request there is every reason for believing that there would have been no loss of life. Both lifeboats had reached the schooner, and both did, in the event, return safely to shore, the *Charles Deere James* in much worse conditions than those which prevailed when she would have done so had the schooner's crew accepted the offer. As we have seen in chapter 9 the carrying capacity of each lifeboat was adequate for the task, and if both had been used amply so.

What would have happened had Captain Dow accepted advice that he should move is much more difficult to assess. Where did the lifeboatmen contemplate that he should go and how? What was the nature of the "assistance" they would have given? As we have seen in chapter 10, the only contemporaneous clue is William George Mortimer's reference to "slipping the ship and going through Broad Sound" or, as it is reported elsewhere, "slip[ping] anchors and run[ning] for a place of safety".[2]

None of the subsequent commentators, including the many critical of Captain Dow's refusal, develops any clearer or alternative explanation of what could have been done. During his visit on Matt Lethbridge junior referred to in chapter 11 the author posed the question to him. He did not believe that the lifeboats could have assisted the schooner to move, but he thought that a competent pilot could have got her to safety – probably by moving to a more sheltered anchorage further into the islands.

When what is in question is attempting to bring a vessel to safety, as distinct from rescuing her crew and passengers, a lifeboat typically assists by towing. The sheer size and weight of the *T.W. Lawson*, in comparison with the power of two oared lifeboats, clearly put that out of the question here. Less commonly, even as light a boat as a gig can assist a vessel in trouble, if not too large, by kedging and winching, as happened in 1888 in the case of the *Maria Stella*, a brigantine of 141 tons.[3] That involves the boat in carrying out and dropping an anchor in the direction in which the vessel in difficulty needs to move, if upwind, and the vessel is then hauled toward the anchor by her own winches. More complex variations enable a vessel to be moved down wind or across. But, again, the *Lawson's* anchors and chains were far too heavy to be deployed by the lifeboats.

We are then left with what William George Mortimer seems to have contemplated, and what Matt Lethbridge believed could have been achieved by a competent pilot – movement to a place of safety by the schooner under her own sails. That had already been rejected by Captain Dow as he ran into the islands, and rightly so at that point, as has been accepted above. But of the reasons for that acceptance the most important, lack of local knowledge, was now no longer relevant, for qualified pilots were available. Of other reasons canvassed the tiredness of his own crew could also be met

....

2   *The Cornishman*, 19 December 1907.

3   *Azook!* by Keith Harris (Dyllansow Truran, Redruth, 1994), at p.112.

because, although the lifeboats could not assist as boats, members of their crews could do so as deck hands. When the schooner's plight had first been realised there was, it was said by Rowe, "no room to stay or wear ship". That related to the possibility of turning back out to sea, but if that were now to be attempted she was already, being at anchor and therefore head to wind, pointing in that direction.

It does not follow that that, or any other attempt to reach safety, would have been straightforward, risk-free, or assured of success. To make for the open sea would, as Mortimer envisaged, have enabled the *Lawson* to avoid the extra complication of recovering her anchors by slipping them, but to attempt that, either along the reverse of the course by which she had arrived, or by turning out through Broad Sound, would probably have necessitated at least one tack. As we have seen in chapter 4 tacking was a difficult enough manoeuvre for her at the best of times, and now she had lost many of her sails by storm damage. Matt Lethbridge's preferred alternative of running further into the islands to seek shelter in St Mary's Road would have avoided that difficulty at the expense of introducing others. Although the *Lawson* doubtless had auxiliary anchors the main anchors already deployed would have been needed to hold her against the impending storm, even in slightly less open conditions, so she would have had to weigh anchor, a burdensome and time-consuming exercise in such conditions. She would then have needed to gain steerage way and turn through nearly 180°, for which she would need a great deal of sea room, in waters strewn with hazards.

The next question is whether the St Agnes lifeboat was right to leave *T.W. Lawson* when William Francis Hicks collapsed. Something clearly had to be done – his life was in danger – but as noted in chapter 9 the exchange between the coxswain and the pilot about what should be done is a reminder that taking him ashore was not the only, or necessarily the first, option to be considered; the other was to pass him up to the schooner for immediate first aid and warming up. Billy Cook, however, who of all people had everything to gain from the lifeboat's continuing to stand by, himself dismissed that possibility in the very act of raising it: "You cannot get up alongside – you'll smash your side in." That must be accepted as ruling out such a move; had any other way of effecting the transfer been feasible it would have been considered.

That brings us to the question what would have happened had the lifeboat not returned to shore with William Francis. Young Jack, probably reflecting on the situation as a mature pilot, years later, was clear about the answer:

> I have thought about it lots and lots of times since; was it or was it not an act of Providence that our man came unconscious when that sea went over us? Was it an act of Providence that saved us because I feel if we had stayed lain up astern of that vessel as soon as we discovered she had parted we should never have left. We should have endeavoured to the last gasp to get all that crew aboard the lifeboat. We should have been in exactly the same position as they were and every one of us would have been lost.[4]

Was he right about that? As to the first part, that the lifeboat would have stayed and attempted a rescue, surely yes. That would have been their plain duty. William George Mortimer, the coxswain, when pressed at the inquest about the decision to leave and the failure to take Billy Cook back with them, "added that if it had not been for the man who was ill they would have stayed on until the last minute".[5] One commentator suggests that "in these circumstances" (the gale which arose) "it is quite probable the lifeboats would not have been able to stand by in any case",[6] but in truth it was not standing by but running for home which was the more acutely perilous. To lie astern in the lee of the schooner's great bulk was comparatively comfortable.

The second part of Jack's answer, that "every one of us would have been lost", is more difficult to assess. If, as seems to have been the case, the *Lawson*, having lost one anchor, dragged the other before eventually striking Shag Rock, that process would have taken a significant length of time, during which the lifeboat's situation would have been much the same as it had been while the schooner was riding at anchor, because although moving slowly in relation to the land she would still be virtually stationary in relation to the wind. If that is right members of her crew and the pilot could have come down over the rope holding the lifeboat, and there might well have been time for them all to do so. What is much more doubtful is

....

4   *From Rock and* Tempest, in *Portfolio*, 5 June 1974.
5   *The Western Morning News*, 17 December 1907.
6   *Wreck and Rescue round the Cornish Coast* by Cyril Noall and Grahame Farr (D Bradford Barton Ltd, Truro 1964) at p. 84.

whether the lifeboat, having cast off, could then, with its extra load, have lived in the seas which were running, especially in the first, most exposed, leg, past the Haycocks at the north point of Annet and into its lee. What we know is that she made a rather longer return journey, carrying one short of a full crew but no passengers, at about 9 pm (and therefore before moonset), in a force 9 or 10 wind, and beached safely in Periglis, but that her performance in doing so attracted apparently justified complaints from her crew of lack of stability. It would be foolhardy to express any certain conclusion, one way or the other, about the consequences of an attempt at 2.30 am, in pitch darkness, more heavily laden, in force 10 or 11, especially if it began just before the *Lawson* struck, and so involved a full semicircle clear of the rocks round the north end of Annet.

The question whether the St Mary's station should have been informed that the St Agnes boat had left the Lawson can conveniently be dealt with next, although strictly it arose only if, or because, the *Charles Deere James* was not being turned round to go out again. It need not detain us, because the answer is quite obviously yes, as the RNLI committee recognising by admonishing William George Mortimer and putting a system in place to guard against any such failure in future. Mortimer's professed reason, at the inquest, that "he did not think it necessary" because "he had not the slightest doubt of the ability of the ship to hold"[7] does not sit easily with his earlier advice to the master that he was not safe. He more likely just did not think of it, and the committee's recognition that in the multiple stresses of such a moment that could easily happen is shown by the steps they took to prevent a recurrence.

Next, did the failure to inform the St Mary's station of the return of the St Agnes boat make any difference? That turns, first, on whether the St Mary's boat would in that event have been re-launched and secondly, if so, how she would have fared. The two issues are in principle distinct, but the first does not seem to have been separately addressed at the time; what the answer to it would have been has to be inferred from the little which was said on the second. It is, however, dealt with by Richard Lethbridge in the book cited in chapter 9; he says that the lifeboat was repaired by midnight and "would have put to sea again".[8] There is also the consideration that her

....

7   *The Western Morning News* (note 5 above).
8   *Behind the Eyebrows* by Richard Lethbridge (Arden Craig Publications, 1994), at p.41.

crew would not have worked flat out to re-step the mast had there never been any prospect of re-launching the boat.

As to the second question, no member of the St Mary's lifeboat crew gave evidence at the inquest; it was the divisional coastguard, Frederick Bradley, who dealt with their activities. Having said that the damage to their boat was repaired "that same night" he was asked by the coroner whether, if she had tried, she would have "got out there again" and replied "I don't believe it possible for any boat to have lived in that sea and wind, either under oars or sails. I don't think it would have been prudent"[9]

That implies that she would not in any event have been re-launched, contrary to Richard Lethbridge's understanding, presumably gained from his grandfather, second coxswain of the St Mary's boat at the time. There is no direct evidence from the St Mary's coxswain, who would have made the decision, and in any event his answer would have been hypothetical, because he never actually had to make it, so there can be no certainty which is correct, but given that there was no recorded complaint by the St Mary's crew of the performance of their boat, that but for Captain Dow's request for tugs she would probably never have left the schooner, and that at midnight the storm was probably not as bad as it later became, it seems more probable than not that she would have put out again. Whether she would have been forced to turn back on leaving the comparative shelter of St Mary's Road is more problematical, but there is a distinct possibility that she would have reached the *Lawson*.

Had she done so, how would she have fared? That is essentially the same question as the one already posed in the case of the St Agnes boat, with the differences that the St Mary's lifeboat was a little roomier, had two more oars, and was heavier and, apparently, more stable. Those differences improved her chances of survival. It might be said that on the other hand she would have been farther from the safety of her own harbour, but in truth, had that become crucial, she could have made for St Agnes and lain up there until the morning. The answer must therefore be that there can be no more certainty about the outcome than had the St Agnes boat been in the same position, but that her chances of survival were rather better.

That brings us to the vexed question whether the St Agnes lifeboat should have gone out again. As noted in chapter 9 the oddity here is that

....

9   *The Western Morning News* (note 5 above).

although fiercely debated at the time, and later, in relation to the point at which the schooner's lights were lost, it was apparently then, and has been since, passed over in almost complete silence, in relation to the point at which William Francis was landed, although conditions then were less extreme. Only the coroner seems to have been alive to the issue. He asked "Why didn't you [return]?", to which William George Mortimer replied "Because we could not get out".[10] It is not just that there was no reported discussion after arrival on land; the whole conversation with Billy Cook, as reported by Jack, proceeded both explicitly ("it'll be impossible to get back again") and implicitly (in Mortimer's invitation to the pilot and crew to come with them and Billy Cook's promise to fire rockets in case of trouble) on the basis that unless called the lifeboat would not return.

That the decision should have been reached so early, and that Billy Cook should have been an apparently unquestioning party to it, seem to be explicable only on the basis of the crew's shared experience of the journey out in a force 5 wind, its increase to gale force since then, and their subsequent successful plea for a dramatic increase in the keel weight of their boat. It looks as if they simply did not trust the *Charles Deere James* across such a heavy wind, and to reach the *Lawson* under sail they would have had to tack, which they could not risk; the boat could be kept head to wind only under oars, and that would have required pulling her for nearly three miles into the teeth of a howling gale, which must have been judged beyond their capacity, at least with no lives immediately at stake and given that despite the availability of the crew of the lighthouse relief gig at least some of the already wet and tired original crew would have had to go straight out again. Nevertheless it remains something of a puzzle that no-one except the coroner seems, then or since, to have questioned the decision.

Despite Freddy Cook's pleas at the time and life-long protestations thereafter the decision not to launch when the schooner's lights disappeared is much easier to understand and justify. (What would have happened if, instead, the promised rocket had been fired as soon as the *Lawson* started to drag her anchor will never be known and need not be hazarded.) Not only was the storm significantly fiercer by then, but the lifeboat, instead of making her way to a lit vessel at anchor in a known position in open water, would have been searching in the dark for a wreck among rocks, with only

....

10   *The Western Morning News* (note 5 above).

the most general idea of where to look and, if she did find it, would have been unable to approach without the probability of being holed or smashed to pieces herself. At that point William George Mortimer was clearly right to refuse.

Chronologically, the last remaining question, another not apparently discussed at the time or canvassed in the literature, is why the *Slippen's* was the only rescue attempt on 14 December. St Agnes could not reasonably have been expected to find the resources to man more than one gig, but St Mary's and Tresco certainly, and probably the other islands too, knew about the wreck by that morning at latest. Although St Agnes was the nearest island it was by no means unusual for gigs from more distant islands to be involved in rescue attempts. The main reason must presumably have been the sea conditions. Osbert's refusal to let both his sons go with him, as recounted in chapter 1, is a stark reminder that the dangers were very real, and gigs from other islands would have had to encounter, at some points, more open water even to reach St Agnes than the *Slippen's* crew met in rowing to the search area, at least on their morning trip.

There remains the central question whether Captain Dow was at fault in failing to abandon ship and in refusing to accept assistance to move from his anchorage when advised to do so on the arrival of the St Agnes lifeboat. We must return to the question of abandoning ship, but that has attracted little attention; it has been the refusal to move which has been seen as the prime cause of the disaster, and from the outset he was criticised for it. One of the contemporaneous newspaper reports described it as a "serious mistake",[11] and many subsequent judgments have been even harsher. But like any other decision it should not be judged by hindsight but by reference only to what Captain Dow knew or should have known at the time, and what he could reasonably foresee as the outcome of the alternatives before him. That involved his weighing the likely consequences on the one hand of staying put and on the other of leaving his anchorage.

The consequences of staying put were obviously that if the anchors held all would be well, but that if they failed the T.W. Lawson would with virtual certainty be lost and her crew and that of the lifeboat (because its departure could not have been foreseen) would have been in great danger of perishing. On that side of the equation, therefore, everything turned on the

....

11 *The Cornishman* (note 2 above).

degree of confidence which Dow could reasonably have in his anchorage. What he said, as remembered by Jack Hicks, was:

> I have got both my anchors down and I've ridden out worse storms than this on the American side. I've had boats on either side of me drag their anchors and go aground but mine have held – I'm alright.

That is, on examination, a very curious reason to give. The second sentence, in particular, would make sense only as Dow's own testimony to the adequacy of the *Lawson's* anchors and chains or, secondly, as evidence of his own skill in choosing just where to drop his anchors. But, as to the first, it was not the *Lawson* which was under his command on the occasions to which he appealed and, as to the second, he was not now in an anchorage of his own choosing or one of which he had any knowledge or experience. Despite the inconsequence of his reasons, however, those two aspects were separate and important elements in any objective assessment of the safety or danger of staying put, and we must consider each in turn.

Ignoring, then, that silly reference to his own (non-existent) earlier experience of using them, did he have good reason for confidence in the adequacy of the vessel's anchors and chains? There was a good deal to be said in his favour. The *Lawson's* two main anchors weighed nearly five tons each and they held the schooner by massive chains.[12] The expected storm was of gale force, but not a hurricane beyond the design capacity of the tackle. Although it was foolish of him to speak as if he had himself been in command at the time he can hardly, as an experienced East Coast master, not have known of the *T.W. Lawson's* history and reputation, and that can hardly not have included occasions when she had had to ride out a storm at anchor. We have seen in chapters 4 and 5 that she had had her mishaps, but none that we know of involved any failure in that regard.

On the second issue, however, of whether there were reasons for confidence in the suitability of the ground taken by the anchors, Dow was, so far

....

12 "Massive" is a safe generalisation, but specific statements about the chains in the sources are difficult to reconcile. In chapter 10 we have noted Mortimer's evidence of being told by Captain Dow that he had 150 fathoms of cable out. One source gives the total weight of chain as 250 tons, or 125 tons for each anchor, which on one standard table (Germanischer Lloyd) would imply links of solid diameter 145 mm and length 870 mm weighing 397 kg (875 lb or 7.8 cwt) each. Jack Hicks, by contrast, speaks of 1 cwt links, which would, if the evidence of length is reliable, imply a weight of some 32 tons for each chain.

as we know, in a state of complete ignorance. The only, slight, reassurance he may have drawn from his exchange with the lifeboat coxswain was that it did not, so far as accounts of it show, include any specific warning on that score. It is possible that he raised the question with Billy Cook, but there is no report that he did so nor, therefore, if he did, of any answer he may have received. Rationally that should have been, and probably was, his main concern in weighing the risks of staying .

If one turns from what Captain Dow said to what he did, the decision to send for tugs casts doubt on his emphatic professed assurance that he was "alright", although it also exonerates him from any suspicion that his refusal to accept assistance from the lifeboats and their crews was moti-vated by the desire to save his owners salvage money. The call for a pilot might, on the other hand, be interpreted as a vote of confidence in his capacity to go on his way in the morning, but in chapter 9 we have seen reasons to doubt whether that was what he had in mind. The other expla-nation canvassed there implies that he wished to assess, with someone who not only had local expertise but would actually be in charge of any move, the practicability of leaving his anchorage in an attempt to find somewhere safer. That would make more sense, but although it throws some light on Dow's real view on the safety or danger of staying it bears rather more directly on how he weighed the other side of the equation – the safety or danger of attempting to move – to which we must ourselves now turn.

There is no contemporaneous evidence of anything said directly by Captain Dow on that subject, only the later assertion by Richard Gillis, probably derived from James Thomas Hicks, and reported in chapter 9, that after Billy Cook had gone aboard "Captain, pilot and lifeboatmen all agreed that nothing could be done". What were, objectively, the possible courses and their probable outcomes has been discussed earlier in this chapter in considering the question what would have happened had the master accepted advice that he should move. There was clearly a substantial risk that any attempt to move would put the schooner in greater danger than she was already in.

In the face of that risk a fair conclusion must be that, contrary to what many commentators, probably the majority, have held, it was within the bounds of reasonable care and skill for Captain Dow to decide that the safer course was to stay at anchor. What has probably been the most potent factor in making that difficult to accept has been the general assumption that failure occurred at the point on which Dow placed his greatest faith – the strength of his anchor chains – but before enquiring whether that assumption is well founded we should recognise that this whole debate ignores the other possibility of abandoning ship.

If that possibility is considered the risks of remaining on the anchored schooner remain as already described, but they no longer have to be weighed against those of attempting a hazardous manoeuvre; leaving in the lifeboats was, by comparison, an almost risk-free option. The consequences, in terms of the possibility or avoidance of a salvage claim, have been described in chapter 9. It seems, to a liberal western landlubber writing in the twenty-first century, in a culture in which human life is assigned a virtually incommensurable value, to have been the obvious course. That it was raised, if at all, only in passing (it will be recalled that it is recorded only in Jack's later story, and there only very briefly), dismissed out of hand and hardly mentioned since, suggests that deep-rooted compulsions were at work, rather than rational assessments of advantage and disadvantage. To abandon ship, except in the face of its immediate and inescapable loss, was the ultimate disgrace, so Captain Dow did not do it and was not blamed for not doing it. He had another opportunity, somewhat more firmly attested, when the St Agnes lifeboat left because of William Francis Hicks' collapse, but he did not take it and was not blamed for that either.

Returning to the main debate, the assumption that the *Lawson* was lost because of failure of an anchor chain has been almost universal. It is only an assumption, because no-one has ever found a broken chain-end. Even if it were true, that would not in principle detract from the conclusion above that Captain Dow was not negligent in his decision not to leave his anchorage, which should be judged only on the basis of what he knew or should have known when he made it. But it is worth examining whether it is true, not only in the general interests of factual accuracy and comprehensiveness, but also because, however irrationally, it colours many people's judgment of the master's conduct.

As noted in chapter 12, recreational diving was in 1907 and for many years after unheard of and unimagined. It is therefore remarkable that there is a firm oral tradition among the families of those in St Agnes directly involved in the *Lawson* story that in the summer of 1908 a diving support vessel appeared in the islands and divers were sent down to make investigations. Even more remarkably the different strands of that tradition concur in telling that they dived, not on the wreck itself but getting on for two miles away, between Gunners and Nundeeps, in the area of the anchorage. If that happened it represented a considerable outlay of time and money in what was then a specialised and expensive commercial activity, and must have had a commensurate commercial purpose. Can such a purpose be envisaged?

The loss of the *Lawson* was not only a personal tragedy for those who died, and their families and friends; it was an enormous financial blow for those interested in the vessel herself and her cargo. We have seen that the schooner herself was uninsured, so the loss of her value fell on her owners. It seems clear from what we know of Captain Dow's later life that the owners never made a claim against him. Whether they considered one against the chainmakers is simply unknown; on balance it seems unlikely that the owners would have had any great stomach for the initiation of such litigation The *Lawson* was on charter, so the wreck no doubt necessitated some adjustment of the accounts between her owners and charterers, and no details of that are available, but it seems unlikely that any dispute there would have justified a diving expedition.

The cargo, however, was a different matter. It was insured, and insurers faced with large claims are well accustomed to casting about for someone else who can be blamed for the loss and made to pay for it, or at least contribute to it. The cargo insurers here could well, in the name of their insured, the cargo owners, have had a claim against the shipowners had they been able to prove that the wreck was caused by the master's negligence, or possibly against the chainmakers (either directly or through the shipowners) if they could show that the chain was faulty, and had there been a reasonable prospect of success in any such claim they would certainly have wished to pursue it, if only in the hope of obtaining an out-of-court settlement.

Although no documentary record of such an enterprise has been traced, there is therefore no difficulty in identifying someone (claimant or defendant, or perhaps both jointly in an attempt to agree a crucial element of fact) with a sufficient commercial motive to mount it, or therefore in accepting the body of oral evidence that it happened. Admittedly no record of litigation has been found, but an exhaustive search has not been possible, and in any event if there was in truth no such litigation that may be because, as we are about to see, there is evidence that the dive itself established that there was no basis for a claim alleging a defect in the anchor chain.

As to what the divers did find, the oral tradition is slimmer. The one intact strand consists of the account given to the author by his father, Israel Hicks' son Charles. It was, however, entirely clear. The divers, he said, found the *Lawson's* port anchor. It had not taken the ground as a stockless anchor should, with both flukes embedded in the bottom and the shank aligned with the direction of pull of the chain. Instead it had chanced to fall into a vertical cleft in solid rock, or between two enormous rocks, and had become wedged there, with the shank upright and the chain pulling almost at right angles to its axis. The shank itself, the main shaft of the anchor, had snapped under the strain.

Is that reliable? Charles was aged just ten at the time, but to an island boy of that age the then current technology of boats and ships was as familiar as that of computers is to most children now. The wreck of the *Lawson* must have been the most dramatic event of his young life, as well as one of the most tragic (he had lost an uncle), and the importance of the finding was as apparent to him as to an adult. He related it as a middle-aged man, somewhat taciturn by nature, and certainly not given to telling tall stories, indeed so impressed with the importance of truthfulness that he could never bring himself to utter the whitest of the white lies which routinely lubricate social encounters. He talked rarely and briefly about the wreck, but about two facts he was so clear and emphatic that they have always stuck in this hearer's memory: that William Francis Hicks went out in the lifeboat without an oilskin, as recorded in chapter 9, and that divers found what is set out in the last paragraph above. His evidence of that should be accepted.

It follows that Captain Dow's confidence in his tackle was not just well-founded in the light of what he knew when he made his decision; it remains so even by hindsight, for the chain did not fail and the anchor itself, by a remote and unforeseeable chance, did so only under forces which it could not have been expected or designed to resist. Some measure of what was involved in such a failure can be gained by considering the likely dimensions of the anchor. No specification of it has come to light, but we know that it weighed about 10,000 lb (just under 5 tons). A standard model of such an anchor would have a steel shank about 8'9" (2.66 m) long and with a cross-section of something like 8½" (216 mm) square. To gain an

A stockless anchor, probably the 15-ton main anchor of the Titanic. Photograph from the Jonathan Smith Collection.

adequate visual impression one needs a photograph alongside something or someone of familiar scale, and in the absence of such a photograph of one of the *Lawson's* own anchors there is offered above one of an anchor made for the *Titanic*. Although the caption does not so state the anchor shown is almost certainly the *Titanic's* largest, weighing 15 tons, because that would have needed a shank some 13' (3.3 m) long, which by comparison with the proud craftsman behind seems about what it is. (Linear dimensions are proportional to the cube root of the weight.) To envisage the *Lawson's* anchors imagine something with linear dimensions about two-thirds of what is seen in the photograph (and compare also the picture at p. 37).

That, then, is the story of the wreck of the *Thomas W. Lawson*. It is not just a story of heroes, although there was what it is no exaggeration to call heroism in the actions of the *Slippen's* crew – not just in Freddy Cook's plunge into the water to reach Captain Dow but in the simple willingness of every member to go out, again and again, in conditions in which, as they well knew, and as Osbert matter-of-factly said for them all, "whether we come back is in the balance".

Nor is it by any means a story of villains, although it is one in which human frailty played its part: the inability of the *Lawson's* navigators to set a safe course into the mouth of the English Channel, the failure of her watchmen to recognise the light of the Bishop and the neglect of the St Agnes lifeboat coxswain to inform the St Mary's station of his return, together, possibly, with the largely ignored handling of the St Mary's lifeboat in such a way as to lose her mast. And there were not just individual frailties but in at least one respect a collective mindset which strikes a modern observer as manifesting a distorted value system; one in which Captain Dow was not prepared to face the ignominy of abandoning ship, even when the St Agnes lifeboat had to leave, and does not seem to have been blamed by anyone for not doing so, despite the fact that he knew that his vessel (and more importantly his crew) was at risk whether he stayed where he was (as he recognised by sending for tugs) or tried to move (as he showed by refusing to make the attempt to do so).

It is certainly not a story of cowards, although it is one in which William George Mortimer, in refusing as coxswain to re-launch his lifeboat, showed a caution which Freddy Cook at least, and perhaps others, thought misjudged. But it is likely that most of the lifeboat crew agreed with him, not from lack of courage, since some of them were in the *Slippen* in the morning, but because their experience in the *Charles Deere James* that evening had convinced them that in that sort of sea she was seriously short of keel weight and therefore inherently unstable.

It is not, we have in the end concluded, although many have thought and written otherwise, a story in which the blame for the wreck and loss of life should lie at the door of Captain Dow for failing to make the attempt to move the schooner from her anchorage.

It is, if (as we do) one accepts young Charles' recollection of the outcome of the 1908 dive, predominantly the story of a great mischance – the wedging of the *Lawson's* port anchor immovably upright.

It is a story replete in "what-ifs" incapable of a certain answer: what if Israel had not been relieving the Round Island light, so that there would have been no need for William Francis to be in the lifeboat or become the cause of its leaving station; what if Captain Dow had, after all, with Billy Cook as pilot, slipped or weighed his anchors and made the attempt to run for safety; what if the St Mary's lifeboatmen had known of the St Agnes boat's departure; what if the St Agnes lifeboat had attempted to go out to the *Lawson* again, either as soon as she could be turned round, manned and launched or when the *Lawson's* light was lost?

In all this it is a story which exemplifies the complexity, even the messiness, of real life, and some of its paradoxes – not least the fact that for all the efforts of the lifeboatmen involved, and the awards bestowed by the Royal National Lifeboat Institution in recognition of those efforts, the Institution had, by its own exacting standards, to record its part in the events of the 13th and 14th December 1907 in the words "No service rendered".

APPENDIX 1

Glossary

Anchor types   See "Stockless anchor"

Back   A wind backs when its direction shifts anticlockwise, viewed from above, for example from north through north-west to west. The opposite is to veer.

Bark   American spelling of barque.

Barque   As for a ship, except that it carries fore-and-aft sails on the aftermost mast.

Barquentine   As for a ship, except that it carries fore-and-aft sails on two or more of the aftermost masts.

Beam   The maximum width of a vessel, or its side.

Bight   A loop, open or closed, in a rope or line.

Boom   The horizontal spar to which the foot of a fore-and-aft sail is attached.

Bow   The foremost part of a boat or vessel. Also the foremost oarsman in a rowing boat.

Bowsprit   The spar projecting forward from the bow of a vessel, to which are attached the feet of the jib sails.

Bow rigged   (Of a rowing boat). Rigged in such a way that bow rows right-handed, with his oar on the port side of the boat, and stroke left-handed, to starboard.

Brig   As for a ship, except that it has only two masts

Brigantine   As for a brig, except that it carries fore-and aft sails on the aftermost mast.

Captain   See "Master".

Counter   The overhanging part of a vessel's stern.

Dead reckoning   Navigation by dead reckoning was necessary when no sighting of the sun or stars could be taken. It involved continuously plotting the vessel's position by measuring or estimating its speed and course from its last known position.

Dipping lug   A sail which is like a square sail in that it is hung from a yard along its top edge, but unlike in that it is not hung square but with the yard at a steep angle, crossing the mast much nearer its lower than its upper end, the sail being shaped accordingly. Although "square", the sail can then function much like a fore-and-aft sail when the wind is before the beam, the yard acting like a gaff, except that when tacking it has to be "dipped" across the mast, so that the mast is always to windward of the sail.

Fathom   Six feet, two yards, or 1.83 metres.

Foot   The bottom edge of a fore-and-aft sail.

Fore-and-aft   A fore-and-aft sail is attached at its luff to a mast or stay and, in its neutral position, as when housed, lies aft from that attachment along the vessel's axis.

Freeboard   The part of the hull above water level, or the height of that part.

Gaff   The inclined spar to which the head of a quadrilateral fore-and-aft sail is attached.

Gunwale   The top edge of the side of a boat.

Gybe   To gybe is to change from one downwind tack, or broad reach, to the other, through the position in which the vessel is heading downwind. That involves difficulties and potential dangers where fore-and-aft sails are concerned; they have to be taken across the centre line, and will suddenly and forcefully flip over as they take the wind on the opposite tack. For square-rigged sails there is no such problem, and where they are concerned the pejorative overtones of the word "gybing" are often avoided by referring instead to "wearing".

Head   The top edge or (if triangular) corner of a fore-and-aft sail.

Housed   Of sails and moving spars: fastened in the neutral, "home", position to which they are returned when the vessel is not under sail.

Irons   See "stays".

Jib   A fore-and-aft sail set on a stay ahead of the foremast.

Ketch   A (usually small) vessel with a main mast and shorter mizzen, having the steering position aft of the mizzen.

Leach   The trailing edge of a fore-and-aft sail.

Lee   The sheltered area downwind of a vessel or shore feature.

Leg of mutton   A triangular fore-and-aft sail attached to a mast but with no boom or other spar.

Luff   The leading edge of a fore-and-aft sail.

Lug   See "Dipping lug".

Master   The commanding officer of a merchant vessel. He (at those dates always a man) was also called the captain, and that was and is the commoner word in America and outside maritime circles, but "master" was the "insider's" word in Britain.

Mizzen   A mast aft of the main mast. In a vessel with four or more masts, it is usually the next after the main mast which is so named.

Pitch   The motion of a vessel around a transverse horizontal axis, so that the bow and stern alternately rise and fall.

Port   The port side of a vessel is the left side, looking forward.

Quarter   A vessel's quarter lies between its stern and its beam.

Reach   See "tack". A reach is "abeam" when the wind is at right angles to the vessel's course, and "broad" when it is aft of that, i.e. coming over its quarter.

Roll   The motion of a vessel round a longitudinal horizontal axis, so that each side alternately rises and falls.

Schooner   A vessel with two or more masts, rigged fore-and-aft overall (but see "Topsail schooner"). More precisely, such a two-master is properly a schooner only if the masts are a foremast and a (taller or equal) main mast. A fore-and-aft rigged two-master with a main mast and, behind it, a (shorter) mizzen is a yawl or ketch.

Sheet   The rope attached to the outer end of a boom (or, if there is no boom, of the lower edge of the sail itself) and run out or hauled in to govern the angle at which a fore-and-aft sail is set.

Ship   A sailing vessel with three or more masts, square-rigged overall, apart from the jibs.

Spar   A length of timber used as a mast, boom, gaff, yard or other part of a vessel's upperworks.

Square-rigged   A square-rigged sail is approximately rectangular in shape and hung from a horizontal yard.

Starboard   The starboard side of a vessel is the right side, looking forward.

Stay   A length of wire or rope forming part of the standing rigging of a vessel, in particular one which holds a mast in position and transmits to the hull the forces generated in the mast by the pressure of the wind on the sails.

Stays   A vessel is "in stays", or "in irons", while tacking, during the period when it is heading dead into the wind, or so nearly so that the sails cannot derive any driving force from it.

Steerage way   Sufficient speed through the water for a vessel's rudder to be effective.

Stern   The aftermost part of a boat or vessel.

Stockless anchor   An anchor must incorporate some means of ensuring that one or more flukes "take the ground", that is to say dig into the bottom in order to provide the holding capacity which is the anchor's function, rather than sliding flat along its surface. The traditional "Admiralty" anchor achieves that end by having a stock, a rod set across the top of the shank, or main shaft of the anchor, at right angles to the line of the flukes, and long enough to ensure that the anchor rolls over into a position in which one of the flukes is forced to enter the ground. The stockless anchor, invented in 1821 and in general use for large vessels by the time the *Lawson* was built, does without a stock by setting the flukes on a hinge and ensuring that although they begin by lying flat on the bottom, projections at the other side of the hinge force them, as the anchor drags, to rotate downwards.

Stroke   The aftermost oarsman in a rowing boat.

Stroke rigged   (Of a rowing boat). Rigged in such a way that stroke rows right-handed, with his oar on the port side of the boat.

Tack   A vessel is on the port (or starboard) tack when the sails are taking the wind from the port (or starboard) side. The noun is sometimes understood as applying only when the vessel is heading upwind (being replaced by "reach" in other situations), and the verb "to tack" accordingly means to change from one upwind tack to the other, through the position in which the vessel is heading dead into the wind.

Tholes   A pair of upright wooden pins or pegs between which the oar of a gig or other rowing boat lies, the foremost of which transmits the pull of the oar to the boat.

Thwart   A rower's bench seat, in a gig serving also as a main transverse structural member of the boat.

Tonnage   Registered tonnage (which is the usual meaning in relation to shipping), is a measure of capacity (100 cubic feet per registered ton), not of weight. When the weight of hull or cargo is described in tons some adjective is used to distinguish it from registered tonnage. As to differing values for the ton or tonne of weight see note (12) to chapter 4.

Topsail schooner   As for a schooner, except that it carries square-rigged topsails on one or more of the foremost masts.

Veer   A wind veers when its direction shifts clockwise, viewed from above, for example from north through north-east to east. The opposite is to back.

Warp   The rope or line by which a boat is paid out from, or hauled in or attached to, a larger vessel or a fixture.

Wearing ship   See "gybe".

Yard   A spar from which a sail is hung. In a square-rigged vessel it is straight and horizontal, is slung centrally in front of a mast and, in its neutral position, lies square across the axis of the vessel, but in other rigs (see "dipping lug") it may be slung at an angle and asymmetrical.

Yaw   The motion of a vessel round a vertical axis, so that it rotates clockwise or anticlockwise (as seen from above), or each alternately.

Yawl   A (usually small) vessel with a main mast and (much) shorter mizzen, having the steering position ahead of the mizzen.

APPENDIX 2

Monetary equivalents
(Reprinted from Chapter 3, pp. 26, 27)

The U.S. cent had started life as the equivalent of a British halfpenny, at a time when there were 12 pence in each shilling and 20 shillings in the pound, so at 100 cents the dollar was worth 4s.2d. (or 21 new pence). Upon independence the dollar was officially defined in terms which made it worth slightly less in terms of sterling, and since both currencies were linked to gold the exchange rate remained essentially unchanged until the United Kingdom abandoned the gold standard in 1931. During the whole of Lawson's life, therefore, it is sufficiently accurate, in round terms, to treat £1 as worth $5. As to internal values both currencies were, in comparison with modern rates of inflation, comparatively stable until the First World War, and it would be an unnecessary complication to distinguish between dates or to attempt greater accuracy than simply to multiply dollars by about 25 and pounds by about 75 to give current (2014) equivalents.

APPENDIX 3

Island surnames

Population of St Agnes, Isles of Scilly, 1841–1911. Key: H = households or, in relation to places of birth, heads of households; P= persons

	1841		1851		1861		1871		1881		1891		1901		1911	
	H	**P**	H	**P**	H	**P**	H	**P**	H	**P**	H	**P**	H	**P**	H	**P**
Incomers																
Coastguards	5	**20**	4	**28**	4	**18**	3	**16**	5	**21**	4	**19**	4	**10**	3	**11**
Lightkeepers*	2	**7**	2	**9**	2	**14**	2	**15**	2	**8**	2	**6**	2	**?**	2	**?**
Curate	1	**1**	1	**2**	1	**5**	1	**5**	1	**8**	1	**3**	1	**3**	1	**4**
Bible Christian Minister	–	**1**	–	**–**	–	**1**	1	**1**	–	**1**	–	**1**	–	**1**	–	**–**
Schoolteacher	–	**–**	–	**1**	–	**–**	–	**1**	–	**1**	–	**1**	–	**1**	–	**1**
Visitors	–	**–**	–	**3**	–	**1**	–	**1**	–	**–**	–	**–**	–	**2**	–	**1**
Other transients#	–	**7**	–	**3**	–	**1**	–	**–**	–	**3**	–	**1**	–	**5**	–	**10**
Total incomers*	8	**36**	7	**46**	7	**40**	7	**39**	8	**42**	7	**31**	7	**22**	6	**27**
Islanders																
Hicks (A)	21	**111**	28	**95**	27	**101**	28	**85**	15	**66**	14	**72**	12	**59**	12	**46**
Legg (B)	6	**29**	5	**23**	6	**16**	2	**15**	3	**13**	3	**10**	4	**9**	2	**6**
Mortimore (or Mortimer) (C)	2	**6**	2	**6**	1	**6**	2	**6**	2	**5**	1	**6**	1	**7**	1	**6**
Humphreys (or Humphry)	2	**7**	2	**6**	2	**6**	1	**4**	1	**3**	–	**1**	–	**1**	–	**1**
Pender	2	**10**	2	**8**	2	**9**	1	**3**	1	**4**	–	**–**	–	**–**	–	**–**
Woodcock	1	**3**	1	**2**	1	**5**	–	**–**	–	**–**	–	**–**	–	**–**	–	**–**
Stephens (or Stevens)	2	**6**	2	**4**	1	**2**	1	**2**	–	**–**	–	**–**	–	**–**	–	**–**
Bickford	4	**10**	1	**5**	–	**–**	–	**–**	–	**–**	–	**–**	–	**–**	–	**–**
Ashford	1	**5**	1	**3**	1	**4**	1	**2**	–	**–**	–	**–**	–	**–**	–	**–**
Edwards	1	**3**	–	**–**	–	**–**	–	**–**	–	**–**	–	**–**	–	**–**	–	**–**

	1841		1851		1861		1871		1881		1891		1901		1911	
	H	P	H	P	H	P	H	P	H	P	H	P	H	P	H	P
Jenkins (or Jenkings)	–	**1**	1	**5**	2	**9**	–	**1**	1	**5**	2	**9**	1	**5**	–	**1**
Ellis	–	**–**	–	**1**	–	**2**	–	**1**	–	**1**	1	**1**	–	**1**	–	**–**
Nicholas	–	**–**	–	**–**	3	**5**	1	**8**	–	**–**	–	**–**	–	**–**	–	**–**
Deason	–	**–**	–	**–**	1	**2**	1	**2**	1	**2**	1	**2**	1	**2**	–	**–**
Thomas	–	**–**	–	**–**	1	**6**	1	**5**	–	**–**	–	**–**	–	**–**	–	**–**
Wingate	–	**–**	–	**–**	–	**–**	1	**2**	1	**2**	–	**–**	–	**–**	–	**–**
Williams	–	**–**	–	**–**	–	**–**	1	**3**	–	**–**	–	**–**	–	**–**	–	**–**
Trenary	–	**–**	–	**–**	–	**–**	–	**–**	1	**4**	1	**3**	1	**3**	1	**6**
Escott	–	**–**	–	**–**	–	**–**	–	**–**	–	**–**	–	**–**	–	**–**	1	**5**
Phillips	–	**–**	–	**–**	–	**–**	–	**–**	–	**–**	–	**–**	–	**–**	1	**2**
Total Islanders (D)	50	**191**	45	**158**	48	**171**	41	**139**	26	**105**	23	**104**	20	**87**	18	**73**
Total Population	58	**227**	52	**204**	55	**211**	48	**178**	34	**147**	30	**135**	27	**109**	24	**100**

Place of birth of islanders

	H	P	H	P	H	P	H	P	H	P	H	P	H	P	H	P
St Agnes	+	**+**	42	**141**	41	**140**	35	**117**	20	**83**	15	**87**	15	**75**	14	**56**
Rest of Isles of Scilly	+	**+**	3	**16**	4	**25**	3	**10**	5	**14**	7	**14**	4	**9**	4	**6**
Elsewhere	+	**+**	0	**1**	3	**6**	3	**12**	1	**8**	1	**3**	1	**3**	1	**11**
Total islanders, as above	50	**191**	45	**158**	48	**171**	41	**139**	26	**105**	23	**104**	20	**87**	19	**73**

Percentage of islanders

	H	P	H	P	H	P	H	P	H	P	H	P	H	P	H	P
Hicks (A/D)	58	**58.1**	62	**60.1**	56	**59.1**	68	**61.2**	58	**62.9**	61	**69.2**	60	**67.8**	67	**63.0**
Legg (B/D)	12	**15.2**	11	**14.6**	13	**9.4**	5	**10.8**	12	**12.4**	13	**9.6**	20	**10.3**	11	**8.2**
Mortimer (C/D)	4	**3.1**	4	**3.8**	2	**2.3**	5	**4.3**	8	**4.8**	4	**5.8**	5	**8.0**	6	**8.2**
(A+B+C)/D	74	**76.4**	78	**78.5**	71	**70.8**	78	**76.3**	77	**80.0**	78	**84.6**	85	**86.2**	83	**79.5**
Born on St Agnes	+	**+**	93	**89.2**	85	**81.9**	85	**84.2**	77	**79.0**	65	**83.7**	75	**86.2**	74	**76.7**
Born in Isles of Scilly	+	**+**	100	**99.4**	94	**96.5**	93	**91.4**	96	**92.4**	96	**97.1**	95	**96.6**	95	**84.9**

* Lightkeepers are recorded elsewhere in 1901 and 1911

Persons who are not heads of households, or related to them, and appear in only one census

+ Not recorded

APPENDIX 4

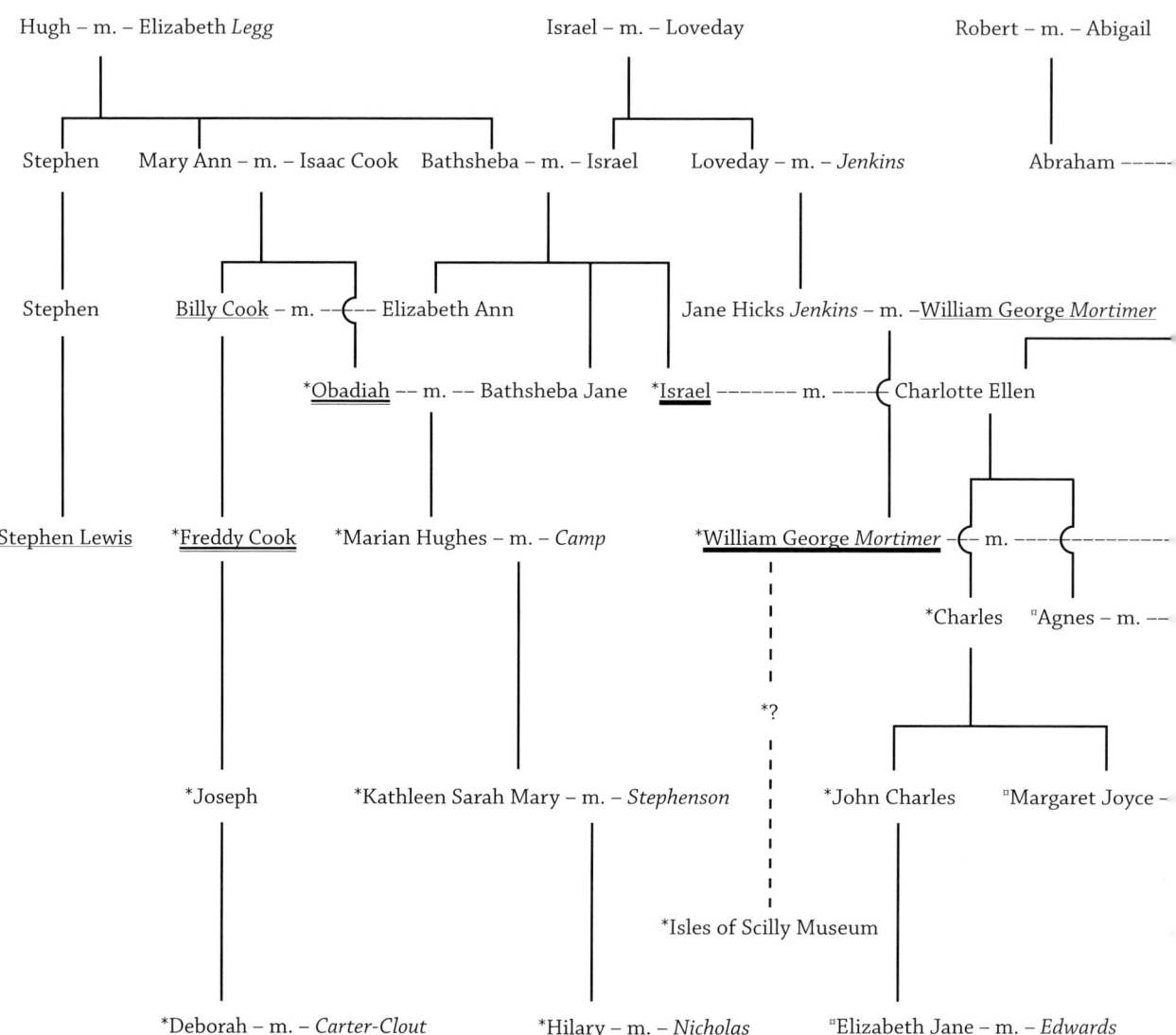

Key:

<u>Crew of lifeboat.</u>

<u>Crew of *Slippen*.</u>

<u>Crew of lifeboat and *Slippen*.</u>

* Successive holders of gold watch/medals.

▫ Successive holders of Edward Rowe's ring.

Notes:

1. Everyone has the surname Hicks, unless another surname is given in italics.
2. Persons featuring in the story are given the names used in the book.
3. Spouses and siblings are omitted, unless (i) ancestors, (ii) links in a relationship, or (iii) bringing a change of name.
4. Forenames are omitted of spouses included for reason (iii).
5. Siblings are not necessarily in order of age.

Family Relationships

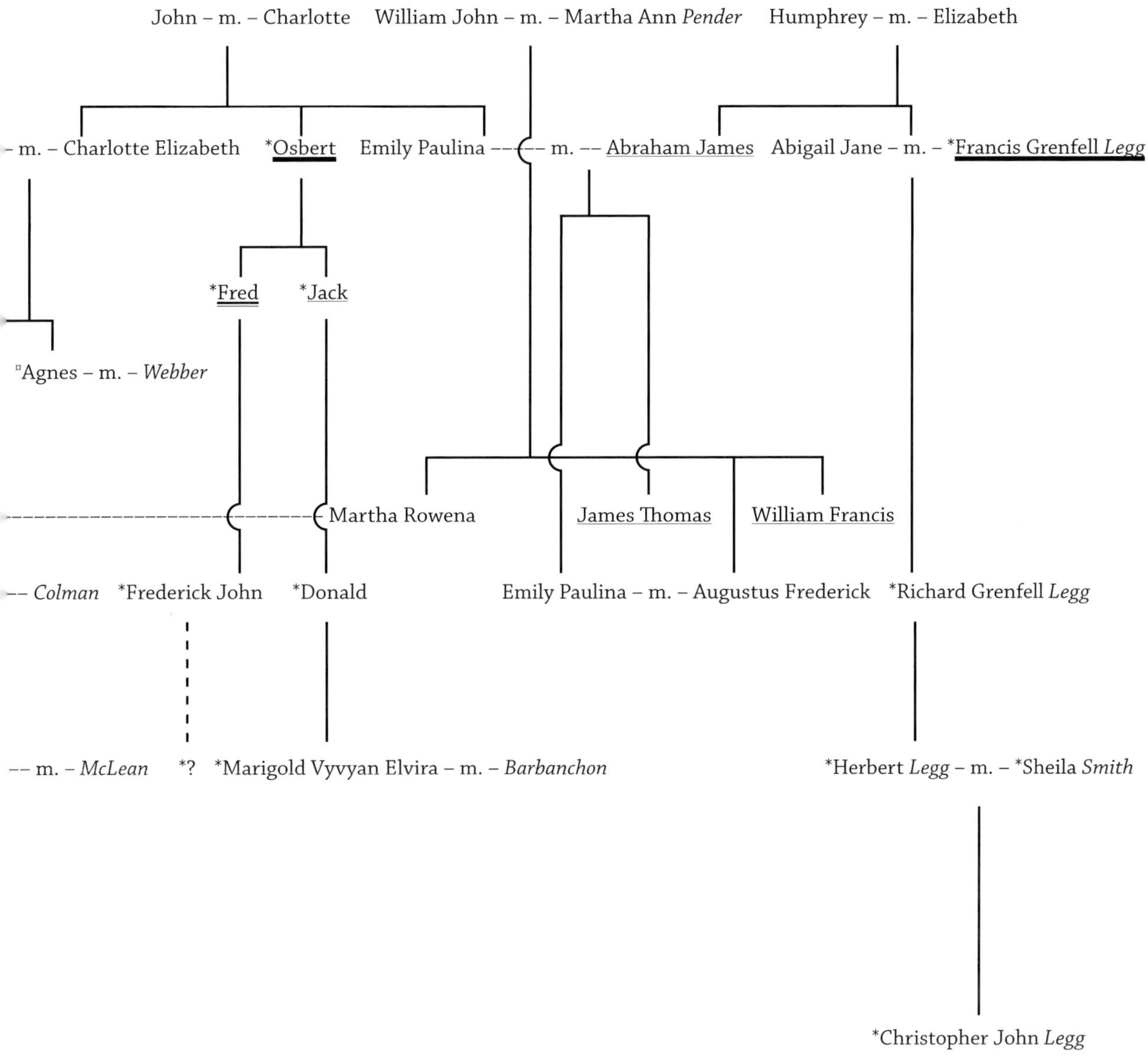

John – m. – Charlotte   William John – m. – Martha Ann *Pender*   Humphrey – m. – Elizabeth

– m. – Charlotte Elizabeth   *<u>Osbert</u>   Emily Paulina – – m. – – <u>Abraham James</u>   Abigail Jane – m. – *<u>Francis Grenfell</u> *Legg*

*<u>Fred</u>   *<u>Jack</u>

□Agnes – m. – *Webber*

Martha Rowena   <u>James Thomas</u>   <u>William Francis</u>

– *Colman*   *Frederick John   *Donald   Emily Paulina – m. – Augustus Frederick   *Richard Grenfell *Legg*

– – m. – *McLean*   *?   *Marigold Vyvyan Elvira – m. – *Barbanchon*   *Herbert *Legg* – m. – *Sheila *Smith*

*Christopher John *Legg*

Relationship unknown:
<u>Benjamin</u>
<u>James</u>

Unrelated: *<u>William *Trenary*</u> – m. – Grace *Nicholas*

*Lilian – m. – *Willey*

*Gerald *Willey*

229

APPENDIX 5

Beaufort Scale

T HE BEAUFORT SCALE OF WIND SPEEDS was devised in 1805, was officially adopted by the Royal Navy in the late 1830s and was for many years the international standard. It has been modified from time to time and has now been abandoned by some countries, but is still in widespread use, with minor local variations. The following is based on the version published by the (U.K.) Meteorological Office, with some simplification, the replacement of knots by mph, wave heights in feet as well as metres and the addition of some commonly used variants under "Wind".

Scale	Limits of wind speed		Wind	Sea	Probable wave height		Probable maximum height	
	mph	*m/s*			*Metres*	*Ft/in*	*Metres*	*Ft/in*
0	<1	<1	Calm	Calm (glassy)	–	–	–	–
1	1–3	1–2	Light air	Calm (rippled)	0.1	0/4	0.1	0/4
2	4–7	2–3	Light breeze	Smooth (wavelets)	0.2	0/8	0.3	1
3	8–11	4–5	Gentle breeze	Slight	0.6	2	1.0	3
4	12–18	6–8	Moderate breeze	Moderate	1.0	3	1.5	5
5	19–24	9–11	Fresh breeze	Rough	2.0	7	2.5	8
6	25–31	11–14	Strong breeze	Rough to very rough	3.0	10	4.0	13
7	32–38	14–17	Near gale (high wind)	Very rough to high	4.0	13	5.5	18
8	39–46	17–21	Severe gale (strong gale)	High	5.5	18	7.5	25
9	47–54	21–24	Storm (whole gale)	Very high	7.0	23	10.0	33
10	55–63	25–28	Violent storm	Exceptionally high	9.0	30	12.5	41
11	64–72	29–32	Hurricane	Phenomenal	11.5	38	16.0	52
12	>72	>32			14.0	46		

APPENDIX 6

Points of the Compass

Compass point	Bearing
North	0°
North by East	11° 15'
North-North-East	22° 30'
North-East by North	33° 45'
North-East	45°
North-East by East	56° 15'
East-North-East	67° 30'
East by North	78° 45'
East	90°
East by South	101° 15'
East-South-East	112° 30'
South-East by East	123° 45'
South-East	135°
South-East by South	146° 15'
South-South-East	157° 30'
South by East	168° 45'
South	180°
South by West	191° 15'
South-South-West	202° 30'
South-West by South	213° 45'
South-West	225°
South-West by West	236° 15'
West-South-West	247° 30'
West by South	258° 45'

Compass point	Bearing
West	270°
West by North	281° 15'
West-North-West	292° 30'
North-West by West	303° 45'
North-West	315°
North-West by North	326° 15'
North-North-West	337° 30'
North by West	348° 45'

APPENDIX 7

Astronomical and Meteorological Data

The Sun: On St Agnes sunset on 13 December 1907 was at 4.24 pm GMT, and sunrise on 14 December at 8.15 am.

The Moon: The moon had been at first quarter at 2.16 am GMT on 12 December and, approaching two days later, would have had visibly more than half of its disc lit. It set at 2.11 am on 14 December.

Tides: The tidal range varied a little over 13 and 14 December 1907, but was in the region of 10 feet, or 3 metres. The predicted times of low and high water were as follows:

13 December 1907	5.06 pm	Low water
	11.27 pm	High water
14 December 1907	5.42 am	Low water
	12.03 pm	High water
	6.17 pm	Low water.

Meteorology There are wind speed and direction readings for St Agnes at 8 am and 6 pm daily, and fuller data for St Mary's at 8 am, 2 pm and 6 pm, including temperature and "weather". Both sets are tabulated below. It will be seen that the two stations agree on wind speeds but sometimes differ markedly on direction, presumably because the readings are instantaneous rather than averaged over a period, and wind direction can fluctuate widely and rapidly on each side of its general set. Directions at St Agnes are given in traditional form (see Appendix 6) but at St Mary's in bearings, so the approximate equivalent is given in brackets in each case.

Temperatures in the table below are air temperatures. As recorded in Chapter 10, the nearest station recording sea temperature was the Seven Stones Lightship, between Land's End and Scilly, where it was 51.5°F (11°C) on the night of 13–14 December 1907.

Date	Time	St Agnes		St Mary's			
		Wind		Wind		Temperature	Weather
		Force	Direction	Force	Direction		
13 December 1907	2pm			5	220° (SW)	49F (9C)	Rain falling
	6pm	5	WSW (247°30')	5	220° (SW)	51F (11C)	Rain falling
14 December 1907	8am	7	WNW (290°30')	7	260° (W by S)	49F (9C)	Half cloud
	2pm			6	260° (W by S)	50F (10C)	Three quarters cloud
	6pm	6	NW (315°)	6	280° (W by N)	49F (9C)	Three quarters cloud

INDEX
(including bibliographical references)

Where the key word is repeated in the body of entries it is sometimes represented by an italic initial, doubled for the plural form.